Also by Thom Hartmann:

Attention Deficit Disorder: A Different Perception

Focus Your Energy: Hunting For Success in Business with ADD (Pocket Books)

The Best of the DTP Forum on CompuServe (Peachpit Press)

ADD Success Stories

A Guide to Fulfillment for Families with Attention Deficit Disorder

*Maps, Guidebooks, and Travelogues
for Hunters in this Farmer's World*

Thom Hartmann

Foreword by John J. Ratey, MD

Underwood Books
Grass Valley, California
1995

ADD Success Stories
ISBN 1-887424-03-2 (trade paper)
ISBN 1-887424-04-0 (hardcover)

Copyright © 1995 by Mythical Intelligence, Inc.

Distributed by Publisher's Group West
Volume discounts may be available: (800) 788-3123

Manufactured in the United States of America

10 9 8 7 6 5 4 3 2 1

The ideas in this book are based on the author's personal experience with ADD, and as such are not to be considered medical advice. This book is not intended as a substitute for psychotherapy or the medical treatment of Attention-deficit Hyperactivity Disorder and the various medications described herein can only be prescribed by a physician. The reader should consult a qualified health care professional in matters relating to health and particularly with respect to any symptoms which may require diagnosis or medical attention.

Dedication

For my children: Kindra, Justin, and Kerith Hartmann;
and my brothers: Steve, Stan, and John Hartmann.

I've learned so much about life from each of you.

Contents

Foreword

John J. Ratey, MD

The germ theory has dominated much of our thinking about disease since the time of Pasteur. The premise was simple: one germ, one bacteria, one pathogen. All one had to do was isolate and kill it. To this day, the same mode of thinking persists: we hold onto the notion that we may master diseases by simply identifying their culprits and eradicating them one by one, with singular expedience and facility.

Just as we cling to the prospect of a simple cause and effect solution with regard to afflictions of the bacterial kind, so too do we conceptualize the treatment of psychiatric disorders as merely a matter of making a diagnosis and fixing it, as if there were a mathematical guide to the Normal. Whether prescribed for an effect of mind or body, treatment typically proceeds from determination of cause to prescriptive remedy. This simple conceptual approach, by virtue of its sense of mastery, understandably holds a seductive appeal. It remains a common public perception and feeds the wishes of medical and mental health care providers.

In the recent past, professionals in the field of psychiatry, resolved to find the "right" pathogen: to identify the traumatic event or deficiency in the support system. More recently, the search focused on the offending chemical imbalance and revolutionary new drugs, such as Prozac, were developed to suspend the imbalance and restore order. Today the attention has been drawn to the genetic culprits. Gene hunters look for the aberrant gene or genes that are responsible for our psychic distress with the notion that once we identify the bad agent we can control our destiny. However, against the backdrop of new discoveries and our current refined understanding, the simplistic Newtonian model has become outdated and no longer sensibly applies. The new model takes into account both the complexity of biological systems of the body and the equally complex systems of the brain. Yielding to a multitude of variables, it is clear that the medical care and treatment of body and brain necessitates more than a simple linear, cause and effect approach. Instead, an approach more congruent with the concept of "complexity" is required.

Christopher Langston, a biologist and a true pioneer and one of the founders of the Santa Fe Institute, has brought the issue of complexity to the fore in biology. He believes that future trends in science will be less linear and more poetic and metaphorical in approach, and will thereby be able to capture the nature of the complex. As we reach the limits of what we can know, a new model of the complex will form, organizing the chaotic mix of seemingly unrelated simplistic elements into a more integrated and comprehensive framework of understanding, approaching a clearer picture of complexity.

One such complexity, Attention Deficit Disorder, or ADD, is a disorder posing a myriad of variables and distinctions. It is very much a nonlinear condition that does not have clear boundaries and sharp delineations. Coming up with a biologic acid test has been impossible and improbable. In the foreseeable future even with yet another revolution in our neuroradiologic capacity we will probably not be able to have the kind of test whose results are reproducible and satisfactory. Thus we are left with the uncertainty of making a diagnosis based on symptoms, as if ADD were a psychiatric syndrome. Further, we need to collect these symptoms over time. ADD is unlike depression which tends to be there all the time and thus can be determined by an interview or through scaled testing. The person with ADD may not show symptoms during testing. Instead we depend on the longitudinal presentation—that is, how the condition has been over a long period of time—recognizing that the condition itself changes in different contexts over time. Even in one of the most sharply defined area that we deal with, genetics, we find the smudge. Gene hunters are finding that there may be a genetic cross between many syndromes—Obsessive Compulsive Disorder, ADD, Oppositional Defiant Disorder, Conduct Disorder, Post Traumatic Stress Disorder, depression and autism.

In effect, Attention Deficit Disorder displays a spectrum of variations, presenting symptoms from a mild impairment to a mild to moderate disability to a virtual handicap that, for some, makes it impossible to function in the world. ADD is a neurologic syndrome expressed in a number of different brain regions, that varies in presentation in almost everyone who has the diagnosis. With no reliable test for the disorder aside from clinical histories, the true nature of ADD is hard to pinpoint. The cause of ADD in most cases is genetic and is believed to be caused by a growing number of different gene abnormalities. Thus, the "ADD brain" manifests through an infinite variety of brain functions, different than the norm, and poses a wide range of symptoms that vary within families and even within individual patients over the course of their lives.

What we are learning today is that even if ADD is initially and primarily a genetic disorder, as it is thought to be in 95% of the cases studied, the environmental contribution, though unmeasured, is judged to be considerable. Taking cues from the nature versus nurture debate, there are those who believe ADD is entirely biological and consequently beyond treatment, and others who believe environmental adjustments can reduce the deficits, enhance the assets, and provide a better life beyond that of predetermined genetic destiny. ADD is a prime example of a spectrum disorder that is biologically determined, yet is often best treated by environmental manipulation through what we call environmental engineering. Which brings us to the contents of *ADD Success Stories*.

After Thom Hartmann's first two books on ADD, the metaphor of the hunter began to provide many ADDers with an acceptable label for their quirkiness and a way of looking at themselves that was full of hope and permission. Just as the diagnosis of ADD itself often helps in replacing guilt with hope so does an appealing metaphor like that of a hunter (which smacks of Robin Hood and Madame Curie) help in giving many people a sense of purpose and direction. This sort of personal mythology can provide a platform that looks to the future with promise and approval—never masking the problems of the ADD brain but instead offering role models to guide the Adder into a more optimistic and foreword-looking journey. While this new reframed version of who they are should never excuse foibles or open the door to self-indulgence, being granted permission to be who they are often drives individuals to reach previously unattempted heights. When the shackles of shame are lifted, the future can be approached with a cleaner, crisper, more energetic viewpoint.

This book, third in a series by Thom Hartmann on the Hunter/ADD brain, presents us with a myriad of real-life examples of how scores of people have developed ways of managing their environment to serve their quirky brains. This book presents the hopes and wonderful shared experiences of those who have triumphed over their "disabilities", turning what was a liability into a valued asset. The positive power in making any diagnosis lies in bringing to light the common problems of a disorder, so that the person may recognize what he or she is up against and begin to make plans to combat what is causing difficulty. As we try to emerge from an age of black and white thinking that engenders stigmatization of all persons diagnosed with a psychiatric disorder, Thom Hartmann's hunter metaphor poetically translates and communicates the complex issues while keeping a positive slant on brain type. As one patient said to me recently, "ADD is not a problem—it is the way my brain functions. I have disadvantages and advantages and I came to get a diagnosis to learn about my brain so that I could gain a vantage point, a platform of stability to go on with the rest of my life." As reflected in this statement, some individuals view their ADD as a handicap, some as a nuisance and some as a gift granting them special talents.

The effect of listening to the experiences of others who have the disorder is extraordinary. ADDers, like individuals in any group who share a common identity, know that they are implicitly understood by those with a similar list of characteristics and foibles. Hartmann presents this book almost as if it were a record of a large support group meeting where each fellow traveler shares his or her frustrations with an inability to perform "normally" and offers insight into how he or she was able to overcome their deficiencies. In many cases the impairment is slight, but nonetheless troublesome, but most importantly the problem is shared by others. One has permission to acknowledge it, learn more about it, and then learn to manage it. This tremendous experience of instant recognition and acceptance is one that many grass roots support organizations engender. The broad spectrum of ADDers and related others on the Internet adds to the connectedness and reinforces the awareness that not only is the person not alone, but that there are many people out there working on similar problems and offering advice and support.

ADD can be thought of as a type of environmental dependency syndrome, which requires more environmental advice and helpful examples than most other disorders. In the neurology literature this syndrome describes patients who develop pronounced and somewhat humorous symptoms of imitation and utilization after experiencing frontal lobe trauma. These individuals depend upon the environment for behavioral cues. They adopt accents of the people they talk with, they imitate gestures and utilize whatever else they notice about those with whom they interact. For instance, if they walk into the examining room and spy a tongue blade they may immediately pick it up and try to examine the doctors throat. If a stethoscope is available they may attempt to listen to the doctors chest. They have little goal directed behavior and thus are severely dependent upon the environment for guidance. In its mild form, this environmental dependency syndrome accurately describes many people with ADD. The treatment often involves setting up an environment in which it is possible to win rather than lose. Treatment of ADDers includes environmentally engineering their lives to try and keep the hunter brain on track. This book is in large measure a presentation of shared stories about individuals who have successfully engineered their environments to help them both overcome and utilize the characteristics of their ADD.

John J. Ratey, MD
June, 1995

John J. Ratey, MD, is an assistant professor of psychiatry at Harvard Medical School and is in private practice. He is co-author, with Edward M. Hallowell, MD, of two books on Attention Deficit Disorder: *Driven to Distraction* and *Answers to Distraction*.

The Men That Don't Fit In
by Robert Service (1907)

There's a race of men that don't fit in,
    A race that can't sit still;
So they break the hearts of kith and kin,
    And they roam the world at will.
They range the field and they rove the flood,
    And they climb the mountain's crest;
Theirs is the curse of the gypsy blood,
    And they don't know how to rest.

If they just went straight they might go far;
    They are strong and brave and true;
But they're always tired of the things that are,
    And they want the strange and new.
They say: "Could I find my proper groove,
    What a deep mark I would make!"
So they chop and change, and each fresh move
    Is only a fresh mistake.

And each forgets, as he strips and runs
    With a brilliant, fitful pace,
It's the steady, quiet, plodding ones
    Who win in the lifelong race.
And each forgets that his youth has fled,
    Forgets that his prime is past,
Till he stands one day, with a hope that's dead,
    In the glare of the truth at last.

He has failed, he has failed; he has missed his chance;
    He has just done things by half.
Life's been a jolly good joke on him,
    And now is the time to laugh.
Ha, ha! He is one of the Legion Lost;
    He was never meant to win;
He's a rolling stone, and it's bred in the bone;
    He's a man who won't fit in.

There's Power in How We Look At Things

Every man takes the limits of his own field of vision for the limits of the world.
    —Schopenhauer, *Further Psychological Observations*, 1951

As I travel around the country and share the Hunter/Farmer model* of ADD, I'm struck by how many people find it a liberating point of view. Although even the Merck Manual recognizes that no one knows exactly what ADD is or where it comes from, "Hunters & Farmers" gives people a *useful* paradigm to describe ADD that helps them see new ways to view career choices, organizational strategies, and even the value of therapy and/or medication.

And that, after all, is the point: to find something useful, something with practical value we can use to improve our situation.

However, I also encounter a small minority of individuals who tenaciously want to embrace a label of "ill" when describing themselves, while other people with ADD—and with symptoms just as strong—are successful in business, school, or the professions. They no longer lose their keys, they have learned to improve their memory—in short, they've *learned to deal with it.*

Let's establish a clear overview:

• The Hunter/Farmer concept is a model.

It's not hard science, and was never intended to be (although more and more scientists are embracing it as a possible working hypothesis). There are dozens of theories about the cause or origin of ADD. They range from prenatal fetal injury to neurotransmitter imbalances in the brain, to developmental "hiccups" where a person failed, for whatever

---

*First introduced in my 1993 book, *Attention Deficit Disorder: A Different Perception* and later discussed in the July 18, 1994 *Time* magazine article about my book and theory.

reason, to learn organizational and focusing strategies at some particularly critical point in childhood.

As more proof accumulates that ADD has a genetic basis, it gives increased credibility to the Hunter/Farmer model and the possibility that ADD was once a useful adaptation that's maladaptive in modern society (much like sickle cell anemia, which protects against malaria in Africa but is a liability in malaria-free America). Recent studies done at the University of Chicago have all but proven that ADD is a genetic condition, and has little or nothing to do with parenting or environment. It's all nature, and no nurture, at least in its baseline state, although the specifics of it are still elusive.

The Merck Manual, the official book of the medical profession for defining diseases, states: "The etiology (cause) is unknown. Several theories advocating biochemical, sensory and motor, physiologic, and behavioral correlates and manifestations have been proposed." The Merck Manual further states: "Diagnosis is often difficult. No particular organic signs or set of neurologic indicators are specific."

In other words, nobody knows what ADD is or where it comes from, and anyone who says differently is not speaking on behalf of the scientific community.

I developed the Hunter/Farmer model of ADD first as a way to explain ADD to my own son, after a psychologist had told him he had a "brain disease." I felt that was a pretty poor way to describe any sort of challenge to a person, and wanted to give him a paradigm for understanding that the challenges he faced would not be crippling to his self-esteem.

Hunters/Farmers explained his problems in terms he could understand, and allowed him to discuss his ADD with teachers and friends without hanging his head. Instead of denying the value of therapy or medication, it made him more enthusiastic about considering those options. Asking, "How can we look at this usefully?" always validates approaches that are already proven effective.

• The Hunter/Farmer model approaches head-on the difficulties people with ADD face in modern society. It brings those difficulties more clearly into focus. It also provides a rational explanation for some of the many techniques that psychologists suggest for working around, overcoming, or working through the ways that ADD can challenge a person's life.

Using the Hunter/Farmer model, I've pointed out the differences between Hunters and Farmers, and recommended that people do what works best for them. In modern society, there are positive and negative sides to both Hunter and Farmer types of people.

• ADD represents a spectrum of severities. Some people with ADD/ADHD are so dysfunctional they require medication or even institutionalization. The high number of people in our jails with ADD is sobering testimony to this. On the other hand, many people with ADD find it less than disabling, and some even celebrate their "Hunterness."

An increasing number of recent books and contemporary scientists point out that rarely in nature do things happen by accident. The science of Darwinian Medicine proposes, for example, that even genetically-transmitted conditions such as asthma, cystic fibrosis, obesity, sickle-cell anemia, Tay-Sachs disease, and morning sickness have evolutionary roots. All were, at various times in human pre-history, useful adaptations.

For example, when medical researchers graphed the nine-month sensitivity of a fetus to birth defects caused by its mother eating toxic foods during pregnancy, they made a startling discovery. The graph overlaid perfectly with a charting of the average reported severity of morning sickness among contemporary pregnant women. Among our hunter/gatherer ancestors, morning sickness encouraged pregnant women to eat only those meals they already knew to be safe, and to avoid experimenting with foods which may contain toxins dangerous to the fetus. While morning sickness has little usefulness now, as we hunt and gather our food at Kroger's, it's still firmly anchored in our genetic material.

Similarly, *Time* magazine ran a cover story in the August 15, 1995 international issue about Robert Wright's book *The Moral Animal*, which looks at human behavior in the context of Darwinian Psychology. The *Time* cover headlined: *Infidelity: It may be in our genes.* Even psychology is being analyzed now in the context of evolution and adaptation. Wright and other scientists and science writers point out that behaviors which may not be useful in a highly ordered and organized modern society or classroom may have been vital, during earlier times, to ensure the survival and propagation of our species.

Just as some pregnant women barely notice their morning sickness while others are bedridden for months at a time, any characteristic passed down to us through the echoing distances of spiraled DNA and ancient human history will manifest in ways that reflect the variety of human individuality. So it is with ADD. It is a complex condition, with many facets and most likely many etiologies. It certainly represents a broad spectrum of manifestations and severities.

This book, being about success with ADD instead of pathology, focuses largely on those individuals whose ADD severity has not rendered them incapable of functioning in society. Certainly they face difficulties, pain, and trials; to deny that would trivialize a dialogue which is critical to our society, and produced the need for this book. Helping individuals overcome the challenges of ADD, however, and set the course of their lives for success is the mission of this work. I will leave it to other authors to write about the spectral ends of severely pathological ADD which push some humans off the edge of social or intellectual function.

• I'm absolutely supportive of special education, medication, the psychiatric and psychological community, and the legal classification of ADD as a disability.

In summary, my goal is to re-empower people to take responsibility for their own lives. This may mean that they seek professional help or medication, or change their life situations or careers. It certainly means that people with ADD should seek out the positive, as well as acknowledge the negative, aspects of their Hunterness.

For people with ADD in today's world, life has handed them a lemon in some ways. A few will choose to drag that lemon around with them, showing it to any poor soul who gets close enough to hear their tale of woe, analyzing how sour and bitter it is. They'll squeeze it, drip lemon juice behind them wherever they go, then say, "See?? I *told* you I'm stuck with a lemon! Look at all this damn juice. Everywhere I go, this happens."

The readers of this book, however, are more likely instead to look for ways to make lemonade: to look for useful ways of viewing the situation, develop interventions that work, and get on with their lives— more successfully than ever before.

And *that* is something worth putting energy into.

After exploring the terrain of ADD, we go to the Guidebook section (Part Two), looking into some specific strategies and techniques for navigating through the land and lives of ADD.

Then we reach the third part of this book, a collection of first-person travelogues—stories told to or sent to me. These are by people who learned ways to either overcome some of the obstacles that ADD throws in their life paths, or how they use some of the unique abilities that ADD confers on people to become even more successful than "normal" individuals.

As most explorers are also Hunters (as defined in this book), these seem appropriate metaphors to frame this sequel to my first book about ADD, *Attention Deficit Disorder: A Different Perception.*

Finally, the fourth part of this book is an extensive national and international Resource Directory, with specific information, addresses, and counselors to help you on your way.

Enjoy your journey!

Part One: Maps

Let maps to other, worlds on worlds have shown,
Let us possess one world, each hath one, and is one.
> —John Donne, "The Good Morrow"
> *(published posthumously 1633)*

The first few chapters of this book give a topographic view of ADD. Where are the hills and valleys, the mountains and rivers, the high points and danger spots? As with the most useful maps, they help the reader understand the terrain, define the difference between forest and savanna, and offer some insights into the best ways through an area.

When early explorers first mapped new territories, such as Lewis & Clark's expedition across North America, or Burton's through Africa, their maps sought not only to define geographic landmarks and borders, but to explain the differences in places and the people they found there: what to watch out for, and what to stop and enjoy. "Here be monsters" is a map phrase that dates back to the Dark Ages, as early map makers warned persons following in their footsteps to be wary.

Mapping ADD involves mapping the interior territories of the human mind and brain, and so you'll find some discussion of that here. We'll look into the possible causes and significance of ADD, and the new understandings of it that the Hunter/Farmer model brings.

1

Are You A Hunter Or A Farmer?

The creatures that want to live a life of their own, we call wild. If wild, then no matter how harmless, we treat them as outlaws, and those of us who are 'specially well brought up shoot them for fun.
—Clarence Day, *This Simian World,* 1920

■ Who are the hunters?

Attention Deficit Disorder (ADD) is becoming very well-known. The popular TV show "20/20" played a segment on it twice in 1994, it's regular fare on the TV and radio talk shows, and publications from *Cosmopolitan* to *The Wall Street Journal* debate its significance on their pages. Rush Limbaugh says it's a non-disease; psychiatrists call it one of the major causes of school, work, and relationship problems in our society. Millions of children and adults are taking drugs to treat ADD, and some physicians speculate that the epidemic of cocaine abuse among America's underclass may represent an attempt at self-medication for ADD by those people who lack access to a psychiatrist.

Diseases and mental conditions often appear as fads in America, from herpes to bulimia to chronic fatigue syndrome, and skeptics therefore find it easy to dismiss ADD as only the most recent incarnation of the yuppie flu. For children struggling with schoolwork, however, or adults who have had dozens of unsuccessful jobs or relationships, ADD is far more than the latest designer disease.

Although much of the country is just now learning about ADD, and it's virtually unknown—even by psychiatrists—in most of the rest of the world, research into the condition has been going on for decades. Robert Service summed up the ADD personality in his 1907 poem, "The Men That Don't Fit In" (which opens this book), and many experts point to Ben Franklin and Thomas Edison as classic examples of people with

ADD. Franklin had over thirty careers in his life; Edison had a huge range of interests and started a vast number of experiments, many of which he never got around to even half-finishing.) ADD has been the subject of thousands of studies, many by the most prestigious scientific institutions in the world, and, for decades, has been among the most commonly-diagnosed psychiatric disorders among children in the United States.

Yet for all the research and diagnoses, all the hype and fanfare, the billions spent on diagnosis and treatment, nobody yet knows exactly what ADD is or where it comes from. "In many ways, it's a wastebasket diagnostic category," says psychiatrist Edward Hallowell. "ADD may eventually turn out to represent several different conditions. And, in some ways, for some people, it may even turn out to have advantages, including creativity and a highly adaptive style."

Advantages?

The National Institutes of Mental Health have shown that the brains of people with ADD have a different type of glucose metabolism, or at least a different rate of blood flow, from those without ADD. This only validates the neurological/physiological basis of ADD, but doesn't explain what it is, how it works, or where it came from. Similarly, researchers at the University of Chicago believe they've come close to isolating the gene responsible for ADD, but they can't say exactly how that gene affects the brain, or how or why it came to be part of our genetic makeup.

Theories abound positing neurotransmitter imbalances, frontal lobe abnormalities, blood-flow differences, and even the influence of excessive television viewing as a contributor to ADD, but, at this moment, nobody knows for sure exactly what ADD is or the mechanism by which it works.

■ Disassembling ADD

At its core, ADD is generally acknowledged to have three components: *distractibility*, *impulsivity*, and *risk-taking/restlessness*. (If you throw in hyperactivity, you have ADHD—Attention Deficit Hyperactive Disorder—which, until recently, was considered to be "true" ADD, but is now viewed as a separate condition. ADHD is the disorder that children were believed to grow out of sometime around adolescence, but it appears that most ADHD kids simply become adults with ADD as the hyperactivity of their youth sometimes diminishes.)

Distractibility is often mischaracterized as the inability of a child or adult to pay attention to a specific thing. Yet people with ADD *can* pay attention, even for long periods of time (it's called "hyperfocusing"), but only to something that excites or interests them. It's a cliché—but true—that "there is no ADD in front of a good video game."

It's also often noted by ADD experts that it's not that ADDers can't pay attention to anything: it's that they pay attention to *everything*.

A better way to describe the distractibility of ADD is to call it *scanning*. In a classroom, the child with ADD is the one who notices the janitor mowing the lawn outside the window, when he should be listening to the teacher's lecture on long division. The bug crawling across the ceiling, or the class bully preparing to throw a spitball, are infinitely more fascinating than the teacher's analysis of Columbus' place in history.

While this constant scanning of the environment is a liability in a classroom setting, it may have been a survival skill for our prehistoric ancestors.

A primitive hunter who didn't find that he easily and normally fell into a mental state of constant scanning would be at a huge disadvantage. That flash of motion on the periphery of his vision might be either the rabbit that he needed for lunch, or the tiger or bear hoping to make lunch of him. If he were to focus too heavily on the trail, for example, and therefore miss the other details of his environment, he would either starve or be eaten.

On the other hand, when the agricultural revolution began 12,000 years ago, this scanning turned into a liability for those people whose societies moved from hunting to farming. If the day came when the moon was right, the soil was the perfect moisture, and the crops due to be planted, a farmer couldn't waste his day wandering off into the forest to check out something unusual he noticed: he must keep his attention focused on that task at hand, and not be distracted from it.

Impulsivity has two core manifestations among modern people with ADD. The first is impulsive behavior: the proverbial acting-without-thinking-things-through. Often this takes the form of interrupting others or blurting things out in conversation; other times it's reflected in snap judgments or quick decisions. Another aspect of impulsivity is impatience.

A prehistoric hunter would describe impulsivity as an asset because it provided him with the ability to act on instant decisions, and the willingness to explore new and untested areas. If he were chasing a rabbit through the forest with his spear, and a deer ran by, he wouldn't have time to stop and calculate a risk/benefit analysis: he must make an instant decision about which animal to pursue, and then act on that decision without a second thought.

Thomas Edison eloquently described how his combined distractibility and impulsiveness helped him in his "hunt" for world-transforming inventions. He said, "Look, I start here with the intention of going there" (drawing an imaginary line) "in an experiment, say, to increase the speed of the Atlantic cable; but when I have arrived part way in my straight line, I meet with a phenomenon and it leads me off in another direction, to something totally unexpected."

For a primitive farmer, however, impatience and impulsivity would be a disaster. If he were to go out into the field and dig up the seeds every day to see if they were growing, the crops would die. (The contemporary manifestation of this is the person who can't leave the oven door shut, but has to keep opening it to check how the food's doing, to the detriment of many a soufflé.)

A very patient approach, all the way down to the process of picking bugs off plants for hours each day, day after day, would have to be hard-wired into the brain of a farmer. The word "boring" couldn't be in his vocabulary: his brain would have to be built in such a way that it tolerated, or even enjoyed, sticking with something until it was finished.

Restlessness, risk-taking, or, as described by Drs. Hallowell and Ratey, "a restive search for high stimulation," is perhaps the most destructive of the behaviors associated with ADD in contemporary society. It probably accounts for the high percentage of people with ADD among the prison populations, and plays a role in a wide variety of social problems, from the risky driving of a teenager to the infidelity or job-hopping of an adult.

Yet for a primitive hunter, risk and high-stimulation were a necessary part of daily life. If hunters were risk- or adrenaline-averse, they'd never go into the wilds to hunt: for a hunter, the idea of daily risking one's life would have to feel "normal." In fact, the urge to experience risk, the desire for that adrenaline high, would be necessary among the members of a hunting society, because it would propel their members out into the forest or jungle in search of stimulation—and dinner.

If a farmer were a risk-taker, however, the results could lead to starvation. Because decisions made by farmers have such long-ranging consequences, their brains must be wired to avoid risks and to carefully determine the most risk-free way of doing anything. If a farmer were to decide to take a chance and plant a new and different crop—ragweed, for example, instead of the wheat that grew so well the previous year—it could lead to tragic dietary problems for the tribe or family.

That genetic predispositions to behavior can be leftover survival strategies from prehistoric times is a theme most recently echoed in the

March 27, 1995 *Time Magazine* cover story on the brain. It pointed out that craving fat, among some people in parts of the world that experienced periodic famine, would ensure the survival of those who were able to store large quantities of this nutrient under their skin. "But the same tendencies cause mass heart failure when expressed in a fast-food world," the authors point out.

Even the genetic inclination to alcoholism may have positive prehistoric roots, according to evolutionists Randolph Nesse and George Williams in their book *Why We Get Sick*. The persistence of an alcoholic in the face of social, familial, and biological resistance and disaster, they say, reflects an evolutionary tenacity to go after neurochemical rewards despite obstacles. This tenacity may in some way be responsible for the continued growth, survival, and evolution of our species.

So the agricultural revolution brought us two very different types of human societies: farmers and hunter/gatherers. They lived different lives, in different places, and those persons in farming societies with the ADD gene were probably culled out of the gene pool by natural selection. Or they became the warriors for the society, now hunting other humans as tribes came into conflict. In some societies, such as Japan and India, this was even institutionalized into a caste system, and history is replete with anecdotes about the unique personalities of the warrior castes such as the Kshatriya in India and the Samurai in Japan.

■ Where have all the hunters gone?

If we accept for a moment the possibility that the gene that causes ADD was useful in another time and place, but has become a liability in our modern, agriculture-derived industrial society, then the question arises: why isn't there more of it? How did we reach a point in human evolution where the farmers so massively outnumber the hunters? If the "hunting gene" was useful for the survival of people with it, why have hunting societies largely died out around the world? Why is ADD only seen among 3 to 20 percent of the population (depending on how you measure it and whose numbers you use), instead of 50 percent or some other number?

Recent research from several sources point out how hunting societies are *always* wiped out by farming societies over time: fewer than 10 percent of hunting society members will normally survive when their culture collides with an agricultural society. And it has nothing to do with the hunter's "attention deficits," or with any inherent superiority of the farmers.

In one study (reported in *Discover*, February 1994), the authors traced the root languages of the peoples living across central Africa. They found that at one time the area was dominated by hunter-gatherers: the Khoisans and the Pygmies. But over a period of several thousand years, virtually all of the Khoisans and Pygmies (the "Hottentots" and the "Bushmen" as they've been referred to in Western literature) were wiped out and replaced by Bantu-speaking farmers. Two entire groups of people were destroyed, rendering them nearly extinct, while the Bantu-speaking farmers flooded across the continent, dominating central Africa.

The reasons for this startling transformation are several.

First, agriculture is more efficient at generating calories than hunting. Because the same amount of land can support up to ten times more people when farming rather than hunting, farming societies generally have roughly ten times the population density of hunting societies. In war, numbers are always an advantage, particularly in these ratios. Few armies in history have survived an onslaught by another army ten times larger.

Second, diseases such as chicken pox, influenza, and measles, which have virtually wiped out vulnerable populations (such as native North and South Americans who died by the thousands when exposed to the diseases of the invading Europeans), began as diseases of domesticated animals. The farmers who were regularly exposed to such diseases developed relative immunities. While they would become ill, these germs usually wouldn't kill them. Those with no prior exposure (and, thus, no immunity), however, would often die. So when farmers encountered hunters, they were killed off just by exposure to the Farmer's diseases.

And finally, agriculture provides physical stability to a culture. The tribe stays in one spot, while their population grows. This provides them with time to specialize in individual jobs: some people become tool- and weapon-makers, others build devices which can be used in war, and others create governments, armies, and kingdoms. This gives farmers a huge technological advantage over hunting societies, which are generally more focused on day-to-day survival issues.

So now we have an answer to the question: "Where have all the hunters gone?"

Most were killed off, from Europe to Asia, from Africa to the Americas. Those who survived were brought into farming cultures either through assimilation, kidnapping, or cultural change, and provide the genetic material that appears in that small percentage of the people with ADD.

Further evidence of the anthropological basis of ADD is seen among the modern survivors of ancient hunting societies.

Cultural anthropologist Jay Fikes, PhD, points out that members of traditional Native American hunting tribes behave, as a norm, differently from those who have traditionally been farmers. The farmers, such as the Hopi and other Pueblo Indian tribes, are relatively sedate and risk-averse, he says, whereas the hunters, such as the Navajo, are "constantly scanning their environment and more immediately sensitive to nuances. They're also the ultimate risk-takers: they and the Apaches were great raiders and warriors."

A physician who'd recently read my first book, and concluded that he saw proof of the Hunter/Farmer concept in his work with some of the Native Americans in Southwest Arizona, dropped me the following unsolicited note over the Internet:

"Many of these descendants of the Athabaskan Indians of Western Canada have never chosen to adapt to farming. They had no written language until an Anglo minister, fairly recently, wrote down their language for the first time. They talk 'heart to heart,' and there is little 'clutter' between you and them when you are communicating. They hear and consider everything you say. They are scanning all the time, both visually and auditorally. Time has no special meaning unless it is absolutely necessary (that's something we Anglos have imposed on them). They don't use small talk, but get right to the point, and have a deep understanding of people and the spiritual. And their history shows that they have a love of risk-taking."

Will Krynen, M.D., noted the same differences when he worked for the Canadian government as the doctor for several native North American tribes, and during the years he worked for the Red Cross as a physician in Southeast Asia. After reading my first book, he wrote:

"I've worked among indigenous hunting societies in many parts of the world, from Asia to the Americas. Over and over again I see among their adults and the children that constellation of behaviors we call ADD. In those societies, however, these behaviors are highly adaptive and actually contribute to their societies' success.

"Among the members of the tribes of northern Canada, such as the caribou hunters of the McKenzie Basin, these adaptive characteristics—constantly scanning their environment, quick decision-making (impulsiveness), and a willingness to take risks—contribute every year to the tribe's survival.

"These same behaviors, however, often make it difficult for tribal children to succeed in western schools when we try to impose our western curriculum on them."

But what sent humankind onto the radical social departure from hunting to farming? Few other animals, with the exception of highly organized insects such as ants, have any sort of a society that is based on anything that looks like agriculture.

J. Bronowski, in *The Ascent of Man* (Little, Brown 1973), points out that 20,000 years ago every human on earth was a hunter and forager. The most advanced hunting societies had started following wild herd animals, as is still done by modern Laplanders. This had been the basis of human and pre-human society and lifestyle for several million years.

Until 1995, the earliest hard evidence of human activity (and hunting activity at that) came from the Olduvai Gorge in Tanzania, Africa, with fragments of stone tools and weapons that dated back 2.5 million years. More recently, University of Southern California anthropologist Craig Stanford is quoted in the *Chicago Tribune* (reprinted 5/1/95 in the *Atlanta Constitution*) as saying that recent research he conducted in Africa indicates that early hominids may have been tribally hunting as early as 6 million years ago.

So for 6 million years we and our ancestors were hunters, and suddenly, in a tiny moment of time (10,000 years is to 6 million as less than 3 minutes is to a 24-hour day) the entire human race veered in a totally new direction.

The reason, according to Bronowski and many anthropologists, probably has to do with the end of the last ice age, which roughly corresponds to the beginning of the agricultural revolution. (Bronowski and most authorities place the agricultural revolution as occurring roughly 12,000 years ago.) At that time, mutated grasses appeared simultaneously on several continents, probably in response to the sudden and radical change in climate. These grasses were the first high-yield, edible ancestors of modern rice and wheat, and provided the humans who lived near where they appeared with an opportunity to nurture and grow these staple foods.

Those people with the Farmer-like patience to grow the crops evolved into the farming societies, and ridded their ranks of the impulsive, sensation-seeking Hunters among them. Those persons who were not patient enough to wait for rice to grow maintained their hunting tribes, the last remnants of which we see today in a few remaining indigenous peoples on the earth. (The Old Testament, for example, is in large part the story of a nomadic hunting tribe moving through the

wrenching process, over several generations, of becoming a settled farming tribe.)

■ The need to reduce uncertainty

Another aspect of the way ADD plays out in a cultural context could
be set in the framework of the need to reduce uncertainty in life,
referenced by various psychological theorists from Adler to Jung.

For those Hunters with a highly-variable sense of time, reducing
uncertainty in the environment takes the form of acting *now*, responding
immediately to each change in the environment. For those Farmers,
however, who experience a linear sense of persisting time, reducing
uncertainty takes the form of trying to stabilize things. These people
will, as surely as the tide, eventually try to get rid of people who like to
change things.

Thus, because Hunter-like people are the agents of change, once
the change they create is adopted by the "stables" (Farmers), this latter
group will historically isolate them, kill them off, or exile them. Britain
did this with the undesirables they sent to America and Australia, and
some schools do this socially in ghettoizing ADD children.

■ Hunters and farmers in modern society

This gives us another insight into the role of the leftover Hunters in
our modern society.

Certainly, most of society is set up to reward Farmer-like behavior.
Our schools are still based on an agricultural model of long summer
vacations left over from times past when the children were needed to
bring in the crops. Stability is cherished, but job-hopping and other
forms of social instability are viewed as alarm flags to prospective
employers or spouses.

The industrial revolution, much like the agricultural revolution,
further extended the culture-shift that caused ADD to suddenly fall
"outside the template," by introducing mechanization using repetitive
(farming) techniques. This helps explain why the "factory" model of
modern public schools so often is anathema to ADD children, and why
experience-based school environments are so useful for ADD kids.

At first glance, it would seem that being a Farmer in today's society
would be very desirable. The checkbook gets balanced, the grass is
mowed regularly, and the bolt gets put on the screw at the factory, day in
and day out.

But it's often the Hunters who are the instruments of social change and leadership. *Societies with few Hunters among them require cataclysmic events to stimulate change.*

Japanese society, for example, which had been agricultural for thousands of years, was essentially stagnant until Admiral Perry parked his Black Ships off the coast and threatened war if the Japanese wouldn't let him trade with them.

That signaled the end of a major era in Japanese society. The virtual destruction of Japan during World War II brought about the second great change in their society. It's interesting to note that in the Japanese language there's no word that cleanly translates into "leadership." The notion of standing apart from the crowd, going your own way, and challenging existing institutions is totally alien to Japanese culture.

Virtually all the major changes in that very Farmer-like society were brought about by the invading barbarians (the translation of the Japanese word *gaijin*, which also means foreigner), and happened from without.

On the other hand, the leader in innovation in the world is the United States. We invented the transistor, although the careful and methodical Japanese refined it. The same applies to radio, television, VCRs, plastics, and on and on. We even invented a form of government which is now duplicated all around the world.

And who are we here in America that we would be so innovative? We are the Hunters: the misfits of British society who were daring and brave and crazy enough to undertake the crossing from Europe to America to conquer a new land. And those Americans not descendants of the first wave of British immigrants or prisoners are the offspring of later adventurers from the rest of Europe, Africa, and Asia.

Society needs its Hunters, no matter how much it tries to suppress them in its institutions and schools. ADD Hunters like Edison and Franklin were responsible for massive social, cultural, and technological change, and even today we find a disproportionate number of high-stimulation-seeking persons among the creative ranks, in every discipline from the arts to politics to the sciences.

For example, Wilson Harrell, former Publisher of *Inc.* Magazine and former CEO of the Formula 409 Corporation, and author of the book *For Entrepreneurs Only* (Career Press, 1994) is one of America's most famous entrepreneurs. After reading the first draft of my book, *Focus Your Energy*, he wrote:

"For generations, we entrepreneurs have been asking ourselves: Was

I born this way, or was it the circumstances of my childhood that led me to the entrepreneurial life? Was it destiny or accident?'...

"[Now we know that] entrepreneurs are entrepreneurs because, down through the aeons of time, we have inherited the Hunter genes of our ancestors...

"Until I read Thom's books, I believed that entrepreneurship was inspired by an insatiable desire for freedom. It's so wonderful to know that it's more, much more. That we are born. That we are genetically bound together. That we can and will pass these incredible genes on to our children and their children's children. That, in spite of politicians and Farmer bureaucracies, the entrepreneurial spirit will live on."

Wilson Harrell views ADD as a net positive, in that it sparks the entrepreneurialism which has made our nation great.

In India there also appears to be a very different view of ADD than is conventional in the United States. During the monsoon season of 1993, the week of the Hyderabad earthquake, I took a 12-hour train ride halfway across the subcontinent to visit an obscure town near the Bay of Bengal. In the train compartment with me were several Indian business-men and a physician, and we had plenty of time to talk as the country-side flew by from sunrise to sunset.

Curious about how they viewed ADD, I said, "Are you familiar with the personality type where people seem to crave stimulation but have a hard time staying with any one thing? They hop from career to career, and sometimes even from relationship to relationship, and never seem to settle down to one thing?"

"Ah, we know this type well," one of the men said, the other three nodding in agreement.

"What do you call it?" I asked.

"Very holy," he said. "These are old souls, near the end of their karmic cycle." Again the other three nodded agreement, perhaps a bit more vigorously in response to my startled look.

"Old souls?" I said, thinking that a very odd description for what we call a disorder.

"Yes," the physician said, taking his turn in the conversation. "In our religion, we believe that the purpose of reincarnation is to eventually free oneself from worldly entanglement and desire. In each lifetime we experience certain lessons, until finally we are free of this earth and can merge into the oneness of what you would call God. When a soul is very close to the end of those thousands of incarnations, he must take a few lifetimes and do many, many things, to clean up the little threads left over from his previous lifetimes."

"This is a man very close to becoming enlightened," the first businessman added. "We have great respect for such individuals, although their lives may be difficult."

Another of the businessmen raised a finger and interjected: "But it is the difficulties of such lives that purify the soul." The others nodded agreement.

"In America we consider this a psychiatric disorder," I said. All three looked startled, then laughed.

"In America, you consider our most holy men, our yogis and swamis, to be crazy people, too," said the physician with a touch of sadness in his voice. "So it is with different cultures. We live in different worlds."

In the Hunter/warrior societies of northern India and Europe, religious rituals were developed which would teach focusing and concentration. These include saying the Rosary in the Roman Catholic tradition, with the beads serving to provide a form of biofeedback, constantly reminding the person to not allow their mind to wander. In Hinduism prayer beads called a Mala are often used, which help in Mantra meditation where a single sound (such as "Om") is repeated over and over again.

That the Hunting societies, with their culturally-ingrained prevalence of ADD-like behaviors and highly distractible people, would create concentrative religious rituals to teach them to focus makes perfect sense. Focusing is something which doesn't come naturally to their people, so it's evolved as a learned behavior in the culture.

In traditionally agricultural societies, however, the meditative techniques are quite different.

From Trungpa Rimpoche and Ösel Tensig I learned Vipassana, or mindfulness, and practiced the technique for ten to fifteen hours a day at Karme Chöling. In this Tibetian Buddhist system, the goal is not to concentrate the mind on one point, but to empty the mind and be fully aware. It's practiced with the eyes open; whenever a thought arises which may become the focus of concentration, we visualized it as a bubble we would mentally reach out and pop as we noted to ourselves that we were thinking. This released the thought and returned the mind to empty awareness.

The goal of this form of meditation is not focus, but its opposite. As Berkeley-based Chilean psychiatrist Claudio Naranjo wrote in his 1971 essay On the Psychology of Meditation, Vipassana and Zen represent "the negative way" form of meditation, and come from the East. Mantra, rosary, mandala, and prayer represent the opposite, Western "concentrative or absorptive meditation."

Thus, the agricultural societies of southern Asia, farmers for millennia with a highly focused society and people, naturally developed cultural rituals which train awareness and distractibility. These systems teach them to resist their natural impulse to concentrate their attention.

Shunryu Suzuki (1905-1971), one of Japan's most famous Zen masters, founded the Zen Center in San Francisco, which I visited briefly in the late 1960's. In the prologue to *Zen Mind, Beginner's Mind*, a collection of his talks published in 1970 by Weatherhill (New York & Tokyo), he writes:

"In Japan we have the phrase *shoshin*, which means beginner's mind.' The goal of [Zen] practice is always to keep our beginner's mind...

"Our original mind' includes everything within itself. It is always rich and sufficient within itself. You should not lose your self-sufficient state of mind. This does not mean a closed mind, but actually an empty mind and a ready mind. If your mind is empty, it is always ready for anything; it is open to everything. In the beginner's mind there are many possibilities; in the expert's mind there are few...

"So the most difficult thing is always to keep your beginner's mind...always be a beginner. Be very, very careful about this point. If you start to practice zazen, you will begin to appreciate your beginner's mind. It is the secret of Zen practice."

(That in the West we have missed this distinction between types of religious rituals and its significance when viewing context- or spectrum-disorders like ADD is largely attributable to the influence of Sigmund Freud on modern psychological and philosophical thought (i.e. Sartre, etc.). He wrote forcefully against religion and its seductions, noting that "the derivation of religious needs [come] from the infant's helplessness and the longing for the father." Carl Jung was the first psychologist of any stature to challenge Freud's view and assert that meditative practice wasn't itself an expression of neurosis, but perhaps even a potential treatment for illness. Erich Fromm later developed these ideas even more fully, but Fromm and Jung are still both largely outside the mainstream of contemporary psychotherapeutic thought.)

A view ranging from world history to entrepreneurship to religion and culture shows the distinctions between Hunters and Farmers. And we see that the institutions of contemporary Western society are rooted in the agricultural/industrial model, making misfits of Hunters. However, there's room for both Hunters and Farmers in this world, and, for both to succeed, we each must learn to honor the other, and not try to position either as being somehow superior or inferior.

■ Is ADD a "disorder"?

Viewing ADD from this historical view presents us with both risks and opportunities.

The primary opportunity is to use a model or paradigm for describing ADD that's not disease-based and doesn't imply brain damage or what many children interpret as some type of retardation. This is particularly useful for adolescents, for whom issues of self-esteem are crucial. Before any form of therapy can work, from counseling to medication, a person must have hope; this model restores self-esteem, thus empowering individuals to change.

The risk is that some in our society will use the Hunter/Farmer model as a rationale to deny help to those with ADD. "If it's not a disorder but just a difference," they'll say, "then why should we pay for special programs in our schools, and why should our insurance pay for medications and therapy?"

But acknowledging a possible source for ADD in our gene pool is not the same thing as denying the damage that ADD can do, or the challenges it presents to an individual in modern society. There's nothing incompatible with a child or adult declaring their "Hunter ancestry" and also taking medication or getting therapy. Those afflicted with sickle-cell anemia don't avoid therapy just because they're less likely to get malaria if they were to return to Africa. If any sort of an adaptation is a liability in modern society, we must treat it as such, in a straightforward fashion, without trying to rationalize about or avoid discussing it.

In this context, the Hunter/Farmer model gives us new insights into why certain medications work to reduce the "symptoms" of ADD, and provides models to restructure school and work environments to better accommodate the unique needs of people with ADD.

■ Schools & workplaces for hunters

When ADD is viewed through the lens of genetic/cultural differences, a range of school and workplace options immediately present themselves. Examination of these in actual practice shows that they work for people with ADD, further validating the concept of Hunters/Farmers (which will be treated in more detail in the "stories" section of this book). For example:

• Smaller classrooms. In most traditional hunting societies, hunting technique is taught one-on-one, and there is a tradition of mentorship (as there was in business in the early years of this century). In farming societies, however, group activities are the norm.

By shifting schools back toward the hunter/mentor model, with smaller classrooms which provide more of an opportunity for one-on-one instruction, many private schools have demonstrated that some of the problems associated with ADD in our public schools disappear. The positive results seen in the United States with "charter schools" and home-schooling further validates this concept.

• *Experience-based learning*. Techniques common in alternative school settings, such as allowing children to interrupt the teacher with questions, encouraging hands-on activities as opposed to rote learning, and not demanding that children remain in their seats for the entire day but allowing them to move around the classroom, have been demonstrated to improve academic performance among the ADD school population.

Contemporary people with ADD often complain about their inability to remember details or take care of minutiae. For example, one ADD writer complained that the Hunter/Farmer model made no sense because, he said, "If I were a hunter ten thousand years ago, I'd probably forget to take my spear with me when we left for the hunt."

This reasoning, however, ignores the different learning styles of people with ADD. If the young hunter-trainee were taken out into the forest or jungle to learn first-hand how to hunt, and thrown into life-threatening experiences, that person would learn—and remember—the tools, strategies, and systems necessary for the hunt.

When I was getting my pilot's license back in 1972, my first flight instructor took me up to 8,000 feet in a small plane after giving me classroom instruction in how to recover from a stall/spin (a deadly combination, where the plane literally falls out of the sky with its nose pointed at the ground). The instructor then put a hood over my eyes so I could only see my instruments, killed the engine, and jerked back the yoke, stalling the plane and then throwing it into a spin. The instructor then whipped the hood off my face and began to beat me over the head with a rolled-up newspaper, screaming: "We're going to die! What are you going to do? We're going to die!"

I will never forget, as long as I live, how to recover from a stall/spin.

While this is an extreme example, the moral is nonetheless clear: the more interesting and exciting we can make learning, particularly for people with ADD, the more learning will take place.

• *Partnering with Farmers*. Many companies, realizing that the majority of their sales staffs' are filled with ADD people, are creating Hunter/Farmer teams. The Hunter is responsible for going out into the field and getting the business, doing the cold-calling, and making the sale. The Farmer in the team handles the paperwork, the scheduling, and the follow-through. Many ADD executives have used this strategy for years, with their secretaries or executive assistants being their teammate. Similarly, many ADD children have succeeded in finding friends or tutors who are more Farmer-like, and who can help them learn algebra or teach them how to study.

• *Teach organizational strategies.* A common complaint about American education is that children graduate from high school (or college) knowing the year that Columbus landed on the continent, but not knowing how to balance a checkbook, how to parent a child, or how to organize their time and work.

Perhaps because these have traditionally been things taught by parents, the schools have often ignored them. But with more and more single-parent and both-parents-working families, teaching such skills in school takes on an increased importance.

People with ADD are often disorganized and cluttered, and can benefit tremendously from learning organizational strategies that teach them how to impose order and systems on their schooling or work.

• *Allocate more resources to gifted children.* Gifted children are labeled as having ADD in alarming numbers. While many of them may have ADD (and many, many ADD kids are also gifted), some authorities speculate that others are simply bored because they're already intellectually way beyond the rest of the class or the curriculum.

While the vast majority of our special education dollars are allocated to children who are struggling to keep up with their grade level, gifted children in the American public school systems receive, on average, less than 1 percent of these funds. Gifted children in public schools often find themselves in a boring and hostile environment. It's small wonder so many of them fail to sit still and ultimately become unenthusiastic about learning.

■ Should hunters take drugs?

To drug or not to drug is a complex question.

On the one hand, there are those who express concern that we've become a medication-dependent society. They point to statistics show that tens of millions of people daily take psychoactive drugs, from stimulants to tranquilizers, in search of an often-elusive functionality. (Prescription tranquilizer sales will exceed $1 billion this year in the U.S., and stimulant drug sales for ADD are close behind.) Like anorexics, they argue, people in our society have a distorted view of their own normalcy, and are obsessively searching for a psychological wellness that, like the bodies of the models in the Calvin Klein ads, is probably unattainable for the average person.

On the other hand, millions of people wouldn't be taking these drugs if they didn't experience some benefit from them. The drugs most commonly prescribed for ADD, for example, are the stimulants: methylphenidate, dexedrine, and methamphetamine, sold under the brand names of Ritalin, Dexedrine Spansules, Adderall, and Desoxyn. (In a minority of cases children and adults are prescribed tranquilizers, SSRIs, or other drugs for ADD.)

The literature of both psychology and education abound with stories showing how administering stimulant drugs to children improves grades, and how giving these drugs to adults improves relationships and workplace performance. Similarly, the most commonly-used non-prescription drug in our society (and in most societies around the planet) is caffeine, itself a stimulant.

If we accept the notion that ADD is rooted in a primitive need to hunt, and that that need is driven by an urge for stimulation, then giving stimulant drugs for ADD makes perfect sense. In the forest or jungle, the hunter (with no access to a hot cup of coffee) required the hunt to produce enough adrenaline to focus his attention, sharpen his decision-making abilities, and help him overcome risks.

In modern society, individuals with ADD often put themselves into risky situations (from business ventures to skydiving to a sexual fling) in order to recapture that adrenaline rush. Many use procrastination as a form of self-medication (the last minute panic that derives from procrastination produces the surge of adrenaline that clears the mind and refocuses the attention).

If we wanted to recreate the brain-chemistry of the hunt without imposing actual dangers or threats, drugs such as the amphetamines and methylphenidate which, in many ways, mimic the actions of adrenaline would seem to make the most sense. And, indeed, these drugs are considered both safe and effective as treatments for ADD. They don't drug the Hunter into a Farmer docility: instead, they recreate the steel-edge mental sharpness that comes with the most exciting parts of the hunt, and sustain that throughout the day.

The downside, of course, is that the *urge* to hunt is lost. It was that urge which drove our ancestors to take the risky voyage from Europe to the Americas, and which drove Ben Franklin to his many creations (from the bifocal lens to the Franklin stove to the United States of America). Today it drives the lives of many entrepreneurs, salespeople, trial lawyers, ER physicians, and pilots, just a smattering of the professions where higher-than-normal numbers of ADD adults are found.

But Ben Franklin, with his many mistresses and roller-coaster life, was often a very unhappy man, constantly searching for the formula which would allow him to get control of himself and his many distractions. (Many of his strategies to reach this were detailed in his diaries, letters, and *Poor Richard's Almanack*, such as, "A place for everything and everything in its place.") If he'd had Ritalin or Desoxyn available to him, he may have had a much more stable existence. He might have even made it beyond the 3rd grade in school, and lived a happier life. On the other hand, perhaps we would now be living in a colony of Great Britain!

■ Paradigm or science?

Whether the Hunter/Farmer model as a way of viewing ADD is ultimately demonstrated to be good science or not may be less than vital. For the moment, it provides us with a way to view this condition that leaves self-esteem intact, accurately models and predicts how and why medications are helpful, and reframes our techniques for working with Hunter-type individuals in schools, the workplace, and in relationships.

Like the (as yet unproved) electron-flow model for explaining electricity, the Hunter/Farmer paradigm allows us to get our hands around a phenomenon, to wield it to our benefit, and to empower the lives of people.

If ADD is part of our genetic heritage, it cannot be an excuse for a person's failings. It's merely an explanation, one that then provides the first steps toward overcoming those obstacles which, in the past, so often caused failure.

2

Change *Is* Possible

I found that the chief difficulty for most people was to realize that they had really heard "new things": that is, things that they had never heard before. They kept translating what they heard into their habitual language. They had ceased to hope and believe there might be anything new. —Ouspensky

■ The brain changes as we learn

New research indicates that it may be possible to substantially modify the functioning of our brains for the better, without the use of drugs. A landmark study by Lewis Baxter and Associates reported in *The Archives of General Psychiatry*, September, 1992 * demonstrates that certain types of behavioral changes can actually produce the same types of apparent brain-structure and neurotransmitter-level changes as do many drugs.

If true, and the research was certainly solid enough to make it into this peer-review journal, then the implications are staggering. It means that the way we act and perform can be modified, by us, and without the intervention of medication. It may even imply, when combined with other research, that the use of drugs to try to solve problems like ADD and OCD (obsessive-compulsive disorder) may be the least effective route, particularly long-term.

To understand how this is possible, it's first necessary to take a look at recent research into how the brain grows, works, and the varieties of the processes of learning and focusing.

---

*("Caudate Glucose Metabolic Rate Changes with Both Drug and Behavior Therapy for Obsessive Compulsive Disorder")

■ There are specific stages of brain changes—before birth and at adolescence

There are three specific stages of brain development that we all undergo, and the first two involve massive die-offs of brain cells.

The first stage is prenatal, while We're still in the womb. The brain grows explosively for the first four months of gestation, with a huge proliferation of cells called neurons. But this growth comes to a sudden stop at about four months, and a second type of cell, the cell axions (thin, long projections through which the neurons communicate) begin to travel all over the brain. They interconnect the neurons at points called synapses (a tiny gap between cells) that allow the cells to communicate.

After a few months of this, the brain is more or less fully formed and ready for the final prenatal stage: the death of billions of brain cells. No one knows for sure why this huge die-off of brain cells occurs, but most likely it has to do with nature's way of making sure there's more than enough brain matter, and then pruning back just before birth. This pruning back of brain cells continues at a very rapid rate until the baby is fully formed and ready for birth, when the essential and functional networks of the brain are in place.

After birth, the second stage begins. This is another explosive growth phase, where the neocortex, the area responsible for higher mental processes, thickens during the first three years of life, while the brain hardwires into it its other circuits. During these three years, the brain will achieve three-quarters of its adult weight, and, after age three, no new synapses will be formed. But soon a second huge die-off begins.

According to Dr. Harry Chugani, associate professor of pediatrics and neurology at UCLA, PET scans (Positron Emission Tomography) of the brains of infants and children show that they reach their maximum metabolic activity at age three. Once that peak is achieved, the number of cells, the number of interconnections (synapses), and the level of activity begins to drop. This slowing down of activity and dying off of cells stays high until about the age of nine years, and then slows down until the brain stabilizes in young adulthood.

While this process may sound "bad"—after all, who would want to know that millions of their brain cells were dying?—it's actually a "sculpting" process, producing a brain that's perfectly adapted for adulthood in the particular world or culture in which it's growing up. The dying off of brain cells could be likened to Michelangelo chipping away bits of stone from a concrete block to end up with David. The unneeded parts of the brain are discarded, and the necessary connections are sculpted, strengthened, and polished.

One vivid demonstration of this is in language. All children are born with brains fully complex enough to speak any language, from the weird "R" sounds we use in English to the varied and complex tones of Mandarin Chinese, to the harsh clicks of the !Kung bushmen. Studies show that when children learn language before the age of nine, they will be able to recover and/or speak the "unusual" sounds of that language for the rest of their life. If they continue to learn vocabulary, they'll be able to one day speak with the fluency of a native-born speaker. Even if it's a second, third, or fourth (or more) language for them, they'll be fluent if it was learned before age nine.

If one tries to learn a language after that age, however, one will never be able to achieve the proficiency of a native-born speaker. The brain cells that would have been dedicated to those particular sounds of that language have already been pared away during the childhood sculpting process of the brain. Instead, we have to use our existing brain pathways and try to modify sounds we already know, resulting in the inability of native German speakers to say "the" (there's no soft "th" sound in German) or native Chinese to say the English word "rice" (there's no "r" sound in Chinese).

This is also the reason why the vast majority of musical or chess or athletic prodigies started their training and careers as very young children. After adolescence it's possible to learn things, but nearly impossible to master them as easily as one would speak a native language. Interestingly, people who learned to competently play the piano before the age of nine will often describe the experience of expressing a new tune or sound on the piano as "speaking" or "singing." They're actually using a part of their brains, associated with that area devoted to language, that the rest of us have lost in this massive pruning process.

This process of brain-sculpting is not all bad, however. As much as it represents a loss, it also represents a gain in the ability to master the skills necessary for survival into adulthood. According to psychologist Jean Piaget, the years from twelve to adulthood represent a time of great maturation. While brain cells are dying off by the millions, children are mastering the ability to focus or concentrate their attention, to fathom abstract concepts, and to define their basic beliefs about how the world is organized and their place in it.

Our basic attitudes are so solidly formed during these few years that researchers at the University of Michigan have learned that, for most people, the political beliefs they acquire during their teenage years are the ones that they will hold for their entire lives. Similarly, as the manufacturers of tobacco can tell you (with their modern cartoon-driven advertising), habits acquired during the teenage years during this massive brain-sculpting are profoundly more difficult to shake off than those acquired after adulthood. This is best reflected in the statistic that over 60 percent of adults who smoke want to quit but say they cannot, and, of them, over 95 percent began smoking while teens or pre-teens. Smokers who started as adults have a far easier time quitting.

■ The brain organizes itself according to the type and nature of stimulation

So the process of maturing is also the process of learning, and this process is driven (or drives) massive, profound, and largely permanent changes in the actual structure of the brain.

Knowledge of this is stimulating new investigations into ways to treat such "brain disorders" as ADD, OCD, and dyslexia. For example, Dr. Michael Merzenich, a neuroscientist at the University of California in San Francisco, is an expert on how the brain becomes reorganized after being exposed to experience, this sculpting and reshaping process. He's working with Dr. Paula Tallall, co-director of the Center for Molecular and Behavioral Neuroscience at Rutgers University, to devise new techniques to overcome, permanently, dyslexia.

They've found that dyslexic children respond to sound in a slightly different fashion than non-dyslexic children, and that the difference has to do with the length of the sound. Dyslexics won't notice a short "ba" sound (40 milliseconds in average length), but if it's stretched out in speech by a computer to the length of 100 milliseconds then the dyslexic brain will hear it. They're working with this technique to re-sculpt or train dyslexic brains to recognize progressively shorter and shorter sounds until new neural pathways are actually wired in the brain to instantly recognize the 40-millisecond sound.

■ It's not so simple as "just making the change"

But changing brain wiring, even for a child, is not often easy or quick, and it's orders of magnitude more difficult for an adult, whose brain is already "sculpted." It turns out that there are two different parts of the brain that deal with new experience, the first in processing it, and the second in storing it. If the experience isn't repeated often enough, it never makes its way into the permanent "storage facility" of the brain. On the other hand, once it's in this permanent place, the "thinking" or processing part of the brain feels free to ignore the information.

The details and apparent biochemistry of this were just recently discovered in studies at the Washington University School of Medicine in St. Louis. Marcus E. Raichele, M.D., professor of neurology and radiology, says that this new mechanism in the brain that they've discovered has to do with preserving energy and helping the brain to work more efficiently than the most sophisticated supercomputers. "This study provides some insight into how the brain goes about efficiently learning to do things," he said in the January 1994 issue of *Cerebral Cortex*.

When the brain is first exposed to a new task, it uses a "novel task" circuit that's specifically designed to handle learning new things. Dr. Raichele and his team use PET scans to observe brain activity in study subjects as they did a simple word-association test: given a noun (such as "fork") they were asked to state the appropriate verb (such as "eat"). When first asked to do this task, the PET scan showed that the brains were working very hard, particularly in the "novel task" circuits.

When people were given the same list over and over, however, the brain actually became less active. After the sixth or seventh exposure to the list, people had nearly totally turned off that "novel task" part of the brain, overall brain activity had dropped dramatically, and the "autopilot" part of the brain had taken over. The switch occurred after, on average, fifteen minutes of practice for any particular task—a time that many people report corresponds with how long it takes them to memorize something using flash cards or other memorization tools.

This is the key to driving a car, eating, and other automatic tasks: we move them, through repetition, into the "autopilot" part of the brain, and thereby reduce overall brain activity, freeing that organ for other, more urgent tasks. Without this function, it would be impossible to drive a car and carry on a conversation at the same time, for example. It's also the reason why, when We're driving a familiar route but with a different-than-normal destination, we often find ourselves at the familiar destination before we realize that we forgot to divert to the new destination—the automatic brain had taken over. It requires a substantial act of will and effort to override the automatic part of the brain, and if the brain becomes distracted with another "front processing" activity, the "autopilot" will take over.

This knowledge is incredibly powerful stuff, and researchers are experimentally using it to "resculpt" the brains of people with behavioral problems such as obsessive-compulsive disorder (OCD).

Proof of that power is found in a study done in 1992 by Dr. Lewis Baxter at Stanford, using PET scans of the brain to study how changes in behavior changed activity in the brain. He and his research associates first showed how the drug fluoxitine (Prozac) could be used to reduce the severity of the symptoms of OCD.

In OCD, a person, when confronted with a "trigger," will begin to obsessively think about a certain behavior that has to do with that trigger until they finally must submit to the obsession and engage in a compulsive activity. The classic example is the person who must wash his or her hands dozens of times a day, whenever They're triggered by seeing a sink, by touching something, or by shaking hands with somebody. Other examples include "evening up" behaviors where if a person steps on a crack with one foot he must hit the next crack with the other foot. Or the overwhelming sexual response some people experience when exposed to pornography.

With the PET scan, Dr. Baxter showed how a person's brain went wildly active when exposed to a "trigger," and how this activity didn't diminish until the behavior was acted out. He also showed that when an OCD person was given fluoxitine, strong brain activity was diminished, corresponding to the observed change in behavior—the person didn't act out the compulsion as frequently.

A new type of behavioral therapy for OCD was suggested back in 1966, however, by Dr. Victor Meyer, called Response Exposure and Prevention (REP).

In REP therapy, a person is exposed to their particular "trigger," and then prevented from acting out the compulsion. In order for this therapy to be effective, it must be repeated dozens, perhaps hundreds, of times over the course of a few days or weeks. After a certain time, new neural pathways are sculpted and the OCD behavior is eliminated.

Because fluoxitine and other drugs could bring about such a rapid and measurable change in OCD behaviors, however (and, perhaps, because manufacturing and prescribing them was/is so profitable), REP therapy was largely ignored in the literature of psychiatry. The torch of interest in it was carried only by psychologists and therapists who did not have the legal ability to prescribe drugs.

When Dr. Baxter measured OCD brains before and after fluoxitine and REP therapy, he found that the changes were identical. People who had undergone a purely behavioral form of therapy had modified the way their brains were metabolizing glucose, and had experienced an identical change in behavior to those who were given the drug, but not therapy.

More importantly, though, when the drugged patients were removed from the drug, their OCD behaviors returned; when the REP therapy patients were tested months later, their OCD behaviors were still gone. With the non-drug REP therapy, they were "cured."

In reporting his experience with REP technique on a 12-year-old girl named Martha who washed her hands an average of fifty times a day, therapist George T. Lynn, M.A., C.M.H.C., of Kirkland, Washington, says:

"Three weeks into daily practice of the method, the number of hand washing episodes a day has decreased by half. By the end of the fourth week, the compulsion is down to a third of baseline. If Martha is like 80 percent of OCD sufferers who have achieved success with this therapy, this type of compulsivity will gradually extinguish and not reappear. Her mother is effusive in praise of the work Martha has done. She is greatly relieved to see the end of their ordeal.

"How and why Response Exposure and Prevention works is not known. In terms of brain function it is clear that obsessive compulsive activity is related to low levels of serotonin in "gateway" centers of the brain that screen out avoidance-approach thoughts from consciousness. The therapy may up-regulate serotonin in these centers and thus inhibit hyperactive communication of danger messages.

"Research on the etiology of depression and Piaget's work in learning theory make a strong case for the power of experience to change brain structure. It is possible that Response Exposure and Prevention therapy and the Habit Reversal protocol used in treating TS, provide a muscular and cognitive experience that is able to change serotonin levels in minute amounts in just the right neurological areas to make a difference.

"Unlike a discrete change that could come as a result of the behaviorists' habit deconditioning, these methods seem to change the whole biochemical system so that a person can generalize change to other compulsions and tics.

"The success of these therapies shows not only that we can heal daunting psychological problems but also that we have the ability to change our own brain's function and structure. This discovery is visible evidence that we have the capacity to move past genetically programmed limitations by force of will and love."

■ What does this mean for today's children?

The correlation of this work in OCD and dyslexia to ADD is clear. Numerous studies over the years have demonstrated that focusing exercises such as meditation or concentration on a particular sound, light, or image will have long-term impact on a person's attention span and ability to perform complex tasks. Proponents of EEG neurofeedback argue that their technology provides a convenient and easy way of training this type of focusing, thus resculpting the developing brains of children. And, if the OCD studies are any indicator, this may also mean that therapies aimed at teaching children and adults concentration and focusing techniques will be far more powerful and long-lasting than simply medicating them.

But stepping back from how this knowledge can be used for constructive and therapeutic purposes, let's consider for a moment its significance in the context of the milieu in which our children are growing up.

In a paper published in the Brown University Child and Adolescent Behavior Letter ("TV and Video Shape the Developing Brain" Dec. 1991, v7, n12, p1[2]), learning specialist and adjunct assistant professor at Cleveland State University Jane M. Healy points out the "plasticity" of young brains. She cites the growing body of research on how children's neurological foundations for analytic thinking, problem-solving, reading comprehension, and sustained attention are the result of "a Darwinian interaction between brain and environment determining which sets of synaptic connections are preserved and strengthened and which are weakened or lost."

This paper points out that the brain can operate on several levels, including a "responding" level and a "thinking" level. Television, because of its use of quick cuts, zooms, pans, and rapid stimulation, pushes the brain into the "responding" level—and then traps it there. All that rapid stimulation eliminates the possibility of reflection, analytical thought, intellectual challenge, or, perhaps most important, sustained and focused attention. She points out how as children's watching of TV goes up to and through the US average of twenty-eight hours per week (can you imagine a child *reading* twenty-eight hours a week?!), there's a corresponding and predictable change in behaviors. There are "shorter attention spans, diminished capacity to stick with' a problem, reduced comprehension of the complexities of language, faltering oral expression ('you know...'), and a crisis in listening abilities."

Television traps the brain in a responding state, and reduces the ability of the brain to sustain focus or concentration. Because it requires no active problem-solving or language expression skills whatsoever (even ordinary conversation requires these), "it does not develop syntactic skills, speaking and writing skills, or the ability to organize the bits of information gained." She points out that video games are similar in their effect on the brain of children, which is why they're so habit-forming to youngsters.

Similarly, Evan I. Schwartz reports in the January, 1995, issue of *Omni* magazine ("The Changing Minds of Children: Growing up in a context-free family) that there is considerable evidence that modern American children have differently differentiated brains from those of their parents or grandparents. College basketball and football coaches find that they can no longer draw circles and x's on a blackboard to represent plays: they must now show videotapes of the play being executed.

Schwartz quotes several scientists who have studied the phenomena, and concluded that watching television causes children to develop strong right-hemisphere skills, at the expense of those skills traditionally handled by the left hemisphere of the brain. These lost left-hemisphere skills include the ability to process language, and to engage in complex abstract thought.

Traditionally, when reading a book or listening to a story, a child must convert the read or spoken words into pictures in his mind. This is the core of both abstract thinking and language processing. Television and video-games, however, have given us an entirely new paradigm. Instead of having to picture the elephants in the story, the child can see them directly on the screen. And They're moving, in a lifelike fashion that a picture in a book could never do. The result is that no "translation" from words to internal pictures is necessary.

So we have now a situation where children who may have already had a genetic predisposition to "Hunter" attentional states are being trained—their brains are being sculpted—to have even shorter attention spans and to be more distractible. The normal cognitive and language skills employed even in ordinary conversation are turned off for dozens of hours each week, and the brain is being retrained not to use these functions.

Economic necessity is driving more and more parents to turn to the TV as a baby-sitter as they both must work, or must work more than one job, and there's no cultural force driving children to read or into other focusing-training activities. The growth of martial-arts schools may be an exception to this, but even many of these don't include the traditional components of meditation and concentration that are at the root of oriental martial-arts. Students want a "quick fix" and resist the idea of self-discipline and focus.

And this is not limited to children.

While the brain is sculpted intensely during the first twenty years of life, it continues to grow and change until old age and death. Animal studies on rats demonstrate that they will continue to develop increasingly dense brain tissue (synaptic connections) up to and through old age if They're in a stimulus-rich environment, but if They're kept in empty cages their brains cease to grow. According to Dr. Dale Purves, professor of neurobiology at Washington University in St. Louis, "The repertoire of our neural connections is probably never complete... New connections are apparently constructed, and old ones removed, throughout the adult years."

■ EEG Neurofeedback

Numerous studies, many done by reputable universities and published in peer-review journals, indicate that the technology of EEG (Electroencephalograph) Neurofeedback can produce measurable and positive changes in the ability of children and adults to control their attentional states.

The way EEG Neurofeedback works is that a machine monitors certain brainwaves at particular parts of the head, and then processes those brainwaves via a computer so they can be fed-back to the person hooked up to the machine. The subject may see a varying size box or line on a screen, or a sort of video game where producing the desired brainwave pattern moves the game along.

There is considerable evidence that permanent changes in the way the brain controls attentional states exists. Some in the field come close to claiming that EEG Neurofeedback can "cure" ADD and many other conditions (particularly those associated with anxiety). However, evidence of how, and to what extent, it does this is only recently beginning to emerge.

It's been well-known for years that a particular brainwave frequency, known as Theta, is associated with wandering attention and daydreaming. It's also well known that Theta can be increased in any normal person simply by increasing the level of carbon dioxide in their brains, as often happens when they relax and breathe in a shallow fashion.

Many EEG Neurofeedback experts, including Dr. Joel Lubar, Dr. Siegfried Othmar, Michael Hutcheson, and Dennis Campbell, are publicly speculating about the primary change that occurs when a person is "training their brain" with EEG Neurofeedback. The regions of the brain responsible for attention, from the cortex to the thalamus, are receiving increased blood-flow. Recent studies have successfully measured indications of this, and imply that this increase in blood flow, if repeated over

40-60 EEG Neurofeedback sessions, may be permanent, or at least very long-term.

The principal side effect of this increased blood-flow is that carbon dioxide is more efficiently removed from brain cells, and oxygen is more efficiently delivered to them. This, in turn, reduces the "daydreaming state" Theta Waves and facilitates an increase in the "paying attention state" of SMR and Beta Waves.

If this turns out to be the case, it would coincide with Dr. Edward Hallowell's assertion that one of the most effective treatments he's found for ADD is daily aerobic exercise. Dr. Hallowell goes so far as to say that in his experience, exercise may even rival medication in its effectiveness with some patients. (And, of course, one of the side-effects of stimulant-drug medication is an increase in metabolic rate and blood pressure—pumping more oxygen into, and more CO_2 out of, the brain.)

Further evidence of this comes from a study published in the January 19, 1995 issue of *Nature*. In this study, psychiatrist Wayne C. Drevets and his colleagues at Washington University School of Medicine in St. Louis hooked twenty-seven adults up to a positron emission tomography (PET) scanner. They compared the participants' brain blood-flow activity when they were told they would receive a small shock to a finger or toe, to the moment when they actually received the shock.

In a high-tech corroboration of Pavlov's work a century earlier, they found that blood flow and glucose consumption in the brain actually changed in the areas corresponding to the toes and fingers when the shock was given, and also when it was only anticipated but not given.

They went a huge step beyond Pavlov, though, in cracking open the window to the mechanism of the brain in this anticipatory process. *The brain apparently is capable of modulating or varying its own blood flow, and does so in such a precise fashion that it can actually reduce or increase blood flow to specific regions.*

It's long been known that the blood vessels of the body are similar in some ways to small muscles: they can expand or contract in response to specific stimulus. When our skin is cold, for example, the capillaries in the surface of the skin will close somewhat, reducing blood flow and thus conserving heat. When we're hot, they dilate to transport more blood to the surface so it can be cooled, producing the flushing we see from exercise or sitting in a sauna.

Apparently, this control over the ability of vessels to carry blood is very specific and, at least in the brain, very tightly controlled by the brain itself on a moment-to-moment basis. When the individuals in Dr.

Drevets' experiment merely anticipated a shock, the PET scan showed an immediate and vivid change in blood flow. These occurred in specific areas of the brain's somatosensory cortex that are associated with the shocked parts of the body or the facial muscles which would respond to the shocks with a grimace.

Does this mean that oxygenation of the brain, via EEG Neurofeedback, drugs, or exercise, is a cure for ADD? Or the corollary, that ADD is caused by diminished oxygen to the brain, or caused by training the brain to produce Theta Waves through some mechanism such as watching television for thousands of hours a year?

Nobody is credibly asserting that either of these are the case, because even after EEG Neurofeedback, or after years of daily exercise, and even after years of stimulant-drug therapy, people born with ADD are still distractible, impulsive, and restless or risk-takers.

The principal difference is that with the drugs, EEG Neurofeedback, or exercise, Hunters are more able to personally take control of their brain states. They can notice when they're becoming distracted, and bring themselves back to the paying-attention mental states that they've learned during the EEG training or while medicated, for example. And they can make the conscious decision to relax or resist impulsive thoughts.

Again, this validates the notion of genetic baseline differences between Hunters and Farmers, and even demonstrates how the brains of Hunters may have been programmed by evolution or nature to seek exercise to maintain their optimal hunting performance, whereas farming and Farmers may represent an evolutionary mutation where the brain no longer needs the body to jolt it with oxygen in order for the thalamus and cortex to feel alive.

So what to do with this knowledge from the cutting edge of 1990's science?

First, it shows us the environmental factors that may be actually destructive to the brains of our children: neglect, TV, lack of intellectual stimulation. And it demonstrates the importance of teaching languages and musical skills at a very early age, something rarely available in American schools (but very common in European schools).

It also shows us that it is possible to change any aspect of ourselves and our lives, if we're sufficiently committed to pushing through the process of change.

Creating new habits, developing new learning styles, increasing our attention span, even the previously-unthinkable eradication of obsessive and compulsive behaviors are all now in the realm of possibility.

Part Two: Guidebooks

He who, from zone to zone,
Guides through the boundless sky thy certain flight,
In the long way that I must tread alone,
Will lead my steps aright.
— William Cullen Bryant, *To a Waterfowl* (1818)

My favorite guidebooks don't just describe the main tourist sites: they also talk about the less-well-known aspects of a place. In this ADD guidebook section, we'll do the same thing.

That ADD has to do with distractibility, impulsivity, and risk-taking is well known and the subject of dozens—perhaps hundreds—of books. The difficulties that children with ADD have in school is well documented, as are the challenges that adults with ADD face in the workplace.

But good guidebooks don't just point out problems, and say: "Watch out for the pothole on 43rd Street," and "Beware of the taxi drivers who'll try to rip you off." Of course they mention the problems of a city or country, but the emphasis is on living well: what to do, what to see, and where to go to have the best time. To enjoy yourself. To be successful at having a pleasant vacation or voyage. And the best books explore terrain that the casual traveler may overlook on a cursory visit.

So the next few chapters are written as a guidebook for your voyage through life as a Hunter. They are meant to maximize your pleasure and comfort, to increase your success, and, to point out a few of the attractions you might have overlooked. Of course, I must warn you of the potholes and the taxi drivers—that's obligatory in a guidebook. But I'll take you to the next step, to the places not often visited by other books or courses, and smooth your journey as you travel.

3

Defining "Success" For Ourselves

Some men succeed by what they know; some by what they do;
and a few by what they are.

—Elbert Hubbard, *The Note Book,* 1927

■ What is success?

The last time I saw Richard Stewart was in 1991, in the Klong Toey slum of Bangkok. He was sitting on the bare wood floor of a hand-made house that consisted of three rooms. A main room downstairs, about ten by ten feet was doubled as living room and kitchen, and a smaller bedroom was upstairs. The bathroom was attached to the back of the house, with a hole in the floor over the open sewer that ran along the back of the row of attached houses. Richard's home wasn't unique; most of the slum-dwellers lived in similar fashion, and the side walls of his rooms were the walls of the houses to his left and right.

We sat on mismatched purple and brown sofa cushions, and in the background a Duke Ellington tape played from a Sony Walkman outfitted with small speakers. Bangkok is a city of some six-million souls, and over two-million lived in the slums around us. Surrounding us were the sounds of babies crying, children playing and shrieking, the deep hum of conversation, traffic, and daily activity, and the smells of raw sewage, sandalwood incense, curry and frying meat. The damp warmth of Thailand's tropical air was thick with sound and smell, and yellow-white light from the noontime sun penetrated the cracks between the mismatched boards that made up the front and back walls of the house, splashing the room with spangles of color.

Richard was a few years under fifty, tall and gangly with thinning red-brown hair, pale skin made leathery by years in the equatorial sun, and lively blue eyes. He wore kakhi slacks and a pale blue, immaculately starched and ironed—if a bit frayed—short-sleeved shirt with epaulets on the shoulders. An out-of-place Brit in Southeast Asia.

"I came here with a BBC film crew," he said, telling me how he'd left behind in England a job as a television documentary producer, a home in London, a summer house near Tunbridge Wells, a used but service-able Jaguar, and a very respectable annual income. "When I met these people in this slum, when we came to poke into their lives and produce a documentary, I was so enchanted by them that I decided to throw it all off and stay." After a few years in the slum he'd met and married a local woman, and she was today working at the local day-care center and school that Richard had helped organize.

Richard wasn't living in total poverty; in addition to his volunteer work in the slum, he'd taken a part-time job at a local radio station as the DJ for a weekend jazz show, which paid enough to buy food, clothes, and the occasional movie. In fact, most of the residents of the slum worked. They were the taxi and Tut-Tut (a local type of rickshaw) drivers, the maids and bellmen in local hotels, the guides at tourist attractions, the waiters and cooks in the city's restaurants, the laborers in local factories that made products for export.

When I commented to Richard about what a sacrifice he'd made by "giving it all up" to live among the slum dwellers, his face cracked with a huge grin. "Ah, but you have it backwards," he said, holding up a hand. "I'm now far wealthier than I was before."

"You have money in a bank account somewhere? You own land?"

"None of the above," he said. "I only own what you see here. But I'm richer than I've ever been before in my life, because every day I wake up glad to be alive and glad to be here, and I go to my work of community organizing and education here in the slum with an enthusiasm I haven't felt since I was a teenager. My life before was a rat-race: now it's meaningful. That, to me, is true success."

■ Success is not about doing: it's about being

Most of us spend so much of every day worrying about and devoting our attention to the things that seem urgent, that demand our attention and drive our days, that we miss altogether the things that are truly meaningful. Few members of our society, on their death beds, will say, "I accomplished everything I knew I should in my life: I fulfilled my purpose in being here on the planet."

Few of us have the time to even consider such issues, because we find ourselves lurching through life from one crisis to another. We're always putting out fires and dealing with externally-imposed demands, instead of deciding what success really means to us personally and then trying to achieve it.

Hunter-personality types of people are constantly confronted with the problem of doing. It seems so natural to *do something*. Because Hunters in this modern Farmer's society are so often bored and under-stimulated by their lives, they put things off until they become crises, or react to things only when they become urgent. This leads to a life filled with steady streams of urgent things that must be done, and wipes out the time for planning, thinking, and gaining insights into the core issues of real, personal success.

Yet planning is critically important. In 1906, William James wrote to W. Lutoslawski, "Most people live, whether physically, intellectually or morally, in a very restricted circle of their potential being." And, in his 1902 lecture on *The Varieties of Religious Experience*, he said, "We can...lay plans as if we were to be immortal; and we find then that these words do make a genuine difference in our mortal life."

Performance expert Leo Tonkin says that time spent planning is usually returned tenfold in improved performance. "That's why we hire architects before we begin construction of a building," he points out. "We need to do the same with every project we undertake, and with the daily events and details of our lives."

But in order to create a plan, we first must determine our priorities. To do this, we must look beyond the urgencies of the moment and examine the core nature of our *purpose*.

Purpose is the essence that must be behind our goals, and then, therefore, behind our plans to reach those goals.

When we think back on our lives, the highest and most pleasant memories we can recall often have little to do with what we were doing. Instead, they're anchored in how we were being, what state of mind we were experiencing, how we were feeling. What the sun felt like on our skin, the feeling of accomplishment, of love, or connectedness with the world around us or with other people.

These moments, when we examine them, hook us back into our sense of purpose. A teacher told me that she felt most fulfilled in front of a classroom when she hit on a topic the students were interested in, and taught it in a way that they could follow. "There's a flow there," she said, "that's hard to describe. But you feel it, and you want it more and more in your life."

Richard tied his sense of purpose into something he was doing, something that would seem to most of us as a form of service or something worthy of praise. When we deeply examine purpose, however, we discover that it exists outside those stale boundaries of doing, even outside notions of doing good in the world or having a positive impact on others.

In the winter of 1978, I spent some time at a monastery in the mountains of Vermont. In the surrounding forest were small cabins, where renunciants went to spend weeks or months in total isolation. They took no books or papers into the cabins with them, and there was no TV, radio, or telephone. Even when their meals were brought, there was no contact with another person: the trays were left outside the door, the tray-bringer knocked and left, and the person inside would wait a few minutes before opening the door to avoid accidentally having any contact with another human.

This seemed, to me, either masochistic or incredibly self-indulgent. What could a person possibly accomplish by sitting alone all day in a cabin? I expressed my thoughts to one of the monks while we were splitting firewood.

"How can a renunciant have any positive impact on the world?" I said. "Particularly if he doesn't even have books or materials to learn with?"

The older man heaved his maul through a log, cleanly splitting it with one blow. "He's having a huge impact on the world," he said, setting up another log.

"By becoming more centered? By learning to meditate and pray?"

"Nope." Another log split down the middle and fell to the ground in two clean, stove-sized pieces. "Although that happens."

"Then what is it? How is turning inward, becoming self-absorbed, anything more than just a selfish act?"

The old monk, his breath white in the clear cold air, set up another log as I stood, leaning on the handle of my maul. He glanced at me sideways and said:

"Once a young man came to the Buddha and said, 'What will I do when I attain enlightenment?'

'What do you do now?' the Buddha asked.

'I chop wood and carry water,' the young monk answered.

'Then when you achieve enlightenment,' the Buddha said, you must chop wood and carry water.'"

I watched him split another log, wondering if he wanted me to split more of the logs and lean on my maul less. When I asked him if that was what he meant, he laughed.

"Don't you get it?" he said as he swung at another log. "We're all connected. Our actions are visible, but our being is what's really important. And that's invisible. The only way we can guess about another person's being is through what we see of him, or our feelings about that person, which is their actions more often than not. But that's not what is really influencing the world. It's our being, not our actions. Whether you're feeding the hungry or chopping wood, what's really important is the place within yourself from which you do it."

"This is really esoteric," I said.

"It could be," he replied, pausing to catch his breath. "But you can make it concrete. A person who is acting out of a grounded, solid, real sense of who he is will have a force and power to his actions that a person who's just doing things to get them done won't. He'll have a more powerful and visible impact on the world. So, on the coarse level, you could say that it's not esoteric at all. But I think it goes a full level deeper than even that. Simply by his living on the planet, and existing in a way that's grounded and rooted in the core of his being, he's influencing the world."

"Because we're all connected," I said, setting up a log for him.

"Yep," he said as he took a swing. "In my tradition, I would say that we're all children of God. A Sufi might say that We're all part of the same cosmic soup. A Jew might talk about our being interpenetrated by the luminous emanations. A physicist would point to chaos theory, that a butterfly flapping his wings in Brazil could create a winter storm here in Vermont. It's all one thing, and when we discover our own being, our own purpose, we help others discover theirs, too."

So success isn't about doing successful things, or even things that will bring us success. Instead, it's about being success-full. And that comes from defining first what we want to be. Who we are. What's at the center of our lives. What excites and drives and animates us.

■ What's at the core of your life?

Many Hunters spend virtually all their time in a reactive mode: responding to emergencies, dealing with things in front of them so they won't forget to handle them later. The result is that they often go years at a time without a serious, introspective life examination. Some have told me that the last time they discussed or thought about such things was in high school or college.

If you fall into that category, consider doing this simple exercise. Fill in the blanks on the following pages, or write down the answers on a separate sheet of paper.

▪ Reality checking

• If nothing were to change in your life over the next five to ten years, and you were to continue on the same path you're following, where will you be?

_____

_____

_____

• How do you feel about that?

_____

_____

_____

• How would you feel about that if you knew that at the end of those five years you were going to suddenly die? What would you do differently?

_____

_____

_____

▪ Purpose checking

• Name three people you personally know who you most admire.

_____

_____

_____

• What do you admire about them?

_____

_____

_____

• What have been the three most fulfilling times of your life?

_____

_____

_____

• "When you think of yourself in your idealized life fantasy," what are you doing?

_____

_____

_____

• What about it is fulfilling to you?

_____

_____

_____

• What gives you the greatest pleasure?

_____

_____

_____

• What legacy do you want to leave behind?

_____

_____

_____

■ Recentering:
If you took the time to fill in answers to those questions, or gave them serious consideration, you can probably now see the areas where your sense of center, your purpose and true goals, are inconsistent with your current life situation.

You may also have some good leads to the direction you could travel in order to align your life with your life's purpose, and to then pursue job, relationship, and lifestyle directions which are consistent with your sense of purpose.

■ Success isn't accidental: it's intentional

The most important point, once the pathfinding is done and the map is drawn, is to remember that success isn't just the result of decisions. It's the result of decisions followed by actions that are sustained long enough, and repeated often enough, to re-wire the brain.

And true success is caused by change based on an understanding of purpose, built on the centeredness of our being. It begins with pain or dissatisfaction with the way life is now, then moves to determine goals, then to develop specific strategies to accomplish those goals. The final step is to then follow through on those strategies.

■ Why just setting goals isn't enough

This is why simple goal-setting often doesn't work, why motivational speeches and books rarely stick with people, and why there are so few people walking around town with a smile on their faces. Most people's lives are driven by opportunity and external circumstances, rather than purpose. And when they do set down goals, those goals are often dictated by surface considerations, such as income level or possessions.

This is one of the traps of our modern society. We're told constantly, both in advertising and through the themes of television programs, movies, and novels, that life is about winning, conquering, competing, or reaching external goals.

But it's the internal states that we must reach, not the external goals. The latter follow the former, not the other way around. As Ram Dass says, "Wherever you go, you take your same head with you."

And this is particularly important for those of us who have the Hunter personality, because We're so easily stimulated and driven by challenge, adventure, competition. All those aspects of external goals very often simply distract us—sometimes for our entire lives—from considering or reaching our purpose.

4

The Greatest Enemy of Success: Procrastination

We are always getting ready to live, but never living.
— Emerson, *Journals*, 1834

Jokes about procrastination abound. The Procrastinators Society issued, in January 1995, its predictions for the year 1994: they were uncannily accurate, of course, implying some odd upside to procrastination. On the other hand, the society has never successfully had an annual national meeting, because everybody puts off their planning of attending the thing to the last minute, by which time it's already over or been canceled.

In small doses, procrastination can be cute. It can even be useful. One of the time management strategies that's often taught to businesspeople is to only read your mail once or twice a week, and then answer it all at once. A similar strategy is to never return a call the first time, or never to take calls when they come in, but to batch them together for a day or two. Then, like the mail, allocate an hour or two to return them all at once. The rationale for the former strategy is that most calls are about "problems" that will simply go away if they're ignored, and the latter is a way of concentrating effort on one thing at a time.

But chronic procrastination, the type that permeates every part of our lives, is a different thing and can be very destructive. It's part of the suggested diagnostic criteria for ADD in adults proposed by Drs. Hallowell and Ratey, and is a constant source of difficulty for virtually every Hunter I've ever met.

▪ Why do we procrastinate?

One of the more widely-accepted theses about ADD is that the hyperactivity often associated with it is not the result of the person being in an over-aroused state. While that's what it looks like from the outside, as we noted earlier, more and more scientists are now postulating that the person is *under-aroused*, that they feel like they're slipping away, drifting off, and having a hard time focusing on the events or details of the moment. They possibly even may feel like they're drifting away from experiencing living at that moment.

In response to this under-arousal of the brain, they behave the same way a non-buoyant swimmer would: they periodically lurch up through the surface of arousal to gasp a deep breath of air. These lurches up through the surface of arousal we see as hyperactive behavior: the person makes an inappropriate remark, jumps up and paces around, starts a fight, provokes someone, makes a joke, speaks out of turn, or somehow creates a crisis.

But none of it's coming from their being over-stimulated in the first place—instead, it's the result of their being under-stimulated. These eruptive behaviors are attempts to bring on an adrenaline surge that will shock the brain into awareness, wake them up, and give them the few moments of focus that's necessary to re-orient them.

This also may explain why so many children and adults with ADD are sugar junkies. Sugar gives the brain a jolt, since it's the raw material that the brain runs on. That jolt pushes them up and through the arousal surface that they feel just above their heads. The unfortunate part is that sugar jolting usually leads to sugar crashing, as the blood sugar is re-balanced by the pancreas and drops back to normal (or, often, even slightly below normal) levels.

It also explains an oddity I noticed when collecting personal stories from Hunters for this and previous books. A surprising number of people (usually requesting anonymity) commented that they were concerned that perhaps they were sex addicts. One woman commented that she masturbates, on average, three to five times a day. Others told tales of promiscuity that they felt helpless to control. And few had any psychological or historical reason to explain it. They weren't sexually abused as children, and felt themselves to be largely normal in most other facets of their lives.

But if an orgasm produces a burst of adrenaline and therefore brings the person to awareness and consciousness, then this, again, confirms this hypothesis. The sexual experience is just another form of stimulation that brings them to a feeling of aliveness. In fact, one police officer and Vietnam veteran wrote that, "I feel most alive when I'm making love: the only other thing that even comes close is when I'm in a firefight."

Joseph Campbell wrote, in *The Power of Myth* (1988): "People say that what we're all seeking is a meaning for life. I don't think that's what we're really seeking. I think that what we're seeking is an experience of being alive, so that our life experiences on the purely physical plane will have resonances within our own innermost being and reality, so that we actually feel the rapture of being alive."

So if all this is symptomatic of a person being chronically under-aroused, then procrastinating as a way of life makes perfect sense. If we put off things until they're a crisis, then that crisis itself provides the adrenaline, the panic, the rush that brings us to awareness and aliveness and allows us to do the work, often in an extraordinary fashion.

This also fits in well with the Hunter/Farmer theory of ADD. The reason the Hunter is out in the woods in the first place is because he's bored and under-aroused: he wants something to hunt in order to get the juices flowing. When confronted by prey, or a predator, he then experiences that moment of aliveness and shifts into a state of hyperfocus to pursue the game. The "attentional deficit" vanishes, and is replaced by an attentional surplus, as he races through the forest or jungle, spear in hand, chasing after his lunch.

The cat is a good analogy from the animal kingdom that most people can relate to, although just about any of the predatory animals will do. A young housecat roams around the house, bored silly, looking for something to play with. It chases things, pokes into corners, and gets into everything. (Remember the cliché, "Curiosity killed the cat.") But if you've ever seen a cat that's found game, standing stock still near a mouse hole or moving slowly through the grass, you are seeing a totally different attentional state. The cat has shifted from being highly distractible, in an open awareness state, to a state of total focus and concentration so intense that if you make a noise she will completely ignore you.

■ Overcoming procrastination

So, assuming for a moment that procrastination is a type of self-medication, a way of pumping up our brain's neurotransmitters, then how do we overcome it? While it's occasionally useful, most people would agree that living in a state of constant deadline panic is less than desirable. It often leads to substandard work because we don't have the time to go back and do the proofreading or double-checking or careful thinking that might have produced a better product or project had we built in enough time to do the job right.

One solution is to stick with a line of work that provides the constant adrenaline jolt, and doesn't require procrastination to bring it about. Emergency room personnel in hospitals, for example, often describe how much they love the atmosphere of crisis that surrounds "incoming wounded." Every patient is new and different, and everyone is in crisis, be it a gunshot wound, an accident, an overdose, or an unknown problem that's life-threatening.

Combat personnel have described the near ecstasy that they experience when in a fire-fight: Hemingway wrote about it, as have hundreds of others over the centuries. War correspondents for news organizations have a special glow in their eyes when they're on the TV screen describing the incoming missiles that we hear exploding in the background.

An old pilot's cliché is that flying means hours of boredom punctuated by moments of sheer terror. If you pick up any of the popular magazines for and about pilots, though, you'll see that the majority of the first-person stories dwell on those moments of terror. That's where the juice is—where the aliveness in being a pilot is found. And when the subject of ADD was brought up in a pilot's discussion on CompuServe, there was a virtual avalanche of pilots self-diagnosing, and then arguing about whether it was a liability or an asset in the cockpit.

Wilson Harrell, founder of the Formula 409 Corporation and former publisher of *Inc.* Magazine, enthusiastically and proudly points out that he's a Hunter. When I asked him how he dealt with procrastination, he said that he'd organized his life so that the things that he'd normally procrastinate about—the paperwork and taxes and correspondence—were done by other people.

"That's why you hire assistants and secretaries," he said. And then he's free to make his living writing (which he says gives him that high-stim jolt...as it does me), giving speeches (another good source of adrenaline), and, now in his 70's, flying around the world as a consultant to businesses with his new Total Quality Entrepreneurship program.

Like the people in the emergency room, or the men who volunteer for the riskiest combat missions, or the cops who walk the beat in the worst parts of town, Harrell has organized his life and his work to keep his stimulation level high.

After all, if you love your work and are stimulated by it, why would you ever procrastinate?

So much procrastination is caused by simple mismatches, people taking on responsibilities that they really aren't suited for. They assume jobs that require farmer-type mentalities, and then find themselves in life situations that lack the regular stimulation to keep their heads above water.

■ Find a coach to hold you to deadlines

Thomas Edison was a brilliant inventor, but he probably qualifies as one of the world's worst businessmen. He kept poor records, made impulsive decisions, and hated the details of business. In his day there was only the tiniest fraction of the red tape that modern businesspeople must wade through, but even that was enough to drive him to take in a series of business partners to handle the details while he went back to his beloved inventing.

This demonstrates the value of having a preceptor or coach.

When you consider the Catch-22 nature of procrastination and its possible solutions, the value of a preceptor becomes obvious. Consider:

• The situation is not yet a crisis, so it's not interesting.

• Because it's not interesting, we can't build up enough enthusiasm to want to dive into it.

• So we put it off until it's a crisis, and then we do it at the last minute.

• But when it's done at the last minute, it's often (usually!) not done as well as it could be.

While this strategy may work for hunting, combat, or emergency room surgery, where there are few other options than to react to things as they happen, it's a lousy way to do the taxes, write a report, or design a sales presentation. And even the surgeon in the ER would tell you that she might have done things differently—and perhaps better—if she wasn't under the deadline of the patient's drifting near death.

So many solutions to procrastination fall under the umbrella of creating stimulation *now*, rather than later.

■ Creating short jobs

A final strategy for overcoming procrastination is to break big jobs into little pieces. In the stories from individuals which make up the back of this book, you'll find several examples of this, from writing books to doing homework. If you know that after about fifteen minutes on a boring job you begin to drift off, then take that two-hour job and break it into eight parts. Do each part at a different time. While this is counterintuitive to the binge-at-the-last-minute-to-get-the-rush strategy that many Hunters have lived their lives by, it can be learned and is a powerful way to overcome procrastination.

5

Learning How to Handle Criticism and Self-Criticism

It is much easier to be critical than to be correct.
—Benjamin Disraeli speech, Jan 24, 1860

■ Learn from criticism...and then let go of the blame

One of the most common and recurring strategies that successful Hunters tell about is how they've learned to handle criticism.

A successful ADD entrepreneur tells the story of how devastated he was in a high school presentation that he'd spent the better part of two months on for English class. He read dozens of books, dug out arcane facts, sifted through quotes and stories and information, all to find what he thought was the absolutely perfect summary to make his point. With great enthusiasm he pulled an all-nighter, writing the final paper, and marched off to school the next day with his head high and the smell of academic victory in his nostrils.

At two o'clock he walked into his English classroom and marched up to the teacher's desk, the paper in his hand. "Here it is," he said, and handed it to her with a dramatic flourish.

She took one glance at it, leaned over the side of the desk, and dropped it into the wastebasket. "You didn't double-space it," she said. "When are you going to learn to read the directions?"

Stunned, he began to protest, to tell her about the hours of work he'd done. She shook her head, as if shaking his words out of her ears, and interrupted him, saying, "You have to learn how to do things right. This will be a good lesson for you. I'm giving you an F for that paper, and there's no appeal because today was the last day you could hand it in."

He went home that night and, at the ripe old age of fourteen, cried himself to sleep.

"I learned two important lessons from that experience," he told me, twenty years later. "The first was that I needed to slow down, to force myself to read directions. In that regard, it was probably a positive experience. But it also almost destroyed my commitment to her, to the class, to the school, and to any future academic achievement. And that was where I learned my second, and most important, lesson: When you fall down, stand back up, dust yourself off, and carry on."

"That sounds easy," I said, "but how do you do it? How could you keep from being angry with her, from blaming her, or, for that matter, from blaming yourself?"

"I have a picture in my mind," he said, "of a man who's walking down a dusty rural road. He trips on a stone and falls, face-first, into the dirt. And then he reaches over to the side of the road, grabs a stick, and begins to beat himself over the head with the stick, yelling at himself about how stupid he was to trip and fall. Between these comments, he's cursing the stone for being there and blaming it for tripping him.

"That's absurd, isn't it? But it's just what many people do. When I imagine that picture, and see how absurd it is to wallow in self-blame, I feel empowered to get on with my life."

Unfortunately, the "absurd" behavior that this entrepreneur described is just what so many people do—particularly those who've spent their lives feeling like they've never quite lived up to their potential. They respond to criticism first by blaming the critic, and then by beating themselves up. They rationalize the former by taking a debating position, finding flaws in the criticism or the critic, and then rationalize the latter by telling themselves that if they beat themselves up emotionally they'll "learn from the experience."

In real life, it rarely works that way. People who pursue this strategy instead just end up bruised and ineffectual, paralyzed by fear of criticism, or by the damage they do to themselves in the name of lesson-learning.

So how can we best handle criticism?

■ The first step is to examine the criticism to see if there's any truth in it.

Usually there is some truth to criticism, and if we can separate out the kernel of truth from the emotional baggage associated with it, we can often learn something useful.

For example, when my first book about ADD was published (*Atten-*

tion Deficit Disorder: A Different Perception), one reviewer wrote a scathing and sarcastic commentary about it. While much of the commentary was off-base or factually inaccurate, he did point out one very real deficiency: my premise of Hunters and Farmers was based in anthropology, but I hadn't gotten the endorsement of any anthropologists or cited any anthropological texts in my bibliography.

So, deciding that he had a point, I sought out people with the requisite knowledge of hunting and farming cultures. I first found Will Krynen, M.D., who, while not an anthropologist, was one of the few medical doctors in the world to have spent years of his career as the physician to an indigenous hunting society, the one of the last of the Native American tribes of Canada. Every year he followed them with his small airplane as they made their annual 1000-mile trek following the caribou they hunted. He told me that when he first arrived, he found that the previous doctor had diagnosed 100% of their children as ADD, and had put their entire school on Ritalin. That was pretty good validation to him of the Hunter/Farmer theory.

Then I met cultural anthropologist Jay Fikes, PhD, who wrote the famous (in anthropological circles) book debunking Carlos Castenada. Dr. Fikes obtained his PhD by studying the few remaining native American hunting societies of the American southwest and northern Mexico. After reading my book, he wrote a ringing endorsement of it, saying that his experience taught him that hunting and agricultural societies were profoundly different, and that the individuals who make them up are profoundly different. There is a startlingly high percentage of what we would call ADD among the members of native hunting tribes.

So that criticism of my book, as sarcastic and stinging as it was intended to be, nonetheless led to a strengthening of the science behind what I'd first presented only as a model or a paradigm. It improved my book and gave new credibility to the thesis that people with ADD really are descendants of ancient hunting societies.

■ **The second step to handling criticism is to let the pain in it roll off your shoulders.**

After learning what we can from our critics, we have to let go of the emotions that criticism arouses in us.

During the Civil War, Abraham Lincoln was attacked by every armchair general in the world: every move he made, every speech he gave, every law he proposed was mercilessly torn apart by his critics. Yet Lincoln endured. When someone told Lincoln that his Secretary of War, Edward M. Stanton, had called him a "damn fool" for one of his orders, he went to Stanton to ask what was foolish about the order. Stanton made his case, and Lincoln agreed, rescinding the order. And then he took the second step: he let the pain of being publicly called a "damn fool" roll off his back. To use the entrepreneur's metaphor, Lincoln stood up and dusted himself off and continued walking along the road.

Lincoln, reflecting on this need to carry on regardless of the emotional sting of criticism, wrote: "I do the very best I know how—the very best I can; and I mean to keep on doing so until the end. If the end brings me out all right, then what is said against me won't matter. If the end brings me out wrong, then ten angels swearing I was right would make no difference." (These words were so inspiring to Winston Churchill that he had them framed and hung in his office during World War II.)

So whether the criticism originates from others or from within us, the two-step process to deal with it is to first learn from it, and then to let go of it, turning the emotions associated with blaming into the process of learning.

Stand back up, dust yourself off, and get back to walking down that road of life!

6

Hunters Meet the Self-Help Movement: On Being a Professional Victim of ADD

The self-help tradition has always been covertly authoritarian and conformist, relying as it does on a mystique of expertise, encouraging people to look outside themselves for standardized instruction on how to be, teaching us that different people with different problems can easily be saved by the same techniques. It is anathema to independent thought...
> —Wendy Kaminer, *I'm Dysfunctional, You're Dysfunctional*
> (Addison-Wesley, 1992)

When I was the executive director of a residential treatment facility in New Hampshire, I worked with a wide variety of psychologists, psychiatrists, and therapists. One man, in particular, was amazing to me.

Dr. Charles, as he was called by both the children and staff (that was his first name) once confided to me that the ethics of his practice were his greatest impediment to financial success. "My goal is for my patients to get better, so they no longer need me," he said. "That doesn't do much for long-term financial security."

With the explosion of media attention directed at ADD, there's a corollary increase in counselors, psychiatrists, psychologists, therapists, and even fortune tellers (I met one in Atlanta, where it's legal and licensed, who says she specializes in ADD!), who are encouraging an odd form of dependency.

Because ADD is a lifetime diagnosis, it can also represent a long-term income stream for a practitioner treating it. The voices of people pointing this out—as a way of discrediting ADD and the people who work in the field—are growing. From Rush Limbaugh to the editorial pages of *The Wall Street Journal* to people within the insurance industry, critics of the ADD diagnosis are becoming more vocal. At the same time, a growing number of authors and speakers on the topic of ADD are becoming more adamant in their assertions that ADD is a crippling disability, about which little can be done beyond medication. In a speech to a group of ADD adults, a psychologist pointed at the audience and said, "You people have an illness. You're sick. Don't you get it? Why do you think we call it a 'disorder'?"

In the midst of it all, though, are the people themselves with ADD. Many of them are receiving the signal, sometimes from people who have a financial interest in promoting that point of view, that they are damaged, defective, deficient, and disordered. In short, they are victims. And, for some people, this is just what they want to hear.

"Eureka!" they say, throwing the notion of personal responsibility or self-improvement to the wind. "I'm a victim of an organic brain dysfunction!"

■ Take responsibility for yourself

At the same time, an increasing number of prominent therapists are taking Dr. Charles' point of view toward ADD. Instead of fostering a lifetime of dependence, they're helping people define a specific therapeutic goal, working toward that goal, and just as in internal medicine, stopping the treatment when the goal is reached.

One example is the "SBT" (Solution-oriented Brief Therapy) approach espoused by students of Milton Erickson and brought into public awareness in 1995 by the best-selling book *Fire Your Shrink* by psychotherapist Michele Weiner-Davis. One of Weiner-Davis's key bits of advice is: "Choose a perspective that offers a solution." That's a great idea, and it's largely what this book is about in the context of ADD: choose perspectives that offer insights, solutions, and a path to the future you want.

Another example comes directly from the world of ADD, and involves one of the most prominent psychiatrists in the field, Dr. Edward Hallowell. Before he became famous from his appearances on network television and co-authoring the best-selling *Driven To Distraction*, Hallowell was the therapist chosen by a good friend of mine, Dave deBronkart. Dave recalls that Hallowell's emphasis was on understanding and on producing results:

"After a few months of regular (but not weekly) visits, one day I came in for my appointment and he told me he didn't want to see me as a patient any more," deBronkart says. "I wondered if I was a 'bad patient' or if he thought I was 'cured,' but, no, he said it was neither. Rather, he felt that he'd done as much for me as he could by way of imparting information, that I now had a good understanding of ADD and what it and I were all about, and that it was now my duty to go out in the world and teach others what I'd learned." (Dave deBronkart is doing just that, by the way: he's one of the most articulate and well-informed laymen who speaks on the topic of ADD, and his speeches are electrifying.)

On the other end of the spectrum is Angela, a 31-year-old aspiring actress in New York City who cornered me after a speech, wanting to tell me her life story. Angela's parents are wealthy, and she visits her therapist every week for her ADD, and has for over ten years. She won't date a man, make a career move, or even go out of town on vacation, without first discussing it at length with her therapist. Angela is stuck. By contrast, deBronkart is unstuck.

And, since her ADD gives Angela such a convenient excuse for all the problems of her life, it liberates her from the need to do anything for herself. "Why bother trying to learn to pay attention," she asked when I offered to teach her some of Harry Lorayne's memory techniques, "when I'm so ADD?"

Why indeed?

Some people say, "Look at all I've been through—I'm a mess, and if I never make anything of my life, it's understandable!"

And then there are those who decide, instead, to get on with their lives.

They got on with their lives

I remember Jonathan. He came into the Salem residential treatment facility where I was executive director when he was fourteen years old. Three years earlier, he'd seemed a normal boy, if not a bit too bright and extroverted for his teachers' liking. His parents one day had found a marijuana plant on his bedroom windowsill. Not knowing what to do, they called the police, who hauled Jonathan off to the juvenile detention facility.

From there, Jonathan was placed in a foster home, but he was now angry, and determined not to give in to what he thought was an inhumane system. He ran away. The police caught him and put him in another foster home, and he ran away again. This time when they caught him, they took him to the state mental hospital for observation. The psychiatrist there diagnosed him as suffering from oppositional-defiant disorder with possible schizoid tendencies, and ordered him institutionalized. For the next two years, Jonathan was in virtual solitary confinement. He spent half of one year tied to a bed, and during the entire time of his institutionalization was daily given huge doses of the powerful tranquilizer Thorazine, which reduced him to a near-vegetative state.

When Jonathan was referred to our program at the age of fourteen, we were told that he was possibly psychotic, that he needed powerful anti-psychotic drugs, and that he might be mentally retarded because all the recent tests done on him showed that he functioned at about an eight-year-old level.

The day Jonathan came into the program, our psychiatrist took him off the Thorazine. At first Jonathan was angry and defiant, but when we learned his history, we understood the source of his anger and worked with him to learn to deal with it. The Thorazine left him with small seizures, a condition called Tardive Dyskenesia, which is a long-term side-effect of having used Thorazine, and, for many people, is permanent. His tongue would leap about his mouth, he'd twitch, and occasionally he'd have a full-blown seizure and throw himself to the floor. Over a five-year period, these gradually lessened to the point where he could disguise them.

Jonathan, it turned out, has a near-genius IQ, as well as Attention Deficit Disorder.

Four years later, still living at Salem, he graduated from the local public high school at the top of his class. He came back several years later to visit, and even wrote a short piece for one of our brochures, as a "graduate" of the program. And he never, ever, thought or said he was destined to be a failure because of his past or his ADD.

Jonathan was a fighter, not a victim. He chose a different path from that of the many people who blame their boss, their spouse, their parents, and, of course, their ADD, for every failure in their own lives.

In Bogotá, Colombia, I met Juan, who was the driver for Elizabeth Blinken, the woman who started and runs the Salem program there. He looked like he was at least half South American Indian, and was well-dressed in slacks and sweater, with a friendly smile and dark brown eyes.

Over dinner during one of my first trips there Juan told us his story. When he was three years old there was a political uprising in the area where he lived and soldiers (he doesn't know if they were government or rebels) came into his house. They took him and the other members of his family into the living room and tied them up, then raped his ten-year-old sister and mother. Other soldiers came and raped them again. When his father protested, one of the soldiers shot him in the chest. It took his father nearly an hour to die, Juan said. Later in the day, the soldiers methodically went through the village and killed every person. Through some bizarre morality that only they understood, they didn't kill the very youngest children, and so Juan was spared. He stayed in the house with his dead parents, sister, and two older brothers, for two days until word of the massacre reached a nearby town and he was rescued.

His aunt took him in, but she soon tired of surrogate motherhood and took him to a state-run orphanage, telling him she'd be back for him in a week. She never returned.

At age seven, Juan escaped from the hellish orphanage, where the children lived in huge rooms and were regularly beaten and raped by the guards. For the next two years he lived as a street child, begging and stealing. He managed to avoid the "hunting clubs" of middle-class teenagers, soldiers, and off-duty police who go out at night in much of overpopulated South America with rifles and shoot street children for sport, often even taking pictures of their "trophies."

But finally, when he was nine, Jose was captured by police and put into another orphanage. Here he was "adopted" as the "foster son" of a family in Germany through one of the many programs where people send a monthly stipend of ten or twenty dollars to a child. This stipend allowed him to attend school for the first time, and he ended up graduating first from high school, then from college with honors, and finally receiving a graduate degree in mechanical engineering.

Juan was not enthusiastic to tell his story; Elizabeth brought up the details after he had spent a day playing tour-guide and showing me around Bogotá. He acknowledge the events of his life, but when I asked him how he felt about it, he shrugged and said, "At least I survived. So many here do not survive, and most of those I knew as a child are now dead. I worked hard to stay alive, and I was lucky."

Juan had a legitimate right to put living and growing on hold and claim victim status, but he chose instead to move forward with his life.

It's rare that I meet an person who was diagnosed with ADD as an adult who doesn't feel frustration and anger about all those lost years, and the pain of growing up as a misunderstood Hunter in a Farmer's world. Yet a quick recollection of Juan's story, or Jonathan's, will help put that pain in a more useful perspective.

Don't be a victim.

Many adult ADD support groups I've visited resemble AA meetings, and some I've seen are run by people who encourage attendees to yell out, cry, or make a great public drama about the pain of their lives with ADD.

It's so easy to fall into the trap of becoming a victim of ADD. In modern America, it seems, everybody wants to be a victim of something. It's so easy, so convenient, so comforting to know that our failures and weaknesses are not because of "us," but caused by a "them.". Being a victim has even become an excuse for murder, as we saw in the initial acquittal in the admitted shotgun slaying of their parents by the Menendez brothers.

But taking the victim position may be the least effective way for a person to deal with their own ADD, and ADD is not alcoholism or the result of abuse.

At a conference in Santa Fe, New Mexico, put on by Michael Hutchison, author of *MegaBrain*, I met with a psychologist who told the interesting story of one of his patients, a man with all the symptoms of ADD who'd been through the Battle of the Bulge in World War II.

He saw virtually all of his closest friends die, and his best friend from high school, who'd joined the army together with him, died in his arms. Certainly, one would think, this man had every right to claim victim status and to even walk around with the shakes or a pint of gin in his hip pocket.

But that wasn't how he viewed it.

"We were working on finding reservoirs of strength that could be drawn from past experience," the psychologist said, "and, for this man, that experience was one of the times in his life when he was the strongest. So now, when he's confronted with difficult emotional experiences or the frustrations of his ADD, that is the experience he brings back to mind, his time during that battle, as the thing that will empower him and pull him through. Because he survived, and was able to tell himself that he survived not because he was a coward or ducked bullets, but because he did the very best he could, and perhaps because his luck was just a little bit better that than of some of his friends. He viewed that battle as a positive experience, in retrospect."

This story illustrates the point of this chapter: *the stories we tell ourselves about the significance of things that happen to us usually create the core meaning of those experiences for us.*

In certain middle-eastern cultures, it's a horrifying and embarrassing experience for a woman to have strangers see her bare arms. If you were to rip off her shirt sleeve, or roll it up to look at her elbow, you could create emotional trauma that could last a lifetime.

In American culture, as a contrast, people walk along the beach in bikinis and swimming trunks without feeling any shame or humiliation.

Yet those Americans who wear swimsuits at the beach may feel negative emotions if they were forced to remove their bathing suits altogether, a state of (un)dress that's "normal" on many of the beaches along the southern coast of France, Monaco, Italy, and Yugoslavia.

So, as much as we have the raw experience of life itself, what we ultimately carry from our living are the stories we tell ourselves about it.

This is not to say that the trauma of growing up with undiagnosed ADD is not painful or even destructive. In a recent EEG Neurofeedback training program for physicians that I attended, there was a lot of discussion about the value of using alpha/theta brainwave training to bring up traumatic memories, and then using it to "discharge" the emotions associated with those memories. This is used as a form of therapeutic personality integration and ego-strengthening.

What was most interesting to me was that virtually everybody in the room (most were psychiatrists or psychologists) had traumatic memories themselves, ADDers and non-ADDers alike, yet all of us were from basically "normal" middle-class families, without histories of severe abuse. Even without the life experiences of Juan or Jonathan, we all had terribly painful experiences we could point to in our past.

How do we deal with difficulties?

The bottom line is that life itself is difficult. And this is particularly true for the Hunters among us, who have suffered through years of trying to fit into Farmer-style schools or jobs, and experienced years of frustrating failures in their efforts.

Nobody gets out of life unscarred, and we all have times and events we can point to wherein we experienced great pain and stress, often as a consequence of ADD.

The issue, though, is how we process those events.

Do we nurse them and lick them like a dog with a wound, causing them to blossom and fester? Or do we choose to resolve them (through therapy, EEG Neurofeedback, NLP, Ritalin, reframing, learning new strategies, etc.), and move on with life?

And, perhaps more important in the broader context, how does our culture, and how do our professionals, encourage us to deal with things like growing up with ADD in a non-ADD world?

Some people reacted to the initial proposal of my Hunter/Farmer model negatively, because they believed it deprived them of their right to claim victim status. More than one person said, "I'm not a Hunter: I'm a victim of a neurological disorder!" and this debate has persisted on CompuServe and the Internet for years since the publication of my first book. These people want a "disease" to be responsible for the way they are, and if that disease is treatable by the medical establishment, so much the better. When they're still disorganized and late for meetings, they can then blame it on the medications not being properly balanced, or on the therapist not yet having completely worked his or her magic, or perhaps even on the therapist's incompetence.

This is where we see the empowerment of individuals inherent in the Hunter/Farmer model, and the disempowerment intrinsic to the words "deficit" and "disorder."

Dr. Lynn Weiss, one of the most insightful writers in the field of ADD, shared with me an important insight. In her opinion many people with ADD are as harmed by years of living undiagnosed and misunderstood as they are by the ADD itself. This includes being told that they, to use Kate Kelly and Peggy Ramundo's brilliant book title, are "lazy, stupid, or crazy." In some cases, Dr. Weiss said, the harm of being misunderstood is greater than the "problem" of the ADD.

In a recent dialogue on the Internet, a teacher with little patience or tolerance for kids with ADD enumerated a long litany of problems she'd encountered teaching ADD/ADHD children. These included defiance of authority, poor test-taking skills, homework failures, and the fact that many of her ADD kids were performing below their grade levels. She blamed this all on the children. And, from her personal experience and in the realm of her perceptual reality, many of her points were correct.

But was it the fault of the children, or of the system they were thrown into which was not appropriate for their learning style?

Pete Wright, the attorney who successfully argued the Shannon Carter case before the U.S. Supreme Court thus forcing public schools to take financial responsibility for educating ADD children, told me of one of his cases. (Pete, himself, by the way, has ADD...and is one of the most successful attorneys—and human beings—I've ever met.) A young boy had been failing for years in the public schools, yet he had a very high IQ and, when he was put in a summer program designed to meet the learning style of ADD kids, he jumped several grade levels in just a few months.

Pete's wife, Pam, a psychotherapist who spent years working with Vietnam veterans, is very familiar with Post Traumatic Stress Disorder (PTSD). When she evaluated this little boy, Pam found that he was exhibiting many of the classic symptoms of PTSD, including sleep disturbance, irritability, temper outbursts, difficulty concentrating, frequent nightmares, and fearfulness. Yet he hadn't been in a war: nobody had beaten or shot at him—there was no history of an actual traumatic event or experience that involved death or fear of death which could lead to a diagnosis of PTSD. He had model parents. So what caused the trauma?

"It was his failure in school, as a result of the school not properly handling his ADD," Pam said. "His teachers told him that he was lazy, that he was defiant, that he had many deficits, and that he had ADD, a mental disorder."

In Pam's view, this young boy's trauma was caused by teachers who understood ADD as a label, but who had little empathy for individuals with ADD. She said that this child's anxiety symptoms, so similar to individuals diagnosed with PTSD, were causally connected to his negative school experiences over a period of years.

One of the problems that people who do not have ADD (like Pam's patient's teacher) experience when trying to define, discuss, or understand ADD is that they're struggling with a reality that is, for them, entirely conceptual and not at all experiential. A person whose experience of life and the world is very "Farmer-like" will look at ADD and ADD people from their own point of view, scratching their head and wondering how these poor people could ever make it through life. Overlay that with a smattering of knowledge of current trends in psychological thought, and their observation/confusion often expresses itself with words like "pathology," "deficit," and "disorder."

For a person who has experienced life with/as ADD, however, the Hunter/Farmer perspective is so gut-level-true that it often evokes an instant and visceral, "Yeah, that's it!" response. (And no, this isn't an attempt to put lipstick on a pig. Experienced personal truth and feel-good self-talk are wholly different things.)

"The only truths we can point to are the ever-changing truths of our own experience," Peter Weiss wrote in 1964 (*Marat/Sade*). Andre Gide in 1921 wrote that "Each of us really understands in others only those feelings he is capable of producing himself."

This is at the root of both the debate over how to present ADD to people with it, and how to respond to it therapeutically and in schools. Several blind men may differently describe an elephant, but only the elephant truly knows its own nature.

Parents of ADD children must ask themselves if they want their kids to grow up telling themselves, and interpreting all their experience through the filter of, the story that they're "disordered." Or would they prefer to know that they're Hunters, facing specific challenges thrown at them by a Farmer's world? And those of us who are the adult ancestors of Hunters must make a similar choice.

Both models acknowledge the struggles and difficulties of life with

ADD. The former, however, often disempowers people and provides them with excuses to hand off responsibility for their lives to others. The latter model demands that we learn as much as we can about our true nature and our deficits, and then take personal responsibility for changing our lives.

Virtually everybody will take on one role or another: we require an identification or self-identity in order to function in the world.

Psychotherapist George Lynn told me about a discussion he had on this topic with Marcia Jacobs, MSW, who is the head of Mental Health Services for the United Nations High Commission on Refugees. She'd just returned from Bosnia, and George said of their discussion, and his thoughts on it:

"A subtle force for maintaining victim status for trauma survivors is the self-identification with the role. Marcia pointed out that people will, on one level or another, ask, 'If I don't have this status (of victim) what fills the void?'

"This harkens back to the fact that if a person feels that his life is meaningless, he will cling to some identity. Living without meaning is terrifying. This is why so many people are dying in Bosnia, for they identify the very purpose of their existence with their cause.

"I think that this gets me back to my suggestion for your book that a Hunter without a mission will see himself as a prisoner of his condition—better this than nothing. This, in turn, argues for techniques that show Hunters how to use their innate intuitive and creative strengths to locate (for want of a better phrase) Right Livelihood."

So the question: Will we spend the rest of our lives as victims of our genes, pointing to them as the cause of every ill thing in our past and dragging that past into our future like the chains on Marley's ghost? Or will we stand up, take a deep breath of the fresh air of the present, and decide to move forward, as Scrooge himself ultimately did?

The choice is ours.

Part Three: Travelogues

"Great ideas come into the world as quietly as doves. Perhaps then, if we listen attentively, we shall hear among the uproar of empires and nations a faint fluttering of wings, the gentle stirrings of life and hope."
— Albert Camus

After the publication of my first book on ADD, I took on the job of head systems operator (Sysop) for the ADD Forum on CompuServe, the world's largest online computer information service. The forum has, at this writing, over 40,000 members in dozens of countries, and has grown to be the world's largest interactive, 24-hour-a-day, international ADD support group.

The publication of my books also brought an avalanche of speaking requests, and I've traveled from Israel to California to address groups of parents, teachers, school superintendents, ADD adults, attorneys, college professors, psychiatrists, psychologists, and even a science fiction convention. At each stop, people invariably come up to me after my presentation with stories from their own lives. They tell me about ways they've used their ADD to be more successful than the Farmers they've known, or describe techniques they developed to overcome some of the problems Hunters encounter living day-to-day in this Farmer's World.

As I was expanding the normal two-hour speech that I give on ADD into a full-blown course on how to be successful in life with ADD, I sent out an electronic mail message to thousands of the members of the ADD Forum on CompuServe. I asked if they had stories from their lives they'd like to share for my course, and ultimately for this book, and also began to solicit and write down stories from people I had met at speaking engagements.

61

Some people eagerly gave me both their stories and their names. Others had stories, but preferred to be anonymous. Some stories were so long and autobiographical that they required shortening to fit in this book; others were so short and terse that a bit of amplification was necessary.

So here we have a collection of stories from fellow Hunters, traveling across the terrain of this Farmer's world. I've tried to organize them in logical categories, although there is some overlap and a few could probably fit in several different areas. Most have been edited in one way or another, and a few were written entirely by me from memory, describing stories that were told to me by people in lecture halls or classrooms.

All are true stories, however, and all offer practical ways to improve our quality of life. And, as we saw in Chapter Two, persistently practicing new ways of living can lead to permanent changes.

7

Personal Life Success Stories

The questions which one asks oneself begin, at last, to illuminate the world, and become one's key to the experience of others.
—James Baldwin, *Nobody Knows My Name*, 1961

■ Physically position yourself to reduce distractions

From Melissa, a junior high school student in Ohio:

When they discovered that I had ADD, my mom didn't want me taking Ritalin or anything because she's one of those natural type of people. She's mostly a vegetarian and everything. So she asked the doctor what else we could do.

He said that I should try to sit in the front row of the classroom.

That sounded kind of stupid to me, but Mom went in and talked to all my teachers (which was really embarrassing) and they agreed, and suddenly I was sitting in the front row of every one of my classes.

What happened was that when I was sitting in the front row it was a lot harder to see all the other kids, because they were sitting behind me. So it was easier to pay attention to the teacher, and when she noticed I was starting to space out, she'd walk over toward me to get my attention.

And this simple, stupid thing brought all my grades except math up by at least one grade. I'm still working on math, and mom says a tutor is what she's going to try next.

Bill works in marketing for a medium-sized company in Los Angeles and learned a similar lesson:

I have an office that's all mine, but for years I always left the door open. I felt that if I closed the door, people would think that I was being antisocial, or that maybe I was goofing off or making personal phone calls or something.

I know there are people who do this sort of thing, but I'm not one of them.

So for years my door was open, and I was constantly being distracted. Somebody would walk by whom I knew and I'd feel obliged to say hello, often leading to a conversation. I'd hear snippets of discussions from out in the hall and nearby offices (there's one guy two offices down from me who talks so loud whenever he's on the phone that we can all hear him). This really cut into my work, although I don't think I realized it at the time.

Then when I learned about my ADD from my son being diagnosed, one of the suggestions my son's counselor at school gave us was that he have an interruption-free environment to do his homework. We'd always made him do it at the kitchen table, but he complained that there were too many distractions there, and that he wanted to do it in his room. We figured this was just an excuse to get out from under his mom's watchful eye. But the counselor suggested we let him try it, and we did, and it worked.

So I thought, I wonder if that would help me at work? And I started closing the door to my office for an hour or two each day, during the time that I most needed to work on the most difficult things or those that required the most concentration.

The results were rather startling. I just about doubled my productivity. I never realized it before, but now that I look around, I think it's safe to say that most people in the workplace waste 80% to 90% of their day, and most of that waste is triggered by distractions. By reclaiming just two hours a day—just 30% or so of my day—I've been able to increase by more than 100% the amount of work I get done. And the quality of the work has improved as well.

I brought this idea home with me, too. When I have projects to work on at home, or when I want to spend high-quality time with my wife or son, I try to find a distraction-free place, or close the door.

So that's my ADD success story, and it's really pretty simple: close the door and work, think, or talk in peace and quiet.

Samuel wrote from Salt Lake City about how he eliminates distractions when talking with his wife:

My wife loves to have the TV on, and she's not distracted by it. But when it's on in the same room, I *must* look at it. It's like it's some kind of a magnet, all those images flickering by.

Because my wife likes the TV on all the time, there's almost never a time when we're together and it's not on. She has one in the kitchen, one in our bedroom, and one in the living room. Sometimes they're all three on at the same time.

Now for years she's complained that I don't pay attention to her when she's talking. When I learned about ADD and realized that I had it, I realized that maybe she was right and wasn't just being hypersensitive. I decided to start working on paying attention to her.

What I found out, though, was that I can't pay attention to her—or anybody else, for that matter—when the TV is on in the room. For me, it's like trying to eat soup out of a bowl when you're underwater: it all sort of mushes together, her and the TV.

So I asked her if she would mind if I turned off the TV when we talked. Of course, she objected to that. So I said, what if I can pay attention to you better if the TV's off? And she decided that it would be a reasonable compromise.

I'm here to tell you that that made an incredible difference. We now have discussions and I'm actually paying attention, because the TV isn't distracting me. It's made a big difference in our marriage, and I've learned a lot about how I pay attention to things. TV and ADD are a bad combination, unless all you want to do is watch the TV!

■ Express your creativity

Dr. Oliver Sacks, the elder statesman for people with neurological differences, has suggested that different brain chemistry might be a requirement for creativity.*

Similarly, many of the people who shared their stories for this book said that *expressing* their creativity was an important part of their lives and of building and maintaining their self-esteem.

From Nancy in Detroit:

I've known since I was in kindergarten, and maybe even before then, that I'm an artist. It was in kindergarten, though, that I first encountered paints, and understood, solidly and down in my soul, that painting and visual expressions are essential to me.

So I paint, and I've been painting for years. I'm pretty good at it by now, and have even made a small living over the years at it.

*"Tourette Syndrome and Creativity," British Medical Journal, December, 1992.

The point of this as an ADD success story, though, is the impact that painting has on the rest of my life. During those times when I'm not painting for more than a few weeks at a time, I find that I become very distractible, spaced-out, and irritable. My fuse gets short and I snap at people. I'm unhappy.

It wasn't until I was in my late twenties with two children that I understood this correlation between my painting and my moods and mental abilities. I'd been so busy being a mom that I'd given up painting for almost a year, and my life was going down in flames. So my husband suggested I start painting again, thinking that it would take my mind off my problems with our kids (who both have ADD, too).

It was amazing to me that when I started painting again, the old me came back out. I felt like a door had been opened inside me, and, as my creative juices were flowing, so was every other part of my life.

I don't know how many other ADD people consider themselves creative, or if there's a connection between creativity and ADD, but I can tell you that for this ADD woman, expressing my creativity several times a week is the best therapy I've found.

Norman in Denver writes:

I like to write. I've never had anything published, but I've been writing since I was a teenager. First it was poetry, and nowadays I'm writing science fiction more than anything else.

I also write long letters to people, and, for a couple of years, used to keep a journal (very sporadically!).

The point of this is that I think that the writing is a good focusing exercise for me.

I set up specific goals for my writing—such as today I'm going to write the scene where the Kurians take over the planet—and then make myself stick to those goals. Because I'm doing it just for me, I don't get in a sweat about it, and while I don't always hit my goals, I've gotten pretty good at it.

Writing feels good for me, and when I'm doing it there's a certain "flow" feeling that I get. Over the years, this has become an anchor for me, a feeling that I like to get from my writing. And when I'm in other situations, like at work or when I'm in an intense conversation with my girlfriend, I'll sometimes pause and click back to that flow feeling, and bring it into the situation when I need some extra strength or creativity. I don't know how to describe how I do this other than to say that I just do it; it's not quite visualization, but I'm able to hook into that feeling.

Most of my friends who are ADD are also pretty creative people, from what I can tell, although I don't think any of them have developed the discipline that I have to write every week. I think it would be a good habit for them, though. I view it as mental weightlifting: I'm strengthening the muscle of my brain, the same as people who pump iron a few times a week strengthen their biceps.

■ Set short-term goals for yourself to keep on task
From Harry in Virginia:

I work on large projects that have lots of pieces (I'm a mechanical engineer), and I'm often responsible for managing specific projects. The problem for me has always been that large and complex jobs overwhelm me, and so, like I did in college, I tend to put off things until the last minute, and then binge them all at once.

A few years ago, though, I learned a different way of doing things. I got this from a friend of mine who's just a much a Hunter as I am, and who's also an engineer (he works for me).

What I do now is that before I begin any project, I break it down into smaller pieces. Then I assign specific timelines to each piece, for beginning and ending them, and try to keep those timelines in terms of days or hours. Weeks are too long for me, and if a component lasts more than a week, I'll look for ways to break it down even further.

Then I write those timelines down in my desk calendar, and they become my "to do" list for the project. Each day I just look at that one part of the project, and I can get that done. This way I don't get the feeling of being overwhelmed that I used to get from big projects—it would sometimes be so strong it bordered on despair—and I can keep things in perspective. It also helps me get things done on time, and, as I'm moving through the project, I'm getting a daily reality check on how my original timeline looked.

I carried this into my personal life after discovering it at work. For example, I'd been putting off cleaning the garage for—literally—twelve years. (Actually, it's been that long since we moved into the house!) It was a disaster area, and there hadn't been room to park the car in there for at least ten years.

So I broke the job down into little pieces: organize the tools, sort things to throw out, put up shelves, paint the walls, etc. I assigned myself one of those pieces, each averaging about an hour's work, for every Saturday morning over a two-month period. And guess what? For the first time in my 52 years on this earth, I now have a clean garage.

My bedroom closet is next.

■ **Practice keeping on task**

From a fellow at a seminar in Portland:

You've heard the expression "a jack of all trades"? Well, that's me. The problem is that really I was closer to the whole saying: "Jack of all trades and master of none." I never stuck with anything, be it a job, a relationship, or even a hobby. Once I "got enough" of something, I was off to something new.

I was over thirty years old when I realized that this was probably because of ADD, and that maybe I could do something about it. So I started noticing when my attention or interest in something was fading away. And I told myself, like they do in Alcoholics Anonymous, just one more day, just one day at a time. Stick to that for just one more day.

I always thought that was a silly saying, or just something for alcoholics. But I can tell you, that living just one day at a time, and catching myself when I start to lose interest and bring it back, or looking for new ways to make things interesting, has been incredibly helpful.

I've been with the same woman for three years now, which is three times longer than I've ever been with anybody. And I've had the same job for that same amount of time, again a record. I still jump around in my hobbies, I suppose, but that's an indulgence I allow myself. This month I'm interested in racing dirt-bikes, but at least now I'm smart enough to know not to buy one because I know in a few months I'll just want to be doing something else.

So I guess, in addition to noticing when I'm drifting away from something, interest-wise, I'm also prioritizing. I'm deciding that in some things it's ok for me to have variety, like my weekend activities, but in other areas I need to work on sticking to things, like my job and relationships.

■ **Practice "original awareness"**

Harry Lorayne, in his books and speeches, talks about a concept he calls Original Awareness. He points out that most people don't really pay attention to what they're doing as they go through life. That's why they're always losing and forgetting things: they didn't notice them in the first place.

I started practicing Original Awareness back in the mid-1970's after I first read Harry's *Memory Book*. I was constantly losing pens and combs. Using his technique, I got in the habit, whenever I set down a pen or comb, of observing myself setting it down. I brought myself into the "now," and noticed what I was doing.

The transformation was incredible. Overnight, or so it seemed, I'd done away with one of the scourges of ADD. And, ever since then, when people complain about leaving things behind, losing their belongings, or forgetting where they put objects, I silently thank Harry for having taught me his concept.

Two years ago, I shared a few of Harry's techniques with Dave deBronkart as we drove up to New Hampshire for a board of directors meeting for the New England Salem Children's Village. He latched onto Original Awareness, and later mentioned how useful he found it. So I asked him to write up his experience, and here's what he sent.

From Dave deBronkart, a lesson on paying attention to attention:

The way I look at it, the whole point of investigating ADD is to produce the changes you want in your life. So I suggest that people gauge the usefulness of an adaptive technique, be it a pill or a mind method, by a simple measure: does it produce results?

For me personally, the most profound, lasting, and broad-based change has come from discovering Original Awareness.

My overall goal, from the start, was to be able to achieve what I choose. An important goal in support of that was to remember what I want to remember. (I'm not obsessive about remembering every little detail, but when I *want* to remember something, that's different!)

Original awareness was immediately useful. Beyond that, it gave me a real "mind pop:" the sudden realization that I could produce substantially different results in my mind just by the way I put my mind on a subject!

When you've come to expect forgetfulness and you suddenly see that you can remember ten things in a row, it's a genuinely transforming experience. My mind opened to all kinds of new possibilities.

As I lived with the method, I began to notice moments when my mind would get tugged off a subject, such that I was no longer fully aware of what was going on. I noticed that it was usually because something urgent was pulling at my attention.

Then I realized that I was most likely to forget something important—like my car or my wallet!—if I was late for something urgent. As I would race to get there, my mind was running ahead. It wasn't in the car with me, literally, "my mind had left the scene."

No wonder I had no recollection of where I put things; in a very real sense, I wasn't there at the time!

One time this resulted in leaving my wallet in a taxi. On several occasions it resulted in my having no idea where I parked my car at the airport. (My ADD counselor, Dr. Edward Hallowell, found this amusing, in an ADD sort of way, and asked "What do you DO when you lose your car??" My answer: "Go LOOK for it!")

But once I realized the problem—"my mind had left the scene"—the problem receded rapidly. I've learned to stay aware of what's going on, especially at pivotal moments. I've learned to notice the feeling of my mind getting off the subject, so I can stop and tug it back. I've learned to detect the feeling of "I'm late for something urgent" and become vigilant about staying conscious. For instance, when I'm late at the airport, I'll make a point of visually imprinting my parking location. I'll put my eyes on the section signs for a full second, even if I'm running.

Finally, all this encouraged me to realize the value of not being late in the first place, which has led me to put more thought into planning ahead. Sure, all my life people told me to think ahead and not to be late; but that had never been an ingredient of the successes I had. In fact a big part of my success has been that I *can* work under always-late, ridiculous deadlines, and I *can* produce results in unstructured situations that make others crazy.

But when I myself started from my own goal—to produce the results I want—and saw how useful Original Awareness can be, the rest followed naturally. So now I've added Original Awareness to the abilities I already had, improving my capacity to move steadily through a project and get the results I wanted.

■ Using Organizers & Calendars

Tim in Detroit learned the importance of calendars:

One of the things that I never could seem to get a handle on was managing my time. I'd forget appointments, miss project deadlines at work, always turn things in at the last minute in school (even when I finished them). I'd constantly forget even the most simple things like my parents' birthdays.

Then, when I was about twenty and had gotten a job as the manager of a health food chain store, the regional manager gave me some advice (actually, it was an order) that changed my life.

One day about two weeks after I'd started the job, he was walking me through the store, telling me things he wanted done before he returned in a few weeks. "Move those vitamins up to eye-level and replace the sign," he'd say, and, "don't forget to check the raisins every morning to see if they have bugs." Lots of little details like that, as well as big things like the procedure to transmit the daily sales to the corporate office headquarters.

About halfway through his spiel, he stopped, tilted his head to one side, and said, "You're not writing this stuff down."

I told him—as I had told people all my life—that I had a good memory and would remember the things. While that was partially true, what was *really* true was that I had always believed that everybody else was just born with a great memory, and I somehow missed out on it. I was good at faking it, though, and so although I knew that I forgot things easily, I didn't want him to know it.

So I was standing there, working as hard as I could to remember the things he was telling me, but knew deep down inside that I'd forget some of them. In the past when that had happened, people would just remind me again, and eventually I'd get everything done. I'd gotten used to people chastising me, and most often they forgave my lapses.

But he wasn't going to let me get away with it, and he also knew something about the rest of humanity that I didn't: *everybody* has a lousy memory, to one extent or another.

He said, "That's not possible. Everybody forgets things, particularly long lists of things like this, if they don't write them down. Where's your calendar?"

"Calendar?" I croaked, thinking of the wall-hanging contraptions decorated with scantily-clad women that my dad used to have on the walls at the garage where he worked.

He marched to the back of the store, rummaged through his briefcase, and pulled out a small pocket calendar with the name of an out-of-state bank printed on the front of it. With a flourish, he slapped it into my hand.

It was about six inches high, two inches wide, and a third of an inch thick: anyplace you opened it, you saw a full week displayed, half on one page and the other half on the facing page. The last dozen pages were for names and addresses.

"That's a pocket calendar," he said. "It's yours now. I want you to keep it with you at all times, and that's now an official part of your job description. If you don't do it, I'll fire you. And I want you to write down everything in your life, from your Christmas card list in the back to the instructions I'm giving you. Write the instructions on the days that I'm telling you to do these things. And every morning and every evening the first and last thing you will do is check that calendar. Along with checking it throughout the day.

"Additionally," he added, now warming to his job of teacher/Führer, "whenever you get an idea during the day about something you'd like to do to improve this store, I want you to write it down in there. Either put it on a dated page, or choose one of those first few weeks of January that have already passed and designate those pages as your idea file' pages."

"Sounds like a lot of unnecessary effort," I said.

He shook his head, half-smiling and half-angry. "You may think so, but this will make you the kind of store manager I need on my team. In fact, I intend to check your calendar each time I visit your store, and if it's not up-to-date, I'll send you home for a few days without pay to get it filled out."

Having no choice now, I started writing down his instructions as he resumed our walk through the store. That night, I went home and filled in the address pages with the names and addresses of a few dozen friends and relatives. I wrote in birthdays and anniversaries, and for the rest of the year, on each Friday's page, wrote "send weekly report to head office" and the other things that my manager had told me I must do regularly.

At the time, it seemed like a stupid waste of time. Within a few weeks, though, I realized that I'd never truly known what it meant to be organized with regard to my time and my schedules. I got more done than I ever thought possible, and I rarely missed a deadline or detail.

My manager pulled two sneak visits over the next month, each time only to check my calendar! He was pleased to see that I was keeping it up, and then let me thumb through his. I was amazed at how every day on every page was filled with things. He even kept track of the money he spent while traveling, saying it would help him survive an IRS audit.

I've been carrying a pocket calendar like that ever since: it's been over fifteen years now. Every year I get a free one from someplace, last year it was American Express. The year before, my bank sent them out. The year before that, a calendar company sent me one soliciting my business. Each Christmas, part of my Christmas Day ritual is to copy my address list and birthdays (I write the birthdays in red, so they jump out) to the next year's calendar, and put the old one in the back of my underwear drawer. That drawer now has a complete record of my past fifteen years, should I ever need it, and I can honestly say that I owe much of my job success to that little calendar that's always in my pants or jacket pocket.

■ DayRunners & Franklin Planners

Sheryl in Chicago takes it a step farther:

I know some people use those little pocket calendars, but that's never been enough for me. My entire life resides in my DayRunner.

This is a calendar that's about the size of a hardcover book, and inside are not only month-at-a-glance pages for the year (where I plan my travel schedule), and week-at-a-glance pages (where I plan my daily activities), and an address book, but also customizable sections.

I buy little dividers for them, and have them labeled with things like *Meetings, Sales Leads, Ideas, Home & Family Stuff,* and *Taxes.* I also created a section in the back called *Phone Log* where I write down people's phone numbers and the substance of important phone discussions I have with them (along with the date): this has been very valuable when I need to refer back to phone discussions. And I have a section in the front called *To Do* which is my list of things that I must do. Every few days I'll tear out that page, as things get crossed off, and replace it with a new page, moving the unfinished things to the new page.

I used to do this with a legal pad, but now, keeping everything in one place, it's much easier for me to keep track of what needs to be done. And since I'm a (very ADD) traveling saleswoman, my lists, calendar, and even address book are always with me. I also have one of those plastic sleeve-pages in the front where I keep my credit cards and business cards.

One tip I learned from sad experience: every few months, make a copy of your pages on a copy machine. I do the entire book every year and stick it in a drawer in my office. And then every now and then, when I remember, I copy the more recently-updated pages, just flipping the thing down on the copy machine and punching the button. That way, if the book is ever lost or stolen (as happened to me once a few years ago), I can easily reconstruct most of it in a few hours.

■ Important versus urgent

Steve in Philadelphia says:

I've always kept a to-do list, and am pretty good about keeping dates organized on my desktop calendar. (I'm so ADD and inherently disorganized, these are survival strategies!)

A few years ago, though, a friend shared with me a concept which has literally changed my life.

I was going through my list of things to do with him, mostly bragging and complaining about how swamped I was.

"A lot of that seems urgent," he said. "But how much of it is important?"

"All of it!" I replied indignantly.

"Not necessarily," he said. "I'll bet a lot of those things that you think are important are really not all that important if you examine them in the context of your life's goals. They just seem important, because they're urgent."

I was lost and asked him to explain.

"When the phone rings, is that urgent or important?" he asked.

"Both!" I said.

He shook his head. "Nope. You only know that it's urgent. The ringing creates the urgency. But what if it's some guy trying to sell you insurance?"

"I guess it could be either."

"Right. Some things are urgent, but not important. Some are important, but not urgent. Some are neither, and some are both."

"So I should only do the urgent and important things?" I said.

"Nope," he said. "That's the most common mistake people make. And what happens is that they end up not doing the important things, because they're constantly dealing only with the urgent/important things. Remember the song Cat's Cradle'?"

I nodded, thinking about the song about the dad who was always putting his son off, and when the son grew up he started ignoring his dad.

"Your family is important to you, right?" he said.

I nodded again, starting to see his point.

"But I'll bet you haven't spent much time with your kids this week, because you've been dealing with so many urgent things. So, instead, write down that you're going to spend time with the kids. That's important, and it needs to be done, too. And you'll find the same thing is true in business, in your relationship with your wife, and in just about every other area of your life."

So now whenever I'm looking over my To Do list, I ask myself, "Is this item important, or just urgent?" And I've learned that my Hunter instinct pushes me toward handling the urgent things first, when actually they're often not even all that important—they're just easy to check off the list, or the most recent thing that was in my face. So now I'm working hard to deal with the important things, too.

■ Kids and laundry

From Martha in Michigan:

This is probably so simple that you won't want to include it in your book, but it's really helped me out and I'd like to share it.

I used to be totally disorganized in my laundry. I did the laundry for the entire family (I have two ADD kids, one twelve and the other fifteen, and an ADD husband, not to mention myself), and everything was always a mess. The kids and my husband both just threw their dirty clothes on the floor, and I had a pile in my closet (which I thought, at least, looked a bit more organized because I could close the door).

Then a friend showed me a system she'd developed for her home, and it's incredible how it's helped here at my house!

She went to K-Mart and bought a dozen laundry baskets, half red and half white. With an indelible felt pen, she wrote on each of the red ones the name of one of her family members, along with the word "coloreds," and on each of the white ones she wrote a family member's name and the word "whites." Then she gave each person in the family their two baskets.

When the person takes off their dirty clothes, they go directly into the baskets: the whites into the white basket and the coloreds into the colored basket.

And then she did something that I thought was both unthinkable and impossible: she told everybody that they were now responsible for doing their own laundry. She did a little seminar on a Saturday morning and showed her kids (her youngest is seven) how to use the washer and dryer, and how to fold and put away clothes. And they did it!

Well, I told her that would never work in my house because everybody in my house has ADD and the place always looks like a tornado hit it. "Just wait until they run out of clean underwear," she said. "They'll do it. Just try it."

So I did.

And it works!

It's really amazing to me how the kids have taken to this. One of the boys has even become a connoisseur of laundry detergents, and he'll only use Tide, so every month or two I have to take him to the store to buy his detergent.

In addition to cleaning up the floors and making our bedrooms look considerably less messy (I suppose I could probably go the next step and use hampers instead of baskets if I really wanted a showcase house, but the baskets are so easy for them to carry to the laundry room when they're full), this system has taught my children about being organized and about personal responsibility. They aren't as quick to abuse their clothes as they were before, and are more careful about spills and stains. And I think this is probably a very good life skill for them as they grow up.

▪ Develop "I always do it this way" rituals for important things

Dr. Edward Hallowell recently told me a story about a man he met in his health club who best illustrates this strategy.

As Dr. Hallowell was getting dressed in the locker room, he noticed that one particular man was shaving, getting his materials organized, and going through the other things that one does to get ready for the day. The man was totally dressed: jacket, shirt, tie, socks, shoes—except for his pants.

Dr. Hallowell, thinking that maybe the guy was so absent-minded or ADD that he'd forgotten to put on his pants, commented to him, "It looks like you're getting ready to leave here. But, in case you hadn't noticed, you're not wearing your pants."

"I haven't forgotten," the man said. "I just always leave them until the very last thing. I've left so many things behind here in the past that I've started doing things in this order. Putting on my pants is the very last thing: it's my cue to double-check that I have everything else. I know I'll never leave without my pants."

▪ A place for everything, and everything in its place

This Hunter survival strategy was first put forth by Ben Franklin, but it was a common theme I read in stories sent to me by ADD adults.

Psychiatrist Stephen Bluestein told me how his mother had taught him, as a child, to always have a specific place in his clothes and on his dresser at home for his money, keys, wallet, and so forth. "It was one of the most useful life-skills she taught me," he commented, noting that he rarely loses such things as an adult, even though he knows he's a Hunter.

Similarly, Dave deBronkart frequently travels around the country giving speeches and doing consulting work on one of his three expert topics: ADD, computer programming, and marketing. "Whenever I enter the hotel room," he says, "I clear the top of the TV. That's the place where everything from my pockets goes, and that's the place from which, when I leave the room, I collect it all back. I've created the habit of always checking the top of the TV whenever I leave the room, and it's been years since I forgot or lost my keys, wallet, money, or the other things that I used to leave behind so often before I started doing this."

Other people wrote me about the importance of having a small hook in the kitchen or by the front door where they always hung their car keys, or a special place for their wallet or shopping list. The moral: A place for everything, and everything in its place is a great motto for ADD folks to adopt.

■ Put important things nearby

Bill in Pennsylvania writes:

Proximity is important to Hunters, which is one reason our desks are often cluttered with paper. All that important stuff needs to be kept nearby, lest it be forgotten!

However this principle can be taken one step further to office and home filing systems.

Following the alphabetical systems of organization I'd learned in school, I'd always put the files in my desk file-drawer and the ones in the filing cabinet on the other side of the office into alphabetical, or subject-alphabetical order. While this was technically organized, I found that I was often not immediately filing things because it would involve having to walk over to the filing cabinet, and there were other things still on my desk which needed to be done immediately. My "to file" pile ended up huge, and sometimes it was months before I got around to it.

That, in and of itself, wasn't so much the problem as was the fact that when I needed something quickly, if often wasn't in the right file—because I hadn't gotten around to filing it.

So I re-arranged my desk and filing cabinet. My desk drawer files now only contain the things that I frequently have to dig out or use. My filing cabinet files are more archival: things I might need months or years from now, or should keep for the IRS or whatever.

I still have a big "to file" pile on my desk, but now there's nothing in that pile that would be among the things I will have to quickly reference in the near future. Those papers get put directly into the desk drawer file, because it's as close and convenient as my "to file" pile.

After I figured this out at the office, I decided to try it at home, and rearranged my closet and dresser drawers along the same lines. The difference was amazing! Hopefully sometime this coming summer I'll get to the garage...

■ Keyless locks for home and car

From Marge in Atlanta:

I can't tell you how many times I've lost the keys to my house or car. I spent one entire year without ever locking my house because I couldn't find the keys, and I never could find the time to go out and buy a new doorknob, or call a locksmith.

Then I discovered keyless locks!

Several of the mail-order catalogs, and some of the larger hardware stores, sell housedoor locks that have a keypad on them instead of using a key. You program in a number (it could be part of a phone number, social security number, birthday, or anything that's easy to remember), and that becomes your "key." I bought one and installed it, and now my house is always locked, but I'm never locked out.

Similarly, I discovered that Nissan makes a car with a keyless entry system. I'm sure that other manufacturers have a similar option available, but I wanted a Maxima anyway, so that's what I bought. I now keep the car keys *inside* the car, so they're never lost. When I get out of the car, I drop the key into the ashtray and close it, and then lock the door as I close it. It's a regular ritual. When I come back to the car, I just punch in the key code for the door, and the car unlocks itself.

Isn't technology wonderful?

■ Permanent lists

Susan in Tucson writes:

I'm hopelessly forgetful and totally disorganized, which is not good when you're responsible for keeping the family stocked with essentials. There are some things that I always need: the staple foods like potatoes and onions, toilet paper, that sort of thing, as well as supplies for the house like laundry detergent.

For years, whenever I'd go to the store I'd just walk through the aisles, relying on the sight of things to remind me that I needed them. That didn't work so well, as I often couldn't remember what I needed, or would sometimes simply overlook things, even though I might have walked right by them.

After discovering a few times—always at the most awkward moment—that there wasn't a scrap of toilet paper in the entire house, I decided I had to start keeping a shopping list.

So I started creating shopping lists every week just before I'd go shopping. The problem, though, was that I'd then have to go through the pantry and refrigerator and figure out what was missing, and again I often would forget things. Not to mention that it was such a hassle that I usually didn't even bother to do it.

Then I got the idea of creating a permanent list.

This is a shopping list of those things that I always want around the house. Most of them are supplies that if I buy a few extra of it's no big deal: I'll eventually use them anyway. My husband, who's an accountant, says this is even a form of investment, because I'm buying commodities which will increase in price with inflation. So the extra toilet paper or canned tomatoes will increase in value as they sit on the shelf at the house.

I typed up my permanent list, which contains about forty items, on the top half of a sheet of paper. My husband ran off fifty copies at the office and brought them back home, and I keep them in a drawer in the kitchen. During the week when I notice I'm out of something that's not on my permanent list, or see some recipe on TV that I'd like to try but don't have the ingredients for, I just open the drawer and jot that item down on the top sheet of the stack. When Thursday evening shopping time comes, I just grab the top list and head off to the store.

I haven't run out of the essentials in over two years, since I started this system.

Frequent Flyer's Note:
A fellow who travels twenty to thirty weeks a year, both nationally and internationally, and is very ADD, related to me a similar strategy for his packing. He has in his pocket calendar a permanent packing list: articles like socks, underwear, toothpaste, etc. "It's amazing how many times I used to arrive somewhere only to discover that I forgot to bring a tie with me, or that I'd left my business cards at home," he said. "Now I do my preflight check' just like a pilot does. Before I leave the house, I pull out my calendar and check my permanent packing list to make sure that I have everything. And what's so continually amazing to me is that even after having done this for several years now, as I read my list out loud and mentally picture where and when I packed each item, I still discover that I'd often have forgotten something if I hadn't run through my checklist."

▪ High tech note taking
From Leo in South Carolina:
My problem is that thoughts and ideas don't stick in my brain. I'm driving down the street and I get this great idea, or I remember that for two weeks I've been trying to remember to pick up new socks at the store, and no matter how hard I try to hang on to that thought, it's gone in a few minutes. It might be another week before I remember it again. And it's not just in the car, of course. It happens during meetings, while I'm working, when I'm home watching TV, or even walking through the supermarket.

I tried carrying a pad and pen with me all the time, but I was always losing them, or forgetting to bring them with me everywhere I go. Plus it's a huge hassle to have to fumble for the pad. And it fills up your pockets, which can be unsightly and doesn't leave much room for other things that might be important. And it's really hard to get the thing out and write on it when you're driving.

The solution for me was this pen that The Sharper Image sells. It has a digital recorder built into it, and holds about forty seconds of ideas. That's enough for me to take home and play back every night.

And because the pen cost me more than an average pen, I haven't lost it. (I constantly lose things, too, but when I have something that's really valuable and important to me, I don't.) In fact, part of my morning ritual is to check that I have my watch on, that my hair is combed and teeth brushed, and to pat my shirt pocket to make sure my recording pen is in it.

So now when I have an idea, I just pull out my pen and talk into it. It's gotten me a few odd looks from people who probably are thinking of Maxwell Smart and his shoe, but it works for me.

■ Windshield car pads

Peggy in Atlanta has a low-tech reminder tool:

The best ADD success tool I've found so far is one of those three-dollar plastic paper-pad holders that stick to the windshield of your car with suction cups and has a pen attached to it with a coiled plastic cord.

It's probably because I spend so much time in my car that it's so useful to me, or maybe it's the quality of the time in the car. I commute to work about a half-hour each way every day, and that half-hour is my opportunity to reflect on the day, to plan, to think, and when most of my really good ideas come up. It's also when I remember all the things I've been forgetting to do.

I tried keeping a spiral pad with me in the car, but it kept getting lost. And there never seemed to be a pen.

So about a year ago I was running the car through one of those expensive car-wash places where they do everything for you, and they had this big rack of stuff you could buy for your car by the place where you pay for the car wash. It included perfumes for the car, things that dangle from your rear-view mirror, license plate holders, and all sorts of stuff like that. And those suction-cup pads.

I'd seen them before in people's cars and wondered if they were any good or useful, and so I figured, what the heck, it's only a few dollars.

Well, that pad has changed my life.

Like I said, maybe it's just because I'm the type of person who gets great ideas while driving in the car—it's sort of like it's my morning meditation and my evening decompression—but that pad has easily cut in half the number of things that I would have otherwise forgotten to do or get.

■ Buy extras of the non-essentials

A few years ago I heard Hugh Lightman speak at a CHADD conference. Besides being a brilliant speaker, he had a really great suggestion for parents of ADD kids, and for ADD adults.

Dr. Lightman pointed out that most ADD kids are constantly losing things: mittens, socks, pens, caps. He lives near Boston, and he said that he was always hearing from parents who were upset that their kids were losing their gloves. And from adults who couldn't keep track of their pens.

Instead of getting upset or angry, Dr. Lightman counseled his audience to use "The Filene's Basement Anti-ADD Technique."

This seemed to startle the audience, so he explained.

Filene's is a department store in Boston. When things don't sell, they move them to their basement, where they're radically marked down. There's all sorts of cheap stuff there, from $600 dresses to $3 mittens.

So, Dr. Lightman suggested, if your kid is a chronic mitten-loser, at the beginning of the winter season go to Filene's and buy five or ten *identical* pairs of the cheapest mittens you can find.

"Why get upset over behavior that you really can't do much about?" he asked, as a roomful of parents bobbed their heads in agreement and sudden revelation. "These kids need positive reinforcement right now: they're struggling just to get by. They don't need us in their faces about losing a mitten when they're failing in math. Just get extra mittens."

This brilliant and simple strategy, which Dr. Lightman conceived as a way of reducing the volume and amount of criticism that ADD children receive (he calls their learning style "fragile"), works well for adults, too. Many of the ADD success strategy stories which I received from adults over CompuServe had to do with buying cheap pens by the box, buying socks by the dozen in an annual binge, and buying toilet paper by the case.

Along these same lines, the only official biography of former President John F. Kennedy, written by William Manchester while JFK was still alive and with Jackie's help and support, noted that JFK constantly lost things. According to Manchester's book, he lost his reading glasses and had to buy a new pair at least once a week, and lost pens and his comb *several times a day* during the 1960 campaign. A large stock of combs and glasses would have been an easy solution, and apparently this is what he eventually came around to.

■ Get to know your own body's rhythms

From Kenneth on the ADD Forum on CompuServe:

"Early to bed and early to rise" was one of Ben Franklin's favorite sayings. He must have been like me: I function best in the morning. I've intuitively known this all my life, but for the past ten years I've been married to a woman who's a classic night person. She stays up until at least midnight every night, drags herself out of bed in the morning to drink three cups of coffee before going to work, and then sleeps literally until noon on Saturday and Sunday to catch up on her lost sleep.

Thinking that the nature of marriage was compromise, or something like that, for years I've been following her pattern. The problem is, though, that I can't store up my need for sleep the way she can. I'm burned out by Wednesday, and by Friday I'm dying.

It took me several years to figure out that there wasn't something wrong with me in this regard. I always figured that if she could do it, I should be able to, too. I took sleeping pills sometimes, because if I get over-tired I have trouble going to sleep (I don't understand it, but it's true). I took coffee in huge quantities in the morning, and then when my ADD was diagnosed I switched to dexedrine. That made it even harder to sleep, but at least I was functional at the office during the week.

Then last year I attended a conference for entrepreneurs put on by IBM. One of the speakers, oddly enough, was a doctor who was a sleep expert. He said that some people can store up their sleep bank account, and others can't. He said that people who need more sleep and don't get it become distractible, impulsive, and grumpy. (That was me!)

It sounded to me, from listening to him, that my sleeping patterns were making my ADD worse, and his information also helped me to stop feeling guilty for not being able to stay up like my wife does.

So I started going to bed at 10pm, and my wife would stay up and watch TV downstairs (she's a Letterman junkie). The difference was amazing. I now wake up in the morning refreshed, looking forward to the day. I don't crave coffee or even use much of the dexedrine any more. And my ADD symptoms are less severe.

At first my wife and I fought about this: I wanted her to come to bed with me at ten, and she thought I was being unreasonable and couldn't understand why I couldn't work the same way she did. Finally we decided that we must just have different body chemistries or something, and she now lets me go to sleep without getting upset. We have an agreement that either one of us can wake the other up to make love, so it hasn't hurt our sex life much; in fact, in some ways it's improved it and added variety to it.

■ Visit "organizing stores" for tools and ideas

From Sandy in suburban Atlanta:

They opened this new store near my house, called Everything's Organized. I've always been major disorganized. The house is a disaster, I can't find the kid's school records, I constantly run out of milk because I forget to make lists, and on and on. My husband is even worse than I am. He's so ADD that he's on Ritalin, and even that doesn't make him organized, it just slows him down enough to be able to have a conversation. But that's another story, this is about how my house was in a shambles.

So I visited this "organizing" store. It's the size of a department store, and the variety of stuff is amazing. They have books on how to get organized. They have trays and baskets and tables, and systems for just about everything imaginable from organizing your books to your spices.

I know that some rich people hire organizational consultants to come into their houses and tell them how to set up systems. Stephanie Winston in her book on getting organized talks about how she does this for people as a consultant. But we could never afford anything like that, and I'd be embarrassed to death to ask any of my well-organized neighbors to come into my house and help me.

But this store was like having a consultant. It was incredible. And the people in the store knew about the stuff they were selling, and the books on how to get organized that they have there are pretty useful, too.

So I went on a shopping binge there, getting racks for my clothes closets and color-coded filing systems and even organizing my pantry. It's been almost a year now, and the house is still pretty well-organized!

My mother in Los Angeles says that there's a store like this near her, too. Apparently, they're popping up all over the country. So my ADD success story is one that many women will appreciate: go shopping!

■ Do the fun stuff last

From Bill, A guy I sat next to on a flight from Phoenix to Cincinnati:

I find that my most destructive procrastination has to do with those things that are the most important, but not the easiest to knock off quickly.

When I walk into my office, there's the stack of mail and phone calls to return. That stack is calling me, like the siren's song, because I can flick through them fast. They all represent a higher level of stimulation and interest than the boring stuff, the report that I have to write, or the marketing analysis that I have to have done sometime in the next two weeks.

But I've found that if I take the important things first, and, among them, the most unpleasant important things very first, I get much, much more done.

The mail then sits at the corner of my desk as a reward to me for doing the job of writing the report or spending an hour on the thing I knew I really didn't want to do.

I also find that once I've finished the hard job of the day, or at least taken a bite out of it as my starting point for the morning, that the rest of the day goes well. I don't have that thing hanging over my head, and I'm not feeling guilty about it not being done.

The little things are always easy, like opening the mail and returning phone calls. They're even fun, usually. But if I do them first, then the rest of the day is a let-down and I find that I'm descending from the fun stuff into the drudge work.

So, by simply flipping the order in which I do things, and doing the unpleasant stuff first, this little system works well for me and makes my days better.

■ Pretend "then" is "now"

Dan in Little Rock has learned how to visualize time:

I was always late for everything. My friends used to call me "The late Dan," as if I'd died. It was a joke in college and at work.

Even worse than being ten minutes late for a meeting or for dinner, though, was arriving late for a meeting or presentation or business trip and discovering that I missed something important.

The problem, I figured out, is that I don't have a good sense of time. There are only two times for me, as you mentioned in your book: *Now* and *Some Other Time*. And I'd learned through my life to only react to the Now times, figuring that I could always put off the Some Other Time stuff until Then became Now.

This habit had done much damage in my life. Between being late for appointments and being unprepared for things, I decided I had to break that pattern. I asked a few friends how they handled it, and one gave me a success technique, which I've been using for a couple of years now. It really works.

What I do is to sit down for a moment and close my eyes. Then I imagine that the Then is Now. If I have to prepare for a meeting in two days, I imagine that it's in five minutes from now. What will I need? And then I walk through the meeting quickly in my mind. What did I forget to bring?

This simple strategy of pretending that Then is Now is very useful for me. Maybe everybody does it, or maybe it's something that's normal for normal people, but I know that most of my ADD friends have never heard about it, and the people I've told about it use it and love it.

■ Exercise to even out metabolism

From Dave in Sacramento:

I've known since I was a kid that there was something weird about my metabolism, because I was always a sugar junkie and I'd get so bored in class that I'd fall asleep. The doctors tested me for diabetes and hypoglycemia, and the tests turned out negative, but I knew something was odd.

I should have figured it out my first year of high school. I tried out for football that year, and got on the team, and all that year I had to exercise after school and on weekends with the team. We'd do warm-up exercises, and then work pretty hard at practice and scrimmage. And that was my best year ever, academically. I should have realized there was a connection.

Now I'm in my mid-thirties, and my wife was hassling me about my gut and that I should start to exercise so I don't drop dead of a heart attack. So first, true to my normal style, I went out and spent about eight hundred dollars on exercise equipment for the house. That lasted about two weeks, and then it became boring.

So I spent a thousand bucks to join a health club. But, after the first few weeks, I didn't go back. It was boring, it was a huge hassle to get undressed and dressed and all that, and I frankly didn't much care for the guys who were regulars there.

Then one night my wife said, "Let's go for a walk." We live in a suburban neighborhood, and so we went out and walked for about twenty minutes. It seemed like no big deal. We had an interesting conversation, probably more of a conversation than we'd had in the past month, because we were alone for twenty minutes with nothing else to do but talk.

Anyhow, she liked that so much that she wanted to do it the next night. And the night after that. It became our regular after-dinner ritual, and we gradually raised the twenty minutes to about a half-hour walk, which I clocked with my car at just under two miles.

The point of this as a success story, though, is what resulted at work and in the rest of my life. I found that I could concentrate more easily. I wasn't so burned out and tired by midday, and I could endure boring meetings without going ballistic!

I'm convinced that there's something that ADD people need that's satisfied by exercise. I don't know what it is; maybe it has something to do with that Hunter idea you have. Whatever it is, I know that when we walk four or five times a week, my weeks are a hundred percent better, in all respects. It even seems to have improved my sex life, although that may just be because my wife and I are spending more time together talking, which I never liked before because after a few minutes I'd want to jump up and pace around. Now I'm pacing around for the full thirty minutes.

Anyhow, it works. And the exercise doesn't need to be at a gym or even difficult. Just enough to get me a bit out of breath (we walk fast) makes a huge difference.

Similarly, Paul Elliott, MD, a physician in Ft. Worth, Texas who specializes in ADD reports:

I have a patient, himself a Ph.D., psychologist, who had referred patients to me for several months before he, himself, realized he had ADD as well.

As we were discussing his history, he reported a typical pattern of irregular and ineffective attempts at college, followed by a determined effort beginning in his mid-thirties.

He commented, casually, that the only way he was able to get through college, including his Ph.D. program, was to exercise one hour at a time, three times a day! To do this, he had to separate his major courses and would jog around the campus, arriving in the classroom slightly out of breath. He said he could perform very well on tests, do very well at taking notes, and follow the conversation of the professor for about 1 to 1 1/2 hours. After this time, he would once again be in his "ADD fog."

Even he had not seen the significance of this. The 60-90 minute period is the amount of time it takes the newly produced endorphins (resulting from the exercise) to undergo their natural, biological degradation and cease their activity. This is another reason that students can often come home from their athletic practice and sit down for an hour or so focusing very well on their homework.

■ Develop "boredom response" techniques instead of drinking, drugs, or acting impulsively.

From a physician who asked that his location not be identified.

All my life I've been easily bored. That's why, when I went into medicine, I gravitated toward surgery: it's exciting stuff. When I'm in surgery, I'm totally in my element, and things are racing along. I love it.

But when I'm not working, life can be boring. And I've done some pretty stupid things in my life to get rid of the boredom. I drank a lot when I was in college. I took a lot of drugs. Even when I finished my residency, I was still taking drugs, sometimes even stealing them from the hospital. And it was all just to turn off the boredom.

I can tell you, this is a hell of a difficulty for a physician. I can get just about any drug, any time. Particularly as a surgeon, it's easy for me to get the most powerful painkillers and I can even get clinically pure cocaine (we use it as a local anesthetic).

At first, I thought maybe I had an addiction-prone personality, and even thought about checking into one of the programs for impaired physicians. But that can be a very dangerous step: people eventually find out about it, and there can be a real stigma associated with it. Besides, when I was working I had no real desire for the drugs; it was on my time off that I'd start thinking about them. This didn't seem to me an addiction pattern, but I really didn't know what to make of it.

Then, about two years ago, a friend invited me to go skydiving with him. I went, and it was the same sort of rush that I experienced during surgery. I was not at all bored, and, in fact, wouldn't have wanted to jump out of an airplane high on any drug.

So I started paying attention to the things that stimulate me and the things that bore me. Social things bore me. Books by certain authors stimulate me. Skydiving and flying (I'm now a certified jumpmaster and licensed private pilot) stimulate me, and next month I'm checking out hot-air balloons. Watching TV bores me. Sex stimulates me (particularly with my current girlfriend).

Noticing these things, I also noticed that when I was doing the things that bored me, I'd start thinking about how good a beer sounded, or even how good four milligrams of IV Dilaudid would feel. But when I was doing the things that stimulated me, the last thing I wanted was the drugs.

So now, when I find myself getting bored, I use that as a cue to shift to something stimulating. And if I'm stuck in a situation that I can't get out of (sitting through meetings, for example), I think of the stimulating things I'll do later, instead of thinking of getting high.

Looking back on the past ten years, I now realize that what I was really battling all that time wasn't just boredom but ADD. The boredom was the most visible manifestation of ADD for me, but there are other symptoms as well. Some of these work to my advantage. I love the stimulation of surgery, and when I'm working on a patient's body I notice everything that's going on. (I really am one of the better surgeons in our city.) The downside was that the low boredom threshold associated with my ADD led me to drugs.

So now I jump out of airplanes and look for opportunities to fly IFR. I'm well past the drug issue (which was really a boredom issue), and am now beginning to tackle some of the other aspects of my ADD, one at a time.

■ Forgive others

From Sarah in Albany, NY:

When I was young my parents abused me. I don't want to go into the details, but it was something that wasn't very pretty.

When I was in my second year of college, I was depressed a lot and not having the best of relationships. So I decided to go see a therapist about it. She got me talking about my parents, and all this stuff about them came out. She encouraged me to get angry at them, to scream about it, to cry. I called them up from her office and yelled at them, and they started crying and got really upset. This therapist told me that if I did all this, my life would get better.

I suppose there was some relief about not feeling so guilty, because when I called my parents they were apologetic about not being the world's best parents, and didn't deny some of the things they did that hurt me. But my life didn't change. I was still down in the dumps. I looked at my girlfriend's relationships with boys and wished I could find Mr. Right.

I went through two more years of therapy, visiting this woman every other week. My insurance paid for most of it, and I kept hoping that it would improve my life. I think one of the things about being ADD is that we latch onto solutions and answers so quickly. Maybe it's because I have such a short attention span that I don't really critically think things through all the time.

Then I bought this book called *Fire Your Shrink*, by a psychotherapist named Michele Weiner-Davis. In this book, the author said there wasn't a single scientific study showing that when people immerse themselves in the pain of their past they get better. In fact, she said, it often makes them worse. And that was certainly my experience.

Ms. Weiner-Davis says that instead of being stuck in the past, we should pull together specific and do-able future goals, then visualize them and work toward them. I know that I'm wildly oversimplifying her book, but it really struck a chord with me.

I left my therapist and found another who was willing to work with me on future goals, instead of constantly revisiting my past. I started out by forgiving my father, and trying to rebuild my relationship with him and my mother. And I've stopped looking for the things in my life—even my ADD—that are pains and roadblocks and difficulties. Instead I now look for the things within me that give me strength, the things I do well, and the things I want to do. I've improved a lot just through this change in direction, and in the past six months I've made some great strides.

■ Join a support group

Hugh in New York writes:

When I first learned about ADD, it was a shock. Both good and bad, if you know what I mean. Good, to learn what had been going on all my life, and bad, to learn that I probably would never become the perfect husband or employee that my wife and boss wanted.

It also raised a lot of questions in my life about what I could or couldn't do. Should I try to get some medications? Should I consider therapy? Would my ADD get worse? Was I doomed?

Since I'm a computer programmer, I've been on CompuServe almost since it started, or at least it seems that way. So I went online and tried the GO word of ADD, and, bingo, found myself in the ADD Forum! What an amazing place: nearly 40,000 people with the same condition I have!

From the ADD Forum, I learned about an ADD support group here in New York. So I attended a few meetings and got to know some of the people there, and that was great for me, too.

It's not like AA, where we're all trying to keep each other from being ADD or something, but more like just a network of friends who understand what it's like to be misunderstood all your life.

Knowing that there are other people out there with ADD, many of them very successful, has been such a help to me. It gave me hope, and

I've learned many valuable tips from the people I've met online and at my local support group.

■ Help other people

This is from a fellow who's a former Dale Carnegie Course instructor in the midwest:

Most people know the Boy Scout's saying about doing a good deed every day.

What most people don't know, however, is that many years ago that saying was slightly different, and, I believe, the older way was the more powerful way.

The old adage said to do a good deed every day in a way that the recipient of it didn't know you were the deed-doer.

This was based on that part from the Sermon on the Mount about not letting your left hand know what your right hand is doing when you do good. We do it for God rather than for the thanks that we might get for doing something good.

I've found that this is a way of bringing power into my life. I don't know what to call this power other than, perhaps, spiritual power. (I imagine the Indians had a word for it.) Whatever it is, I know that when I do good for other people and they don't know that who brought it about, I get a feeling of empowerment that's almost euphoric. Not just the rest of my day goes well—the rest of my week or month goes well.

Think back: when was the last time you went out of your way for somebody in a way that they'd never be able to thank you for or even know that it was you who helped? This is a very rare experience, because you have to work at finding the opportunities.

Sometimes they're right in front of you: the person who left his lights on in the parking lot, for example, with the doors unlocked. Other times it takes some creativity. I was once visiting a family that was having a hard time, as the husband had been recently laid off from work. When they were out of the room, I slipped a $100 bill into their family Bible, where they'd probably find it in the next few weeks but have no idea how it got there. And I called a few people who I thought might be good job prospects for the husband out of work. I convinced one of them to call him in for an interview, on the condition that my name not be used.

So many of us with ADD find that life can be a struggle. We forget things, we misplace things, and we generally have a harder time in this world than our Farmer counterparts. This can be very disempowering and demoralizing.

But I've found that helping others gives me the inner strength to push through just about any sort of adversity. And I agree with the founders of the Boy Scouts that if everybody would do one anonymous good deed every day, the world would be a very different, and much more pleasant, place to live.

■ Have a "clutter place" that you periodically clean out

From Tom in Rochester:

My wife is neat and organized, and I'm not. This causes some conflict about our bedroom, in particular, because I tend to leave things in piles and she wants everything organized.

So, after a few years of hassling about it, she finally hit on a solution: she went to the furniture store and bought me a shift-robe (an old-fashioned type of portable closet) and a bookcase with doors on it. She put them both on my side of the room.

"I don't care if you have a mess," she said, "so long as I don't have to look at it."

So now, when my shift-robe and bookshelves reach a critical mass where things are spilling out and falling all over, I take a weekend day and binge cleaning them up. The rest of the time, I just keep the doors closed, and our room looks, to her, like a nice and clean and organized place.

I know, by the way, that I'm not unique in this. Lots of guys do this with their garages or work areas.

■ Train your attention span: Meditation

Brian in Charleston:

I've found that daily meditation has been very useful for me in training my attention span. I started a few years ago with that course from the Maharishi, called TM or Transcendental Meditation. Then our company had a guy come in who was an efficiency expert and he said it was really just a matter of learning to relax. He told us we could do the same thing as TM but instead say the word "one" in our heads, instead of a mystical mantra. That way there was no religious overtones to it for those who were offended or put off by that.

I tried it both ways, and decided that for me I preferred the TM way, but another guy I work with who's a very solid Baptist didn't want to have anything to do with TM because he said it was based on Hinduism.

He tried the "one" technique and it works for him. So either will work, I'm pretty sure.

The biggest benefits for me are these three:

1. I've learned how to relax. By meditating every day, I feel that I now have a calm center in my life, and when things are getting really hairy, I just remember what it feels like to be in that meditation state and I recover my balance. I don't get upset as easily, for example. It's taught me to take things easy.

2. I believe it's improving my concentration span. Although I'm ADD I prefer not to take drugs. I found that when I took Ritalin and Dexedrine that I couldn't sleep, so I gave them up after just a few weeks. But meditation seems to give me more ability to concentrate at the office on things, particularly numbers, which have always intimidated me. Now, when it's time to do my department's budgets, I just dig in with the other guys and stick to it.

3. I get more ideas. I keep a notepad on my desk at home, and meditate sitting in my favorite chair at that desk. Often during my meditation, thoughts will come to me. They're sometimes things that I forgot to do days, weeks, or, in one case, even two years earlier. Sometimes they're ideas for new ways to do things at work or at home. Sometimes they're insights: suddenly I understand why I upset my wife the night before, or what that guy at the office meant two weeks ago when he said thus-and-so.

When these ideas bubble up, if they're keepers, I write them down. Actually, I discovered that it's essential to do it this way. When I first started meditating I wasn't using the pad, and I'd get a great idea and then spend the next ten minutes (I meditate for twenty minutes every morning) trying to remember the idea, which makes it nearly impossible to meditate. So I started keeping the pad there just to be able to write down and then let go of ideas and get back to my mantra. Now that I realize the value of what's on that pad, and really look forward to seeing what my unconscious mind is going to spring on me each morning as I go up to my study to sit down and meditate.

■ Put a notepad by your bed for ideas

Lamar in Knoxville uses a notepad to catch nighttime ideas:

I'm an independent sales rep with a three-state territory, and my best thoughts come during the night: things about people I should be sure to visit, or new customers for my manufacturers' products, or ideas to suggest to them, or whatever.

I used to wake up all the time with these great ideas, in the middle of the night, or sometimes as I'm first waking up in the morning, but I never had a good place to write them down. And no matter how hard I tried, I could never remember them later.

So I was in the K-Mart (I'm pretty sure that was where I got it, a few years ago) shopping for something entirely different, and I saw this note organizer. I figured what the heck, and bought it.

It's a little plastic holder that keeps a stack of paper, has a place for a pen, and when you push a button on it, the top pops up and a light comes on to illuminate the paper. There's also a little digital clock on it; the whole thing cost about ten dollars.

Now when I wake up with an idea, I just reach over and push the top, the light pops up, I grab the pen and write down the idea.

That thing has paid for itself at least a thousand times over.

A fellow in Portland, Oregon told me this story:
When I was in college I took a course in psychology, and, of course, we studied dreams. We learned Freud's ideas about them, and Carl Jung's, and other scientists'. It was always a fascinating subject for me.

About that time I started keeping a dream diary. I had a little notebook next to the bed and whenever I woke up, I'd write down what I was dreaming.

I first noticed when I started doing this that I started remembering more of my dreams. Used to be that I'd be lucky to remember one when I was waking up: now I can often remember three or four from the entire night.

Then I noticed when I started writing down my dreams, as I read through the dreams from the past week or two I could see where my mind was trying to tell me things. It may be because of that class I took that I'm reading more into this than there is there, or that I'm experiencing placebo effect and making it all happen myself, but I really think that in my dreams, my unconscious mind tries to tell my conscious mind things. It tells me about conflicts and upsets and even reminds me about mundane things like not forgetting to send my niece a birthday present.

I've been doing this on-and-off for years now, and really find it useful. My dream diaries are all in a box in the garage, and sometimes I'll even dig them out and read back through some of my old dreams. It's amazing to me how closely they track what was going on in my life, and the powerful memories they can bring back to me.

I think this has to do with ADD because I believe that lots of us with

ADD are pretty scattered and often out of touch with our feelings and sometimes even out of touch with our lives. This dream diary is a great way to reconnect, to get back in touch with those things. I've found it very useful.

■ Budget in "blow-out" time

Mark on CompuServe wrote:

I have to have my Saturdays. During the week I'm a good boy at work, and with my friends and family, but on Saturdays I allow myself to totally veg out. I don't clean the apartment. I don't answer the phone very often. Sometimes I'll even have a few beers in the middle of the afternoon (maybe three or four times a year, usually when there's a good game on TV). Sometimes I'll go out of town, or take a drive in the country with the top down, or just read a good book.

Whatever it is, I'm beholden to nobody. It's my day. I make absolutely no commitments for Saturdays.

I got this from my parents, who kept trying to be Orthodox but rarely kept it together for more than a few months at a time to really keep a kosher kitchen and keep the Sabbath. But the idea of that one day off, even though I don't do it in a religious way like they did, is something I think is really important to ADD people.

We get so wound up during the week, that if we don't take a day off we just go nuts. I think Moses himself must have been ADD (look at all the things he did impulsively), and he knew (or maybe they're right and God knew), that people, particularly us Hunters, need a day off each week.

So my best success strategy has been to take that day off and do whatever I damn well please with it.

■ Pick "positive addictions" like exercise

Susan in Boston looks for endorphins:

Like a lot of the ADD people I know, I have what some people would call an addiction prone personality. I get hooked on things really easily. When I was a teenager, it was pot. Then I got into alcohol and pills. That lasted a few years until I ended up in a hospital at the ripe old age of twenty-two. I think during most of that time I was also addicted to sex, and maybe even to love.

Two years ago, a friend who was reading this book about how the brain works told me about endorphins. She said that they're chemicals that float around in the brain and make us feel happy. Some drugs, and sex, and even being in love, increase the amount of these endorphins in our brain, and make us feel good. She said that even chocolate does this, somehow.

My friend also said that exercise will cause the brain to manufacture or release more of these endorphins. You can get high from it, she said, just like with other things that aren't as good for you.

Well, I was about twenty pounds overweight at that time, and she wasn't exactly Miss America either. We decided that it would be a good excuse to try to get some regular exercise, so we joined this aerobics class.

At first it was hard work for me. I'd get out of breath, and I hurt. If Sheila wasn't hassling me to go along with her and stick with the program, I'm sure I wouldn't have continued. But she did, and I followed through. After about three weeks of going to this class four times a week, I stopped hurting. I noticed how good I was feeling after the exercise. Before I started exercising, I was always walking around feeling this undercurrent of "I need." I couldn't tell you exactly what it was that I needed, but there was that needy feeling, and I could shut it up for a while with booze or sex or whatever, but that wasn't such a good idea.

Now, I exercise every day. I do it at home in the mornings after I wake up (I jog for about 3 miles), and play tennis on the weekends, and Sheila and I still go to the club three times a week.

The change, for me, has been incredible. I'm addicted to the exercise, I have to tell you, but I think that's an ok thing to be addicted to, so long as I don't overdo it and injure myself. But in the rest of my life, I don't feel that "I need" feeling anymore. I can take or leave things like drinks, men, or whatever, far more easily.

I don't mean that exercise is some instant answer to all of life's problems. But it has been very, very helpful to me. I find that I'm far less impulsive than I was before, and even my short attention span has improved. I don't get fidgety after a half-hour or so of reading anymore. Sometimes I'll read for hours at a time on the weekends or at home in the evenings, which is something I could never before in my life do. My appetite is under control, and I think I look better than I have since high school.

■ **Be aware of your tendency to hyperfocus, and redirect it to positive things, rather than self-punishment or negatives**

From Bill in Kansas City:

I'm a binger. All my life I've binged on things. In school, I binged my homework. I used to go through a different set of friends every six months or so. I went through relationships like that, too: very intense for a few months, then I'd lose interest. I understand that this is the hyperfocus part of my ADD.

One of the unpleasant parts of my binging is that I'd also binge on self-criticism. While I was growing up, my mother was always telling me how I wasn't living up to my potential. My father was more blunt: he just called me stupid. But we all knew that I had a very high IQ, even if I did start flunking out of school around the 8th grade, and never graduated from high school. (I got a GED, and, at 24, binged two years of college; now I'm an engineer with a radio station.)

There was always this voice in the back of my head, usually my father's voice, criticizing me every time I did anything. Every time I broke up with a girl, every time I changed jobs, every time I didn't follow through on something or did something wrong, I'd even find myself criticizing myself for mistakes I made in traffic.

This self-criticism would sometimes run in very large binges, too, sometimes for weeks or months. During those times, I'd get very depressed, be really hard on myself, and that made it even harder to do a good job or have good relationships. This then gave me even more junk to criticize myself about.

I tried going to a therapist about my self-criticism, but all he wanted to talk about was my parents and my childhood, and I thought, this is dumb, this is what I'm trying to escape. Why wallow in the mud when you want to clean yourself off? I tried it for a while, let him get me all worked up and cried a few times. I spent one afternoon hitting his desk with a newspaper and shouting at my father, but it didn't do a thing for my self-criticism. If anything, actually, it seemed to make it worse.

(I'm not talking about hearing actual voices in my head, by the way. I'm not like the Son of Sam. But I'd be saying things to myself, and adopting my father's tone of voice, even, when I said them to myself in my own head. I think many people do this.)

But at least this therapist got me interested in the idea of changing myself, and maybe learning ways to do it. So I started attending seminars and classes at the local New Age center. Most of them were way too weird for me, and I found myself sitting in the room silently criticizing the person speaking, and then criticizing myself for being there wasting my time and money listening.

But one guy said something that changed my life, so I suppose it was all ultimately worthwhile. He said: "We can't always control what happens to us in life. But the one thing that we can control is our reaction to the things that happen to us."

I thought about that for a week, at first making fun of it in my mind, then finding ways to criticize it, and then finally realizing that it was true. So I decided to change the way I reacted to things.

I know this sounds stupid, that you can just decide to change things. And my therapist would have told me it was impossible, although I'd dumped him by then anyway. But I did it anyway. I did it by giving myself reminders (I put PostIt notes on my bathroom mirror), and by putting some effort into it.

Whenever I noticed that I was being critical, I'd force myself to find something good to say to myself, too. I applied this to everything: my criticisms of other people as well as those of myself. That way I was doing it all the time.

So I'd say to myself, "That was pretty stupid, the way you could have made it through that yellow light but instead you hesitated and didn't." Then I'd notice that, and say to myself, "But many people would say that that's good driving, to be so cautious, and, besides, you'll get to your destination soon enough anyway. It's no big deal, and probably was the right thing to do." Or something like that.

The area where this was even easier was with my ADD behaviors. I used to kick myself around the block for them, for interrupting people, or forgetting things, or whatever. Now I just tell myself that it's ok, that that's just because my brain's wired differently, and it doesn't mean that I'm a bad person, or defective. I'm just different from other people, and I have a lot of strengths, too.

I really binged this for the first few days, which then made it a little easier to stick to it as a habit. I found that when I do it regularly, I don't criticize myself so much. And even when I do it now, another voice inside me says that I'm ok.

The biggest result of this is that I'm happier. I don't mean that I'm happy-talking myself into being happy, like some of those idiots at the New Age center (there I go again). Well, they may have been idiots, but they had some good ideas once in a while, too, and one of those ideas has really improved my life. I am actually happier. Because I don't criticize other people and situations so much, I've discovered that most people aren't really so bad or so dumb. And life isn't so bad, either. Because I'm criticizing myself a lot less, I feel ok about myself more, too.

I'm probably not doing a good job of articulating this for you, but at least I'm trying and I hope you understand what I'm saying. I think this is a useful technique for anybody with ADD, and maybe even for people without ADD.

■ **Don't be harsh on yourself about your ADD tendencies: make jokes about them**

Kathy on the Internet writes:

I didn't learn that I had ADD until I was twenty-four, about two years ago. Prior to that time, I'd always figured that my problem was that I was blonde. You know all those jokes they tell about blondes? That's me.

I'm forgetful, distractible, impulsive (I used to be a pushover on first dates, unfortunately), impatient, and always interrupting people. After being told for so many years that I was just a typical blonde, I'd come to believe it, that there was something genetic or whatever about blondes. I'd always be relegated to the dumb blonde jobs, and viewed as a dumb blonde by men.

When I learned about ADD, I realized that my problem wasn't about being blonde, it was about having ADD. I'm a Hunter, as you describe in your books, and, looking back, I see that I come from a long line of them. My mother and father, my mom's parents, my brother, at least two of my cousins—you get the picture.

So at first, when I learned about my ADD, I really struggled with trying to become a different and more normal person. I took Ritalin for a little over a year, and it helped me in college but I didn't like how it would make me feel a bit jittery and then I'd crash, craving sweets by the end of the day like there was no tomorrow. And when I didn't take the Ritalin, I was more distractible.

I think, though, that two things have really helped me the most. The first is understanding what ADD is and how it affects me. I now know what my challenges are, and I'm working on them one at a time. I have my impulsivity under control, now, for example, to a very large extent. And I've learned other coping strategies. That year on Ritalin taught me a lot about what I was capable of.

But the second thing, and, I think probably the most important, is something I learned from my days as a dumb blonde. (I have an IQ of 147, by the way.)

Back in high school, whenever I'd space out or lose something like my car keys or forget my homework, my friends or teachers would make jokes about my being a typical blonde. I learned very early on, probably around the 7th grade, that if I got upset about those jokes, they'd just make more of them.

On the other hand, if I made jokes about myself, and went along with their jokes, they were more willing to forgive me my foibles. Making jokes about myself allowed me to just be me, knowing that I wasn't quite like everybody else, but not sobbing about it or playing the part of the victim.

I've applied this now to ADD. My friends who know about my ADD now hear me make jokes about my ADD, instead of my being blonde. With others who don't know what ADD is, when I forget something or am late or whatever (and, really, it's happening less and less), I revert back to my blonde jokes.

A good sense of humor is a powerful tool. It helps me keep my self-esteem intact, and deflects upset or anger on the part of others. I highly recommend it as an ADD success technique.

■ Schedule activities with friends

Most of us in the business world are so harried, particularly if we're the typical workaholic Hunter, that we end up with little time for friendships. Bill in Atlanta tells how he got around that:

I've known my friend Tom for about fifteen years, but over the past few years we'd just sort of drifted apart. We're both entrepreneurs, and putting in seventy-hour weeks is normal for both of us.

But about two years ago, after Channel 2 ran a news report about this adult ADD support group here in Atlanta, I realized from the news show that I probably had ADD, so I went to the next meeting of the group the following Thursday. I was amazed to see Tom there. It was his first meeting, too, and he was there because he'd seen the same show (as were about 100 other people; the place was packed).

Afterwards, we went out for a beer and caught up on each other's lives over the past few years. It was great. So we agreed to meet the following month at the support group meeting, and then go out for a drink afterwards again.

We only attended the meetings for five months. After that it started to get pretty repetitive, and neither of us really consider ourselves sick, we didn't agree on the emphasis of some of the people there. That's not to say that we don't have problems with ADD, but I guess we're just not group joiner types or whatever.

Even though we stopped going to the meetings, we kept up with our second-Thursday-of-the-month meetings. Now we get together for dinner, and then go out and do something. We've been bowling, went to a strip bar, attended a symphony, been to a few movies, and went to a shooting range. We try to come up with new or weird things that neither of us has done before, just to keep our lives interesting. And we keep each other apprised of what's going on in our lives, and sort of coach each other along when it comes to business, our personal lives, and ADD.

I'd forgotten what it was like to have a best friend: I haven't had one since high school. But Tom's definitely my best friend now, and it's amazing to me what a difference it makes just to have this once-a-month regular get-together.

■ Get in the habit of "double-checking"

Dave in Boston has developed a useful habit:

I used to lose things constantly. Car keys, wallet, money clip, pens, business cards—you name it, I've probably lost it at least once.

Then one time I was in Dallas with a guy from my company to attend a trade show, and we were sharing a hotel room. As we headed out of the room to go downstairs for breakfast, he stopped by the door and patted his shirt pocket, his front right pants pocket, and his back right pants pocket.

"What're you doing?" I asked him. It looked like he was preparing to do a dance.

"Double-checking," he said. "Whenever I go through a door, that's my signal to double-check."

"For what?"

He patted his shirt pocket. "My digital room key, business cards, show badge, and pen." He patted his front pants pocket. "My cash." And his back pocket: "My wallet."

"You always do this?" I said.

"I have since I was a little boy," he said. "My mother used to make me do it every day before I left for school, and the habit stuck."

So I thought that was a pretty good idea, and started doing it myself. And now I rarely lose anything.

■ Find your personal positivity patterns.

Rob Kall is a psychotherapist in Pennsylvania who puts on the annual EEG Neurofeedback conference. At the 1995 conference in Key West, I had breakfast with Rob and he shared what he considers to be one of his most powerful techniques for helping people become successful:

Rob told me that we all have a lifetime of experiences and memories which can either strengthen or weaken us. We've had times when we failed, when we did things about which we feel guilty, and which we wish we could do over or avoid. We've been hurt, we've hurt others, and we all carry a little child's voice inside us which repeats the words of parents and others about how weak, small, powerless, and incompetent we are.

"We all also have had positive experiences throughout our lives, successes ranging from sparkling moments to major life events," Kall said. These are the times when we've accomplished our goals, done things we're proud of, reached beyond what we thought were our limits, and experienced our own strength and resiliencies.

Rob told me that in his early therapy practice, he often did as he'd been trained in school: look for people's areas of weakness, their woundings, their repressed traumas. But the problem, he found, was that when he explored these experiences with people they became weakened, disempowered, and leaned even more on him to help them process and integrate the information contained in those memories.

So, instead, he started looking for what he calls people's "Positive experience resources."

He'd ask people to remember the times in their lives when they were unusually strong, when they were outstandingly capable, when they rose above adversity, and when they were genuinely happy. These positive experience resources can be a wellspring of strength for people, he told me, and they're often totally overlooked in many traditional pathology-based therapeutic models.

"Even when you're dealing with people's weaknesses and pains," he said, "if you've helped them re-connect with their internal strengths then they can bring those strengths to the job of resolving the pain and pushing through the weakness. People can improve many of the skills related to positive experience behaviors, ranging from experiencing good feelings and the sensations of the moment more deeply, to learning to stay with a positive experience flow state for a longer more concentrated period of time."

Many of the ADD adults I've interviewed in the writing of this book have told me stories of a particular teacher, person, mentor, coach, peer, or parent who was significant in their lives. When I ask for details, more often than not, what I hear is that that significant person helped the ADD adult—as a child—to discover or nurture an inner strength or positive experience resource. Whether it was praising them for how well they could paint, or play the flute, or play baseball, that experience of success—and the grounding of the experience in their lives by having it validated by another person—became the basis for other future successes.

Kall recommends that instead of bemoaning our ADD fate and complaining about our weaknesses, we should instead look back into our lives and try to find those patterns of positive experience of which our inner strengths are composed. Remember the times when we could do something well, and revisit those memories often. Dwell on accomplishments, rather than failures; on strengths rather than weaknesses; on the times we took control of our lives rather than the times we were victims.

"Learn your patterns of positive experience and duplicate the successes," he said. "Be brave. It takes courage to be happy. There are countless things you can do which you haven't done yet. Gently, realistically, challenge your resources and start moving forward."

This isn't just happy-talk, Kall insists, pointing to dozens of similar examples from Charles Darwin's less famous book *Expression of Emotion in Man and Animals*, to Bill Moyers' PBS series *Healing and the Mind*. It is, instead, a powerful technique to build our internal and emotional strength.

We find in these success memories a power which will infuse the rest of our daily life. Our willingness to undertake new projects and efforts, our belief in our ability to accomplish things, and even the speed with which we heal emotionally (and physically, according to Moyers and others) from traumatic events in contemporary life, are determined by the strength of our emotional underpinnings. And those underpinnings are found in our memories of our times of greatest strength and competence.

■ Helping children experience competence and success

This story is from Sandra, the mother of a teenager in Southern California:

I hate the current teenage skateboard culture. They wear baggy pants, engage in a dangerous sport, have weird haircuts, and listen to music that seems, to me, obscene.

On the other hand, they're kids. When I was a teenager, I remember that I and most of my friends rebelled. So I'm assuming that this skateboarding stuff is really just a form of teenage rebellion. It's part of a child becoming an adult: carving out for themselves a separate identity in the world. This is an early experiment at that, but I seriously doubt my son will be a skater permanently.

Another mother I know has reacted to her kid wearing baggy pants and all by trying to whip him into line. She punishes him, berates him, makes fun of him and his friends, and does everything she can to get him to stop. His response has been to talk back to his parents in a vulgar and rude fashion, to ignore his schoolwork, which further infuriates his parents, and, ultimately, to run away from home.

I figured, though, that this teenage rebellion could be an opportunity. My son has struggled with ADD all his life, although it was only diagnosed last year. Therefore, he has a lifetime of failure experiences and frustrations. But he's good at skating, and he thinks he looks good in those idiotic clothes.

So I encourage him. I listen to his stories of doing double 180 flips, and tell him how coordinated that means he is. It also shows that he has good concentration and learning skills: skateboarding is not easy. I allow him to keep his self-respect intact by not criticizing his clothes or appearance, and will even occasionally compliment his appearance when he's dressed in a bit less radical fashion.

The result of this is that he and I have become closer, and he's improving in other areas of his life. He tells me intimate stories about his other friends: I know which kids in the neighborhood are using drugs, who's having sex, who's flunking out of school, and who's being beaten by his father. He tells me about what he's doing, within limits (of course, I realize there are some things that no teenager will ever tell a parent). When I think he's making bad choices I tell him in a non-critical way, framing it in the context of how it will effect his future.

This has, I believe, given him a basis for feeling like he can do things competently. After two years of skating (and my gritting my teeth and smiling), he now has a part-time job. His grades in school have improved, and he's thinking about college and careers. And he's more often than not dressing normally. He only skates on the weekends now, and has even commented to me a few times about how some of the skater kids he once thought were so cool and such great role models are really losers.

And the other kids in the neighborhood? What I see is that those kids who are successful at skating, but whose parents are denying or denigrating or dismissing that success, are working even harder at it. Their hair and clothes get weirder and weirder, and they're taking greater and greater chances in their skateboarding. In my opinion, what's happened is that they're experiencing success, and they know it intuitively, even though their parents and most of the rest of society doesn't acknowledge it. And that feeling of success is such a good and empowering feeling that they want more and more of it.

But they're locked into skating as the only source of their success, because their parents haven't taken the opportunity to acknowledge it and then use that as a reference point or metaphor to show them that they can be successful in other areas.

I was watching one of those daytime talk shows the other day where they have weird guests, and they had on some guys who were career criminals. They'd killed people, robbed them, mugged them, and all sorts of things. But they seemed proud of themselves: they were successful.

I'm not a psychologist, but I think that success is a very important thing to people. If the only success somebody can experience is as a break-in artist, they'll latch onto that for the rest of their lives.

So, for my children, anyway, I'm trying to use their unconventional successes as a way to talk about all kinds of success, it's a tool to give them the self-confidence to try to become successful at things like school where they've had trouble before. And so far it's working.

■ The link technique for memory

Don, a dentist from Maryland, tells how he remembers things:

I attended a seminar last year where the instructor taught us a technique for memory that was first developed by one of the ancient Greek philosophers, Socrates or Aristotle, I forget which. He used it to remember his speeches. More recently, the former stage mentalist Harry Lorayne has been teaching an improved version of it, and I see his ads on TV and keep meaning to buy one of his tapes.

But I use it for lots of things.

It involves turning anything you want to remember into an absurd picture in your mind, and then linking that with something else you want to remember.

So if I want to remember a list of things I have to do, I turn each thing on the list into an absurd picture. If I have to remember to do something when I get home, I think of it and hook it to an absurd picture of the front door in my mind, so when I get home and see the door I'm reminded to do that thing. Like if I want to remember to call Bill when I get home, I'll imagine Bill hanging upside down from my front door, with a huge crowd of people around yelling and cheering.

This technique really works well, even though I'm hopelessly absent-minded. The key is to make the pictures really huge, really absurd, and, totally outrageous.

■ Build a spiritual component into your life

Monica found an anchor in the sea of life:

I think one of the big problems for those of us with ADD, particularly women, but maybe men, too, is that we feel adrift so often. We don't know what we want, we can't make up our minds, we're always changing our goals.

My life has always been like that. Only recently I've realized that it was ADD causing it, and now I'm trying to do something about it.

But the reason I'm writing is to tell you about the one thing that has helped me through all those years when I had no idea what was going on with me, and didn't know anything about my ADD. That was my spiritual life.

When I was a child, I was raised Catholic. As a teenager, I rebelled against that, and declared myself an agnostic. In college, I checked out the Quakers and the Unitarians. Now I'm back with the Catholic church, although I don't imagine that's for everybody.

My recommendation, though, is that people with ADD secure an anchor in their lives. I think that something that's greater and more powerful force than us, something we can put ourselves in the hands of, is the best anchor. For me that's my relationship with God, Jesus Christ, and the Church.

I think that whether a person's Jewish, Muslim, or whatever, they should practice their religion. I even know people who are atheists, or animal rights activists, or into politics, who have made that into their religion, and that's probably ok, too. At least they know what they believe, and are anchored in something.

I thank God that my parents took me to church as a child, because it's been the constant and stable thing in my life, all through my life. I encourage you to tell people to take their kids to church, or to say bedtime prayers with their children, or to go to church themselves, or to practice some sort of religion at home. I think it's one of the best things for those of us with ADD who are so easily cast adrift in the sea of life.

■ Pocket voice organizer

Many companies are now selling pocket voice-activated organizers, which will keep track of phone numbers, to-do lists, etc.

Several members of the ADD Forum on CompuServe have experimented with these systems and gotten good results. One said, "I haven't forgotten an appointment in months now, whereas I used to forget them all the time." Another noted that the Voice Organizer "is the perfect mix of high-tech (I love toys!) and practical product; it keeps me organized, and keeps me interested."

Digital Voice Organizers are available in most of the high-tech catalogs; The Sharper Image catalog often features them prominently.

■ Digital Personal Information Managers (PIMs), Personal Digital Assistants (PDAs) and computer aids

Ian on CompuServe likes to use a program called Sidekick on his PC to keep track of his responsibilities:

I thought about buying a PIM but after some thought decided against it. I lose calculators, coffee mugs, keys regularly—heck, it's supposed to be one of our main "symptoms"! I knew I would lose one of these little devices so I didn't buy one. If you do find an ADDer who has used one successfully please let us all know because I would dearly love to know how they managed to keep it attached to their body!

I think you'll find a lot of ADDers, however, who use the more regular computer-program organizers to great effect - you can't take your Pentium 90 to the rest room and accidentally leave it on the little ledge on top of the urinal.

As for computer organizers, I use Sidekick for Windows, which is great because it remembers the things you haven't done, and will remind you every day until December 31, 1999. It'll also play a silly tune to add to the impact of the reminder.

Steve on CompuServe uses a Macintosh program called First Things First:

First Things First is a neat little reminder program that runs invisibly in your Macintosh, until it's time for something you've programmed into it. Then, no matter what you're doing, a little window pops open with the reminder, in your face, where it's unmistakable.

I've put into it all the birthdays of just about everybody I know, asking it to remind me two weeks in advance of the birthday. I first did this about three years ago when the program first came out, and my friends and relatives who used to think of me as the Absent Minded Professor are now all amazed every year when they get a combined birthday and stay-in-touch card from me.

I could use FTF to organized my schedule more deeply, but for that I prefer a paper system, using the DayRunner brand of calendar/organizers. That way I don't have to wait for my computer to boot up to discover I'm late for a meeting, and don't have to worry about a hard-drive crash. I bought the most expensive leather version of the thing, knowing that if I did that it'd both last longer and I'd be more likely to avoid losing it. I've had my DayRunner for three years, too, and it helps tremendously.

A fellow named Rick showed me his new Newton PDA at the CHADD annual show in 1993 in San Diego and said:

This is the first time in my life I've really felt organized. I can do just about anything with this thing, from writing memos to sending faxes to pulling up people's phone numbers and even having it dial them into a phone's microphone.

I particularly like the fact that it reads my handwriting. It's not always perfect, but it's a lot better than having to deal with a keyboard because I never learned how to type particularly well.

The only downside is that it's kind of large, about the size of a can of pop. So I have this geeky leather pouch that's attached to my belt, the way my dad says he used to carry his slide rule when he was in college, and I keep it in there when I'm not recharging it.

Sgt. Hugh Echols uses a PDA (Personal Digital Assistant) to help him keep track of obligations and directions:
I have a tendency to "hyperfocus" on things at times. The alarm (which can be set to go off up to 59 minutes ahead of the activity) can break me out of it so I can at least get to places on time.

By including directions to people's houses I rarely visit in the "Notes" sections of the appointment book(s), I can be sure to find my way when out of town. Since the "notebook" section of the PDA allows for "ink" drawing (with easy correction) I can make quick notes and drawings without worrying about typing on the teensy-tiny keyboard.

Having a to-do list always available is an obvious help.

And, because the whole thing fits in my pocket I'm less likely to forget it than if I were using a paper-type planner.

Donna uses a PDA to keep her life organized:
I am using a teeny Casio BOSS 4600 for all my appointments and phone numbers, and it works like a charm! I have a Dooney & Bourke bag which has a built in wallet in front, so everything I have to carry with me (the wallet stuff, a lipstick, blush, checkbook and register, and the CASIO) is always in one compact place, strapped across my chest like a machine gun cartridge belt.

I must say, the Casio Boss has been an absolute life saver: no papers hanging out all over, everything in one little place, and the BOSS is always with me.

I lead a very hectic schedule as a managed-health-care marketing rep, so, believe me, I need all the organizational help I can get!

Meanwhile, I am testing a Sharp Zaurus, the newest in the line of Sharp Wizard products, and it looks like it may replace the BOSS for me. The Zaurus shows great promise, though it's pricey. However, you can fax from it via cellular and all the rest, and it has a flexible and intuitive operating system. I suspect they'll always be improving these things, and that's only good news for all of us!

■ Redirect your cravings

Frank in Kansas City has found a way to deal with his impulsive cravings:

There are some things in life that I'm a junkie about. Sex, sugar, new toys (especially stereo equipment and new computer enhancements), and sometimes just some wild-ass thing that I see on TV or in some catalog.

Used to be that when I'd get it into my mind that I wanted something, nothing could stop me from getting it. Now, instead, I ask myself if it's a useful craving. If it's not useful but it's not destructive, I'll usually indulge myself just to get it over with. Things like grabbing a quick candy bar or masturbating fall into this category.

If it's something that could get me into trouble financially, or emotionally, like jumping into a new relationship with a woman, for example, then I'll run through my list of other things that I like to do, and try to go for one of them instead. Maybe go to a movie, or get some friends together for a party.

What I've found is that my cravings are deep, somehow underneath everything. I don't know exactly how to describe this other than to say I think they're coming out of some essential part of me: they don't really hook into the specific desire that they seem to be attached to at the moment. If I can find something more useful to crave (even something at work, like a new project), the first craving will diminish or even disappear.

I don't know if this will work for everybody, but it does for me. I still make a lot of mistakes along these lines, but at least now I'm aware when I'm making them, and they're far less frequent.

■ Learn to postpone gratification

Tom in New Hampshire takes it a step further:

I think the worst part of ADD is hyperfocus. When I'm hyperfocusing on something, and it's something I want, I just go nuts. I've gotta have it. I went through it with tropical fish, with woodworking tools, with computer stuff, and I go through it all the time with food, booze, and sex.

Then a few years ago, I went to an AA (Alcoholics Anonymous) meeting with a friend. I was drinking a lot, and he was a recovering alcoholic and he thought he'd pegged me as an alcoholic, so I went along with him to check it out.

I got two things out of that meeting. The first was that I probably am not an alcoholic: I've always been able to take or leave booze, and mostly just drink when I'm bored. I've never been so drunk I've blacked out or anything like that.

But the second thing I got was the most useful. AA has this saying about living life one day at a time, and they use that as one of their ways to deal with the craving that many alcoholics have for booze. The idea of saying that you'll never, ever, ever again do something (like drinking) is pretty overwhelming. But just about anybody can say that they won't drink for just one day.

Although drinking wasn't my problem, I knew that lots of other things were.

So now, when I'm hit with a craving or impulse, unless it's something really important (this can become an excuse for procrastination if you're not careful), I say to myself, "I'll wait just one day and see if I feel the same way." Sometimes I have to wait "just one more day" for a week or so before the craving settles down to the point where I can look at it dispassionately and really make a rational decision about it. This is particularly useful when it comes to buying cars, computers, and houses, all things I've bought in the past on an impulse!.

So my ADD success strategy is to take life one day at a time, and wait to see if my feelings stay high on something long enough to make me pretty sure that I really should get it.

■ Train your attention span

Nigel in Dublin, Ireland tells how he learned to focus his attention:

I was always a very distractible child. In school I suppose I was fortunate that I grew up in rural Ireland, and so was in a small classroom, but still I was a difficult child for my teachers. They often commented to my parents about how easily I'd drift off, or my attention would wander, or I'd interrupt the class with totally off-subject comments. I remember one teacher in particular who used to berate me with a litany of clichés like, "Nigel, an empty wagon always rattles," or, "Even a fish wouldn't get caught if it kept its mouth shut."

Somehow I made it through school, and even through university, although it was a struggle. I'm very bright, probably a genius IQ, and that raw horsepower was probably the only thing that got me through.

Then, in 1984, I heard from a friend about the Maharishi Mahesh

Yogi, the man who'd taught meditation to the Beatles. One of his top guys was coming to Dublin to set up a Vedic Medicine center, and since my degree was in medicine I was interested. I went to a lecture, read some of their literature, and finally enrolled in a class in Transcendental Meditation.

At first it was difficult. The meditation practice involves sitting for twenty minutes at a time in a quiet place with your eyes closed, repeating a single sound called a mantra over and over. It's not the "emptying your mind" that some people mistakenly think: meditation of this sort is very much a focusing of the mind. And my mind rebelled; I'd drift off to sleep at the most inopportune times. Or else my mind would begin long thought-trains. Five minutes would have passed before I realized that I'd forgotten to say my mantra but had, instead, been thinking about a conversation I'd had the day before or some such thing.

I stuck with it, though, largely because my girlfriend, who'd joined at the same time as I, had become a fanatic enthusiast.

And after a few months, I began to notice the change.

At first, I thought it was a negative change. I noticed that I was fidgety, that my mind wandered when I didn't want it to, and that thoughts of an impulsive nature would often intrude into my mind even when I was working in our clinic. My first conclusion was that I was seeing an increase in these sorts of mental behaviors.

Then, however, I realized the truth: I was, for the first time, actually slowing down enough that I could see how out-of-control and wild my mind actually was. These things weren't happening more often; I was just aware of them now.

This self-realization was the beginning of an amazing transformation for me. Now that I was aware of my mental states, I could begin to take control of them. This isn't to say it was easy: I daresay nothing I've ever done in my life was more difficult, at least at first. But now, after a few years of daily meditation, I find that I'm almost always aware of the state my mind is in, and that I can shift that state if I choose to.

I must add that my story is by no means unique. I've heard the same tale told by dozens of people who went through the meditation course. And this isn't placebo effect or self-fulfilling expectations, I don't believe, because it wasn't until well after I began to get these insights that I felt compelled to discuss these things with my peers.

Since that time, I've had the opportunity to discuss with many of my patients their experience with Catholicism and doing the rosary. This being a largely Catholic country, it's difficult to find somebody here who's never said their Hail Marys', but few people have ever done it daily for years.

Those people who have, however, I've made a special point of asking about their experiences. And their reports are similar to my experience: they've trained their minds to be more aware of their attentional states.

■ Other altered states

In February, 1995, I attended the annual EEG Neurofeedback conference sponsored by psychotherapist Bob Kall and held in Key West, Florida.

In discussions with dozens of people including physicians, psychologists, psychiatrists, therapists, and others who had themselves experienced long-term use of EEG Neurofeedback (long-term meaning 20-60 sessions lasting from 30-60 minutes each), I heard a number of stories similar to Nigel's experience with meditation.

Dr. Thomas Brownsback, a licensed psychologist in Allentown, Pennsylvania who uses EEG Neurofeedback in his practice, told me that this experience of becoming aware of brain states, and then—through that new awareness—gaining some control over them, is one of the more common stories he hears among his patients.

In another direction, Drs. Timothy Leary and Richard Alpert, when they were professors of psychology at Harvard University in the early 1960's, noted that their initial use of LSD caused them to discover that, as William James had noted decades earlier, the brain is capable of experiencing a variety of states of consciousness. Many of these we are normally unaware of, and we rarely learn to exert any control over them.

While this insight into other states of consciousness was revelatory for Leary, Alpert, Huxley, and others, they were unable to translate it into their daily lives. Alpert, who later changed his name to Ram Dass, writes and speaks about how he spent years in frustrated attempts to control his brain states through the use of psychedelic drugs, only to eventually discover that such substances weren't the answer: they only suggested possibilities. He turned to meditation and prayer, and claims great benefit from these more traditional practices.

On the other hand, the last time I saw Dr. Leary, in 1992 when he spoke at a convention in Atlanta where I was also a speaker, he was sitting in the speaker's lounge nursing his third of fourth drink (it was scotch, as I recall). The only other time I'd seen him was in San Francisco in 1968, and he seemed then to be a profoundly different person from the man I met in 1992. The introspective, intuitive visage I'd seen decades earlier was replaced by the dull glaze of pain soothed by alcohol.

People respond in different fashions to the discovery of the possibilities of controlling the brain. While Alpert embraced it and dove into the spiritual life, Leary was thrown into prison for years for possession of a marijuana cigarette and this brutal and dehumanizing experience apparently forever diminished his desire to be more, rather than less, aware of his own aliveness.

A more common, and more appropriate, use of drugs to learn to overcome distractibility is told in the following story.

■ Learn to pay attention to paying attention

Stephen is a high-school student in Atlanta, and tells how using Ritalin gave him an insight into how he experienced the process of paying attention:

Through my first years of school I was the class clown, always cutting up and having a great time, but I was also able to keep my grades together. I mean, my parents weren't complaining, and, while my teachers always said I wasn't living up to my potential, they didn't flunk me, either.

Then I hit the 8th grade.

I've talked with a few other ADD kids on CompuServe's ADD Forum, and we all agree that this is called "hitting the wall." It happens to different kids at different grades, and probably has to do with how tough your teachers are or how big the school is or whatever, but the wall for me was the 8th grade. That was the year when I couldn't fake it anymore. I had to start paying attention in class, and I had to start doing my homework.

The problem was that in all those previous years of school, I'd always been able to just slide by, paying attention half the time, catching things here and there, and doing well enough on tests that I could get by, even if my homework was sloppy or done at the last minute. For that matter, before the 8th grade, I never really had much homework.

But in the 8th grade I had to start studying, as I said, and the problem was that I'd never learned how. I literally didn't know how to pay attention in class, and I didn't know how to do my homework. And I couldn't figure it out.

So my mom took me to our doctor, who said I had ADD and gave me Ritalin. I didn't notice much difference from it, but everybody around me said that they did. The one thing I did notice, though, was that now I could pay attention in class. At first it was a shock. Wow! After an hour of boring biology class, I was still listening to the teacher! It seemed that time was moving smoothly for me, and I wasn't bored. This had never happened to me in my life.

I told my mom about it, and she said that I should pay very careful attention to what it felt like to pay attention. I know that sounds kind of dumb, but she was right. With the Ritalin, I could pay attention, and by paying attention, it was sort of like training wheels I guess, I learned how to pay attention to whether or not I was paying attention.

Now I'm a junior in high school, and while I still have a prescription for Ritalin, I only take it if I have to study for a really hard test or something like that. I've learned how to pay attention. I don't mean it's easy. The Ritalin still makes it easier. But I know how to do it now without the drug, and I think that is a very important thing. That will be important when I grow up and go out in the real world and try to get a job or go to college. So for me, taking Ritalin was a good experience.

■ If medication is necessary, develop a system for taking it

Richard in Seattle shared this idea to solve an apparent Catch-22:

How are you supposed to remember to take medication that helps you remember to take your medication? I recently ran across a product seems to be working for me in this regard.

It is a medication dispenser that has a timer built into it. You set the time and day. Then you set the times that you are supposed to take your medication.

At the appointed time, the alarm rings for about 5-10 seconds. The display flashes to indicate that the time has arrived. The display shows the time and day of the last time that the dispenser was opened. The flashing continues until the door is opened.

The model that I have has a belt clip. Usually I slip it into my pants pocket with the clip over the top of the pocket. No one really pays any attention when the alarm goes off since everyone figures it's a beeper.

If you didn't notice the alarm, the next time you look at the display you'll know that the time has passed. In addition you know the last time that the dispenser was opened which is probably the time you last took your medication.

A word of caution is warranted here. If you are taking Ritalin (or its generic, methylphenidate) do not put too much in the dispenser at one time. The manufacturer of Ritalin, suggests, in their literature, that it be kept at less than 86 degrees F. The temperature in a person's pocket can easily exceed that limit. Make sure to use up the tablets so that they don't degrade and lose potency.

■ Experiencing time evenly

Several people I heard from said that they experienced time perception changes or an "evening out in their sense of urgency" when they underwent EEG Neurofeedback training, which feeds back to people their own brainwaves in a way that proponents say will help people learn to control their attentional states. In Dr. Nina Tassi's book *Urgency Addiction* (Signet, 1993), she talks about how many people in modern society experience a distorted sense of time. This is a characteristic I've heard repeated from virtually every ADD person I've interviewed and brought up the subject with. Time, for them, is either going too fast ("on the hunt") or too slow ("bored").

In Dr. Tassi's book, she suggests that what she calls "time-distorted people" can be trained, by techniques that include budgeting rest time, meditation, and other systems, to experience a more even sense of time. This allows them to overcome their urgency addiction, she says.

If this is true, and EEG Neurofeedback turns out to be a high-tech form of accelerated meditation, then it may well be a way of helping people experience time differently, and thus to control their impulsivity, cravings, restlessness, and even distractibility.

Shirley in Houston tells the story of how this technology helped her child:

I was living many parent's greatest nightmare. I had a beautiful daughter of fifteen who was on a downhill spiral of self-destruction. We had been to two doctors. The first, a psychiatrist, told me my daughter had a severe personality disorder that would cause her to either commit suicide at an early age or else burn out by the time she was forty. There was, he said, nothing he could do for my daughter, but he could teach me and my husband coping mechanisms to make our lives as normal as possible. The other doctor, a psychologist, spent six months with my daughter, in private sessions, and I saw no improvement at all.

My daughter had become suicidal, was active sexually, constantly ran away from home, had failed ninth grade twice, and was even kicked out of summer school. She wore black constantly, no makeup, and her hair was always in her face. She slept or locked herself in her room all day, and wouldn't talk with her family.

I came to some very hard decisions. Some call it "tough love"; I call it the only option left if I were to save my daughter from self-destruction. I presented her with three options (she was at the point where she would no longer go to counseling of any kind). They were:

1. Volunteer for a one-year program in East Texas for troubled youth.

2. Be assigned a ward of the state.

3. Attend EEG Neurofeedback training sessions, which I had heard might be useful for her.

I gave her thirty days to make up her mind, and those were the longest thirty days I've ever spent. Fortunately for me and her, she opted to go with the EEG Neurofeedback.

During our consultation with Dr. Nancy White, Dr. White informed me that my daughter had Attention Deficit Disorder, and explained what it was to both of us. I remember seeing tears stream down my daughter's face. She was relieved and sad to know, after all this time and all that she'd been through, that there was help and hope for her future. Because of this diagnosis, Dr. White decided that Beta training would be the best therapy, and my daughter would need to attend sessions three or four times a week for a total of about ten weeks.

It was a one-hour trip to Dr. White's office. My daughter would sleep to and from the office, four days a week. At first she was angry about everything. However, after the 11th or 12th session, she began talking to and from the sessions. One day she told me she would like to go shopping. We went to her favorite country western store. I, from habit, started looking over the clothes, picking out her favorite colors: dark browns and blacks. However, to my surprise, she started picking out bright, colorful clothing—the brighter and more colorful the better.

As the sessions went on, my daughter's personality seemed to change significantly. She started joking around. She would stay out of her room and talk for long periods. Her grades even started improving. By the time she finished thirty-five sessions she was a new and beautiful young woman.

Two years have passed since the sessions have concluded. My daughter has completed enough summer school sessions and correspondence courses to graduate on time with her classmates in 1995. Because of her past, she's had to struggle academically during the past two years. It's taken great courage and persistence. But every time she came across an obstacle (and there have been many), she's found the inner strength to pick herself up and charge through it with great discipline and courage. Even when she felt like giving up, she would pull from the resources inside her and win.

She fully intends to complete college and become a veterinarian or psychologist. She continues to set new goals and sees new possibilities that, before, were unachievable dreams. I now have a new, wonderful, loving daughter with a life full of new beginnings.

.   .   .

Similarly, psychologist Thomas Brownback reports about one of his EEG Neurofeedback patients:

She'd tried to reduce her chronic tardiness by setting her clock ten to fifteen minutes ahead. This strategy was mostly ineffective for her, however, because when she looked at her watch, she'd tell herself that her watch was set fast.

After neurotherapy, however, she found that she was rarely late for things, and had better control of her sense of time.

In addition to using Ritalin or EEG Neurofeedback to change a person's sense of time and their flow through it, some professions actually train people to change the way they're sensing the passage of time and their attentional states. Sgt. Hugh H. Echols, an Officer on a Federal Site in South Carolina, frequents the ADD Forum on CompuServe and he recently left this message to a woman who commented on how she was able to keep her cool because of her ADD hypervigilance and hyperfocus when a knife fight erupted in her school:

From: Hugh H. Echols

To: Andrea

Andrea, regarding your experience with the knife fight, you may be correct in your assessment that ADD assisted you in that situation. In law enforcement we teach our Officers a concept called "the awareness spectrum," which is a way of describing how a person is perceiving and reacting to his environment. The awareness spectrum starts at WHITE and ends at BLACK.

Condition White: A person is engrossed in what he is doing and is oblivious to what is going on around him or her. He cannot react to his environment without significantly refocusing his mental processes.

Condition Yellow: The person is relaxed and aware of what is going on around him, he or she is prepared to act or react to his/her environment, but there is no threat.

Condition Orange: The person is aware of a threat and is preparing for a *proper* action/reaction.

Condition Red: The Officer is actively involved in concluding/mitigating an active threat.

Condition Black: Pure panic; the person cannot react effectively because his mental processes are too muddled to properly perceive his environment.

Most Americans live in condition white and go immediately to condition black. It is a significant step in an Officer's training when we can teach him to operate in "condition yellow."

After thinking about ADHD, the fact that we often can't seem to shut out the world, I think it may not be possible for an ADDult to drop into condition white, unless he or she were "hyperfocusing" to that extent. It is an interesting concept and may explain why so many ADDults do well in law enforcement.

hmmmmmm.

Stay safe,

Sgt. Hugh H. Echols

■ Visualize the person you want to be, and determine what will be necessary to get there

Harry owns an advertising agency in Michigan:

When I first got into the advertising business, I didn't know much about it. Of course I'd gotten a degree in advertising, and I could recite textbook theory, but I really didn't know what worked in the real world. I had no idea whatsoever about how real advertising agencies work.

My first job was as an account executive, which is a fancy word for salesman. I sold advertising, prospected for accounts, all that sort of thing. But I really wanted to be on the creative end. I'm a pretty good writer, and I figured that writing copy was my forte.

There was another guy in Detroit who freelanced for a lot of agencies; he was famous locally for the advertising copy he wrote. I wanted to be just like him: the guy was brilliant, and he also made a lot of money.

So I invited him to lunch one day and asked him a million questions about his life, his business, and how he wrote copy. I guess he was flattered by my interest, because he shared with me all sorts of tricks and techniques. We started getting together for lunch every few weeks, and he sort of took me under his wing.

I started to use some of his ideas and helped my clients write ad copy. In many cases, they liked my copy better than that our copywriters had produced.

The end of this tale is that I quit the agency and went out on my own. I go out of my way not to compete with the guy who taught me the business, and, even at that, I'm doing very well. We've talked about collaborating a few times, but both know that we work best alone. We're still both independent freelancers, although someday we may open an agency and hire some AEs to do the grunt work of bringing in the clients. In the meantime, though, the reputation of our work has been solid enough to build us both up to the point where we don't have to worry about where the rent check is going to come from.

And, of course, I'm a Hunter as you describe in your first book. It's what drew me to the advertising business, what I believe is responsible for much of my creativity, and certainly what forced me to go out on my own. And so is the freelancer I mentioned: he's probably even more ADD than I am.

The lesson here, though, is to find a good role model. Find a person who shares your personality characteristics and who's successful in the world. Then screw up your courage, swallow your pride and buy him or her lunch and ask that person to give you the secrets of their success. Who knows, you just may end up rich and famous, too!

■ Study the lives of other unique people

Beth in Fargo writes about her love of biographies:

As I was growing up, I put together my life skills the way some people assemble a jigsaw puzzle. It's probably because I was ADD and didn't know it, but I always had a feeling that I was different from other people, and also that I was missing some secret formula or important bit of information. If I could just find that special thing, or those things, I could then finally start to pay attention in school or keep my room clean or whatever. So I embarked on a search for life skills, looking for the qualities that I should build into my life and personality. I knew they were out there! I figured the best source of them would be found in the lives of other people, so I embarked on my search by reading biographies.

From just about every famous person's life, I could find at least one lesson—one thing that I could do in my life, or one way that I could improve myself as a person.

I learned about persistence from the story of Thomas Edison, about passion from the biography of Elizabeth Barrett Browning, about compassion from the story of Florence Nightingale (the lady with the lamp), and about courage from the life of Joan of Arc. There were hundreds of lessons over the years, and I loved (and still love) reading the stories of real people who'd lived and struggled, and overcame those difficulties to become not only successful but famous. (I'm convinced that, for example, Marie Curie was ADD herself.)

Now that I have my own children, I mourn the loss of role models in our modern society. I was watching TV with my 10-year-old daughter the other day, and, frankly, was horrified by the way the children on this TV show were acting. And I see her picking up some of those behaviors.

So I've started reading her biographies, whenever I can, and cut back on the TV. It's not always easy, because the only time she sits still is in front of the TV, but I've found that reading to her before bed works pretty well. And she's learning lessons, just like I did, from these people's lives.

■ Find mentors in all areas of your life

Steve in Cheyenne writes:

After getting out of high school (I was too ADD to ever consider college: I just barely made it through high school, even though I'm way above average in intelligence), I had a lot of different jobs. I tried just about everything, from being a bouncer in a strip bar to driving taxis to waitering to working as the assistant manager of a store in a mall.

Then I got a sales job in a company that sells computer parts, and met my mentor.

This man, I'll call him Ralph, was brilliant. He owned the company, and was every bit as ADD as I was, although this was about eight years ago and back then nobody knew what ADD was in adults. But he was successful with his business, and he really knew how to motivate people and get things done.

After working for him for about a month, I went to him and asked if he'd be my mentor. He laughed and told me about how he'd had a mentor himself, a man who'd taught him about how to run a business, and so he guessed he owed it to him to pass it along.

The first thing he did was cut my pay and change my job. This wasn't going to be easy. I went from sales, with lots of income potential, to being his gofer (as in "go fer this" or "go for that"), running errands and doing things that a secretary should do. But he told me that if he was going to be my mentor, then his job had to be to train me to be like him and to do what he did. Since there was only room in his company for one of him, when we were done with the process, he expected me to go out and start my own business with what I'd learned from him. In a way, I was paying for my own college education (the school of hard knocks and gofering) by taking the pay cut and working so hard for him.

He taught me everything he knew. How to hire and fire people. How to understand bookkeeping and work with accountants. How to develop product and bring it to market. How to know good advertising from bad, good salespeople from failures. How to keep yourself motivated. What to delegate (he said this was the hardest thing for any entrepreneur) and what to do yourself. And on and on.

Then, after a year, he graduated me. He told me that I was fired, and gave me an unexpected $10,000 as seed money for my new business.

I now own a company which installs desktop publishing and electronic prepress systems in other companies, and I'm making very good money. And I owe it all to Ralph.

About six months ago, by the way, a young guy who'd just dropped out of college came to me. He said that Ralph had sent him, and that he wanted me to be his mentor. So now I have my own gofer for a year...

■ The "Mirror Technique" from Claude Bristol

Don in Chicago writes:

When I was nineteen years old, I found a book on my father's bookshelf that was published back in the 1920's. I don't know if it's still in print, but it changed my life. It was called *The Magic of Believing*, by Claude Bristol.

In that book, the author had a number of techniques for reprogramming your own mind. One of the best, for me, was what he called the Mirror Technique.

When I'm facing some particularly difficult task, I stare at myself in the mirror, and tell myself how I can pull through it. How I can do it. I acknowledge all the hard things, and also talk to myself about the rewards. I stand up straight and look myself in the eye, and give myself orders.

This probably sounds really stupid and you might not want to use it in your book, but it really works for me. In Bristol's book, he talked about a man who used this technique to even make himself sober when he was drunk. I've never tried that, but I'm convinced it's such a powerful technique that it would probably work for that.

■ Reprogram yourself with reminder cards

Ron in Seattle uses cards to reprogram himself:

When I was a kid, a teacher in high school asked me what I wanted to be when I grew up. I was struggling with school (now I know it was my ADD), but anyhow, I said that when I grew up I wanted to be an attorney. It kind of just popped out. I guess I'd thought about it a lot, but I'd never really said it out loud. And, really, I didn't think there was much of a chance. At that time, I wasn't even sure I'd be able to graduate from high school.

We were sitting there after class, because I had flunked a test and had to take it over, and he'd started up the conversation with me.

When I said attorney, this teacher pulled a small pile of business cards out of his shirt pocket. They were from a Mexican restaurant in town that always had a stack of them on the check-out counter next to the matches, toothpicks, and gum.

On the back of six or seven cards, he carefully printed the words SUCCESSFUL ATTORNEY, and handed them to me. "Do you have a wallet?" he asked.

I did, as I'd just gotten my driver's license, and told him so.

"Put one of these in your wallet, on top of your driver's license under that plastic window, so every time you open your wallet you'll see it. Put another on the mirror in your bathroom so you'll see it whenever you get up and before you go to bed when you brush your teeth and comb your hair. Put one on the dashboard of your car when you get one, where only you can see it. Put one on the wall next to your bed. Stick one inside the door of your locker here in the school."

"Why?" I asked.

"If you don't have a vision of your destination, you'll never get there," he said—and I remember those words exactly to this day. Then he added, "those cards will help you keep the vision alive and vivid."

I did what he suggested, mostly because I didn't want to piss him off, as his class was the one where I had the greatest chance of failing that year.

Today, I'm a successful attorney. I'm ADD as hell, and have two great paralegals who are good Farmers working for me to keep things on an even keel. It was tough work going through law school and I had to take the bar three times before I passed it. But I'm a successful attorney, I win more cases than I lose, and I'm making good money.

I can't tell you absolutely that those cards had anything to do with it, but, honestly, I think that they did. For years, there wasn't a day that went by when the words "successful attorney" weren't run through my mind, and that had to have an influence on me.

And even today I have one of those cards in my wallet.

8

Social Life Success Stories

The noblest service comes from nameless hands,
And the best servant does his work unseen.
                                    — Oliver Wendell Holmes, Sr.,
                            The Poet at the Breakfast Table (1872)

■ The conversational power of listening

Dennis in Anaheim, California shares this story:

I think I've discovered the secret of being a great conversationalist.

About two years ago, I had a capped front tooth that fell off. My wife and I had an important dinner party to go to with my boss and his wife, and I couldn't get out of it, so I stuck the cap back on with some of that one-drop super glue stuff. But I was scared to death that in the middle of dinner, it would fall off and I'd have this huge hole in the middle of my teeth.

So, during dinner I ate very carefully. And instead of talking, I listened. My boss's wife, it turns out, is very active in The Junior League. I'd heard of it, but didn't really know anything about it. And in the past, if somebody had mentioned something like that, it would have been a cue for me to launch into a discussion of all the organizations I've worked with over the years, from the Boy Scouts to the local zoo. (I have a lot of interesting stories from my life, and tell them well.)

But because I was afraid that if I talked much I'd knock that tooth off, I decided to listen to Betty tell her stories about the Junior League.

It was an interesting evening, and I learned more than I'll ever need to know about the Junior League and Betty's activities in the community. But the lesson came the next morning at work.

My boss called me into his office and thanked me for joining him and Betty for dinner the night before. And then came the surprise.

"I never thought of you as a great conversationalist," he said, "but last night you were wonderful. After you two left, Betty couldn't stop talking about how much she enjoyed talking with you and what a brilliant conversationalist you were."

Of course, I was stunned. I hadn't said more than a few hundred words all evening, and they were nearly all questions (to keep her talking, so I would have to). And they both thought I was a brilliant conversationalist!

By this time I'd been to my dentist and had my tooth fixed, but I decided to try out the listening strategy on a few other people. I tried it on my clients first (I'm a salesman), and was amazed by all the things that I was able to learn from and about them. But, again, even more amazing, I was stunned to hear from them later how much they enjoyed our "conversation," when, in fact, I'd worked very hard to try to keep it to mostly a monologue by them.

What this taught me is that people would rather talk than listen. I should have known this before, because it's so true of myself. But I didn't realize that everybody is like this, even shy people, and now I know that if you listen to people, and listen aggressively, they will think that you're a brilliant conversationalist. And, I suppose, you actually will be!

■ Learn to ask questions
From Steve in Atlanta:

I learned something from a sales training seminar that has really helped me out. I'm ADD and it shows up by my always blurting out my comments and opinions and interrupting people.

So I went to this sales seminar, and they said that the best way to sell is to ask questions: that way you learn what your client wants or needs. You then can use his own words to tell him how your product will fulfill his needs or whatever.

I started doing this with sales prospects, and learned something else about asking questions. If you listen carefully to people's answers, they'll tell you what is important to them. Not just with their words, but with their tone of voice and their body gestures.

So I started asking people questions about the things that seemed important to them. Pretty soon people were telling me all sorts of things that they probably wouldn't have bothered to let me know about otherwise. I was learning enough about their businesses so that I could sell to them really well.

But there was another benefit to this. I also started doing it with my personal life.

I started with my wife. It was really hard at first, but now it's becoming second nature. When we're talking and I see that she's animated about something, I'll ask her for more details about that. She then goes off on a tangent, and I learn something new; she knows that I'm really listening to her.

It was incredible for her, too. The first time I tried this, we had about an hour-long conversation. Normally, with my short attention span, I would have been out of there in ten minutes, but the challenge of looking for those little signs of what was important to her kept me there. I kept asking her questions especially about those things that made voice got loud or higher, or when she started gesturing. Suddenly, after about an hour of this, she stopped and gave me a funny look. "What are you on?" she asked.

"Huh?" I said.

"Have you been smoking pot or something? Did you finally go see the doctor and get that Ritalin you've been talking about for months?"

"Nope," I said. "I'm just enjoying listening to you."

"You're kidding."

"Of course not! Why would you think I'm kidding?"

That led us off on another tangent. When we were finally done she told me that after being married to me for five years that was the first time since courting her that she really felt I cared about what she had to say.

Of course I nearly always care about what she has to say, but because I'm usually so busy interjecting my own opinions, or wanting to move the subject along, or wanting to get up and do something else, she never *felt* as though I cared about her.

I use this technique all the time now. I told a friend of mine about it, who's ADD himself, and he told his CHADD group about it. A week later, he told me that there was a shrink at the meeting who said that that's called "active listening," and it's one of the skills that they teach psychologists in school.

I wish somebody had taught me that in school!

A police officer in Phoenix says:
One of the basic techniques of interrogating a witness is to watch for their emotional cues. When they start to squirm, or their eyes move

around the room, or whatever, then you know that you've hit a button with them.

This is a good skill to have in general life, too. While an interrogation with a suspected perpetrator can get brutal, you can just as easily look for those emotional cues in normal conversation and use this information in a positive way.

If you just observe people as they talk, they'll tell you what they really want to tell you, what they're really interested in.

Most people just don't bother to watch for the cues. But even for a distractible guy like me it wasn't that hard to learn.

■ Make notes instead of interrupting

Karen in Columbus, Ohio wrote to me over the Internet:

I'm a field tech support rep for a big software company. When I go out on a service call, I always carry one of those little spiral-binder notebooks in my purse, along with a pen. As the client is describing their problem to me, I make notes. Of course, I've been doing this for years, and this is pretty normal stuff for tech support.

But I've learned a new trick from this old technique.

Listening was never easy for me, because my mind is always blazing along at a million miles an hour. I kept interrupting people before they even had a chance to finish answering my last question or finish telling me all about their computer problem.

The reason I'd interrupt them was because I knew that if I didn't, I'd forget what I was going to say. I'm extremely forgetful, and if I paid attention to what they were saying, I'd forget what I was going to say. On the other hand, if I kept my mouth shut and didn't interrupt them but just kept repeating in my mind what I was going to say next, I'd often totally miss the point that they were trying to make.

So I started writing down my thoughts, the things that I would have said if I were going to interrupt them. That way, I could go back to listening to them without worrying about forgetting what I was going to say or ask; it was written down. And, more often than not, they don't realize that I'm writing down my thoughts or what I'm going to say. Instead, they think I'm writing down their words or thoughts, which is usually even more flattering to them or makes them think that I'm the world's most conscientious tech rep.

This worked so well on the job that I tried it at home. Usually I don't let my Farmer husband get a word in edgewise: I'm always blithering along, blurting things out, and interrupting him. He makes jokes about it to his friends, that I'm like that woman in the Lockhorns cartoon.

When we're talking about something important, though, now I pull out my pad. By "important" I mean it could be about where we're going to go on vacation, or about our sex life, or even dumb stuff about how his day went at work. And I take notes of what I'm going to say, so I don't have to interrupt him while he's talking.

Honest to God, my husband doesn't make jokes about me to our friends any more and our relationship is better than ever. And none of my clients know that I'm ADD or whatever it is that I am, because I don't interrupt them any more and I'm always on track with the conversation.

I used this with some girlfriends a few weeks ago at a baby shower, instead of just blurting stuff out, so I could listen better. One of my friends asked if I was taking notes for blackmail (they were discussing something pretty intimate about one of the girls' husband's and how she was thinking of leaving him). I really wanted to jump in with my opinion, but I just knew I should let her finish, so I took out my pad and wrote down my comment. It was kind of embarrassing at first to tell them why I was taking the notes, and I thought they'd all think I was nuts. But they all understood when I explained it, and now several of them are doing the same thing!

It's always amazing to me how many people out there are ADD and don't know it, and they just run around interrupting you at every chance. If more people would carry around a little notepad, we'd all probably live in a more peaceful world.

■ How to remember names

Mark in St. Louis shares a strategy he learned from a sales training seminar:

I could never remember names. World's worst memory. I could meet somebody and, seriously, thirty seconds later forget what their name was. If there were several people, forget it!

Then I went to this sales training seminar (I sell new cars) and learned something that's changed my life, both personally and professionally. I can now remember all sorts of people's names. Not only that, but I can remember them for a long time, so if somebody comes back in the showroom after a week while they've been shopping around, I can walk right up and greet them by name. That really knocks their socks off!

Here's how it works:

1. Listen. I know this sounds obvious, but most of us don't listen to the other person's name when they're introduced. We're so busy worrying about what we're going to say, or if the person will notice the stain on our shirt, or whatever, that we just don't listen to them when they tell us their names. So, first, listen carefully.

2. Repeat it back. I say something like, "Pleased to meet you, Bill," and then go from there.

3. Comment on their name. This is a way of planting it in your mind. I'll say something like, "Oh, Bill like in those things I get too many of in the mail?" You know, try to make a joke or whatever. I tell them that I had an uncle or aunt with that name (when it's true), or whatever I can think of to comment about their name.

4. Connect the name to the face. The way I do this is to look for a feature on their face that's noticeable. It might be a wart or thick eyebrows or thin lips or lots of wrinkles or whatever, something that'll be there for a long time, though. Pimples don't work because they usually go away.

And then I make an exaggerated picture in my mind of that feature connected with their name. If Bill has three thick creases running up from his nose between his eyebrows and into his forehead (I met a guy yesterday like this), I imagine thousands of bills stuffed into those cracks.

I know this doesn't sound very flattering, and sometimes it can get really gross or funny. Guys named Dick, for example, are very easy for me to remember. But I'm never going to tell them about how I remembered their name, and it's not meant to be mean or anything. It's just that when I make a wild picture in my mind and then see it on their face, that creates a permanent memory. It's locked in forever.

I talked about this last month at my Adult ADD support group. Most of the people there interrupted me (no surprise there, right?) to tell me that what I was describing was something that isn't possible for a person with ADD, that it was too much work, it took too much concentration, and all that sort of BS. But I stuck to my guns: I can do this with or without my Ritalin, and if I can do it anybody can do it.

The next month, three guys came up to me to tell me that they'd been doing it, and hadn't forgotten a name all month. I think that this works well for people with ADD because we're so creative and have such visual imaginations.

■ Plan for social or family time

An entrepreneur in New York writes:

I have four daughters. The oldest is now twenty-four, and the youngest is twelve.

For the past twenty-four years, I was always saying to myself that "next week" or "next month" I'd spend time with my kids. Well, it never happened. There was always something, usually having to do with the business, that got in the way. (And, truth be told, a lot of what the kids would want to do was boring to me anyway. I don't like to play Go Fish, and I hate the zoo. I'm a high-energy, high-stim guy, and even amusement parks get boring to me after a half-hour.)

Then it hit me about six months ago. My oldest "little girl" has grown up, moved away, gotten married, and I still don't know her. I know my business associates better than I know my own kids.

We still have two at home, and one at college who's not yet married. So now I've set aside every Saturday just for my family. It's damn hard to do, this kind of self-discipline, but I made the commitment to them all, and I also asked them if they'd help me keep my commitment. That's been the most helpful part, because the girls and my wife now remind me every week.

And I'm discovering that my kids are really interesting human beings. They're every bit as interesting as my business associates, and we've worked out things to do together that we all enjoy, from watching TV together to going shopping to playing Trivial Pursuit. When I find myself getting bored, I either push through it, or try to get us all doing something else that will keep my interest.

I've lost my first child, and will probably die never really having known her all that well. I'm not going to lose the rest.

A writer in Philadelphia adds:

I just wanted to suggest that many people, particularly those with ADD who may not have the best self-image or high self-esteem, should plan social time in their lives.

I joined a women's business group here in Philadelphia, for example. Before that, because I make my living as a freelance writer for magazines, I was almost always at home in front of the word processor. I had contact with many people—perhaps hundreds a year—as I was doing interviews and research for articles, but no social life.

Joining that women's club was one of the best things I ever did. It got me out of the house, got me thinking in new directions and doing things in new and different ways, and created an instant circle of friends for me. Now, two years later, I'm closer to some of those women than I have been with anybody since we moved away from Chicago when I was twelve and had to leave my best friend.

■ Repeat back to people what they said before going on

From a psychologist in Oregon:

In school, one of the techniques we learned to use with people when doing psychotherapy is to repeat back to them what they just said. There are two ways to do this: one is to use their own words, which makes them feel like you're listening to them (an important thing). The second is to repeat back to them what you understood them to say (which is where you identify miscommunication, and can often help them to see things in a different way).

I lead an Adult ADD support group, and I've shared these techniques with my group's members. From the feedback I've gotten, it's apparently one of the better social skills that people with ADD can cultivate. It both teaches them to listen, and also helps in conversation.

I taught them to use phrases like, "*So you're saying* that people should always buy used cars instead of new cars?" Or, "*It sounds to me like what you're saying* is that used cars are a better value than new cars. Is that right?"

Of course, since the people in my group are all ADD, they had to come up with dozens of variations and new and different ways to do this, but they all seem to work. And, for many of them, the reports that I'm hearing are that this simple strategy has vastly improved their functioning, both on the job and in their personal lives.

■ Become phobic about gossip

From Steve in Michigan:

My father always used to tell me, "If you can't say something nice about somebody, don't say anything at all." He used to jump all over me when I'd criticize somebody or complain about people, telling me about beams in eyes (referring to Jesus' parable in the Sermon on the Mount) and all that.

It was good advice, I suppose, but I always ignored it. I love drama, and, looking back on my life, I now see that I love to be in the middle of things. I remember one time when I was pretty sure that a woman I worked with was having an affair with another guy in our office. I dropped the hint to her husband, and all hell broke loose. I rationalized it at the time as being "the honest thing to do." I admit that I was enjoying the drama. She was confiding in me, as was her co-worker, and I was dropping hints to her husband without letting them know.

Well, what happened was that this woman got so upset when her affair was exposed and her husband sued for divorce, that she killed herself. Until she took all those pills, it was like a game for me. But now, looking back on it, I'm ashamed of myself for having done it. I was just looking for some quick thrills, throwing myself into the middle of another drama.

I was a pallbearer at her funeral, and I cried all that day and the day after. I've never told anybody before that I had a hand in her death, but every night I go to sleep knowing that her blood is on my hands. I often dream about her and all the pain I caused her by helping turn her mistake into a big drama.

And since that time, I've followed my father's advice. I still crave excitement, but instead of getting it from gossiping about other people's lives, I get it now from other things. It was right after her suicide that I learned about ADD, too, and got diagnosed myself, and started taking Norpramine for it. I don't think that was what made the change in me, though, because I've quit taking the drugs and I still don't talk about people behind their backs anymore. I've learned a painful lesson, and probably hurt a lot of other people before Karen killed herself.

So now, if I can't say something good about somebody, I don't say anything at all.

■ Don't be a "blamer"

From Annie in Louisiana:

All my life I've felt like I was under siege. I'd daydream in class, and the teachers would yell at me for it. I remember one teacher who actually threw a book at me. I ran out of the room crying and begged my mom to take me out of school, but it was only fourth grade and she just made me go back the next day.

My father was very critical of me, although I suppose that's probably true for lots of children. But, for whatever reason, I became very good at pointing the finger of blame at other people. I blamed that teacher for throwing that book at me. I blamed other teachers for not being able to keep my interest in class. I blamed my mom for not loving and supporting me enough, and blamed my dad for being too critical of me. I blamed my little brother for everything that went wrong in the house, and usually my parents believed me.

When I hit college, I found all sorts of new people to blame. There were incompetent teachers, professors who were more interested in hitting on me than teaching me, and even the cops who had a speed trap that I hit three times in a year. I blamed them for having the speed trap.

In my relationships, when things went wrong it was always his fault and never mine. When I got a job and things went wrong, I even went to the length of writing down things other people did wrong so I could prove that I wasn't the one to blame. I'd carefully word memos and correspondence so if somebody else looked at it they'd know that the blame was with somebody other than me.

I was an expert blamer.

It took me two divorces, a major estrangement from my parents, and being fired three times, before I finally got it.

I'd read this article in *Cosmopolitan* about ADD and really identified with the woman they described in the article. Wow, what a revelation—and something new to blame! I had ADD and everybody had failed to diagnose it. It was all their fault.

So I went to see this psychologist a friend of mine recommended, who does something she calls "Ericksonian Therapy." I don't know exactly what that is, but after she listened to me for a half hour describe all the people who were to blame for my life being in shambles and my being unhappy, she asked me a really odd question: "What's your favorite thing to do?" (She never once mentioned anything about my habit of blaming other people: I'll get to that in a minute.)

I'd been a tomboy all my life, and I told her that my favorite thing to do was to go to baseball games. Any sort of sporting event, really, but I love baseball, even the minor leagues. (It's a great place to meet guys, too.)

She said, "Who's your favorite ball player?"

"Will Clark," I said, who plays for the Texas Rangers and was with San Francisco last year. He's a good player, a good person, and, in my opinion, very cute.

"What's his batting average?"

"It was .283, last season."

"Which means what?"

"That he hit the ball 283 times out of a thousand at-bats." I explained to her about how batting averages are calculated, and how they change during the season.

She seemed real interested in this, and we talked about it for about ten minutes. Then she said, "When Will strikes out, whose fault is it?"

"His, of course," I said.

"It wouldn't be the pitcher's fault, for throwing a good ball?"

"No, a good hitter should be able to hit just about any ball that's thrown into the strike zone. It's his fault when he strikes out."

"Isn't it interesting," she said, "that he strikes out more than he hits the ball, and he's still your favorite player?"

"Everybody strikes out more than they get a base!" I said, thinking that this woman must be really dumb about baseball.

"Yeah," she said, "I guess that's true."

We talked a little more about baseball, and then got back to me, and she listened to me complain some more, and then I paid her and left, with an appointment for two weeks later. I felt that maybe she wasn't a good therapist, because she didn't have me lay on a couch and didn't ask much about my parents and all that stuff. But I figured I'd give her a month or two before I'd start blaming her for being a lousy shrink.

But the weirdest thing happened. The next day at the office, at my new job where I was a writer for a small PR agency, my boss came in with a news release I'd written. He pointed out three mistakes in it. He wasn't angry or anything, just pointing them out, but in the past I always would have figured out an excuse, and found somebody to blame. In fact, one of the mistakes was because the client had given me the wrong information: I could have legitimately blamed them.

Instead, though, as if in a dream, I heard myself say, "Well, nobody bats a thousand. I'll get this fixed right away."

He smiled, thanked me, and left the office.

During the next two weeks, I don't think I blamed anybody for anything. I took responsibility for my mistakes, helped other people correct theirs, and must have said at least a hundred times, "Well, nobody bats a thousand."

What's really funny, though, is that I didn't realize at the time that I was doing that. What I did notice, though, is that all of a sudden everybody at work liked me. My boyfriend became a different person: much more approachable and affectionate. And I even had a nice conversation on the phone with my mother.

So, two weeks later, there I am again in this shrink's office. And she asked me how the past two weeks have gone, and I tell her that people around me are all changing. I'm wondering if they've all started taking Prozac or something. And she laughed and said that it seemed that probably I didn't need to see her much any more, and maybe we should just get together in six months to touch base.

At that moment, it all suddenly fell into place for me. I realized that in some sort of sneaky way, she'd made me realize that it's ok sometimes to be wrong, and to accept the blame for it. I'd started doing that, and the world hadn't ended. God, what a revelation that was.

"Did you hypnotize me?" I asked her.

She laughed again and said no, that she'd just helped me get a new frame of reference.

So my success story is to stop blaming. I don't blame other people any more, don't blame life's circumstances, and don't blame my ADD. I'll never bat a thousand, and that's ok: even Babe Ruth couldn't do that, in baseball or in life.

■ Always criticize yourself before others

Dale in San Francisco learned how to give criticism without giving offense:

Being the ADD person I am, I tend to blurt things out. I'm smart, and often know the solutions to other people's problems, even before they do. I figure things out quickly. And often what I'm figuring out is how somebody else screwed something up.

Used to be that I'd always just tell people what I was thinking, particularly when I saw how they were doing something wrong. After all, that's how I talk to myself about myself. But people would take offense, get upset, and for years I couldn't figure out why other people were so sensitive, and so stupid for not wanting to know how to change and fix whatever it was they were doing wrong.

Then I went to work for Billy. I work as a waiter in a nice restaurant here in San Francisco, and it's always easy to make mistakes. You drop glasses and they break, you mess up orders (we take them from memory here, but that's another story), sometimes you say the wrong thing to people, and so on. Being a waiter pays well, but it can be a very difficult job. I don't think most people realize how hard it is.

Billy owns the restaurant, and he's my boss. And when I first started working here, I noticed that there was something different about the way he criticized me and the other waiters and the cooks and the busboys and everybody. He'd never say, "You made so-and-so mistake." Instead, he always would preface his criticism with a very short story about how he'd once made the same mistake himself. Then, after this moment of self-revelation, he'd go on to tell us that we'd done the same thing and he didn't want us to do it again.

When he was offering opinions about things, instead of just a straight correction or order, he'd often preface his comments by saying, "I may be wrong—I often am, you know—but I think that..."

By criticizing or correcting us this way, he totally took the sting out of it. I was amazed by how some of the most prickly and sensitive guys who work here as waiters would take criticism from Billy that would have infuriated them from somebody else. And it wasn't because Billy was the boss: these are guys who've told dozens of former employers where they could shove their job. It was because the way Billy corrected you always made you feel he understood the problem, that he wasn't judging you, and that he wasn't putting himself above you.

After a few weeks of working for him and seeing how consistently he used these techniques, I asked a couple of the other guys how they felt about it. "Isn't he just trying to manipulate us?" I said. "Isn't he just trying to butter us up so we'll take his orders without a fight?"

Several agreed that that might be the case, but so what, they said. When he's right, it's stuff that needs to be said, and at least he's saying it in a way that doesn't hurt.

I was amazed. I expected that people would think that he was being a manipulator, that his prefatory comments were gratuitous and maybe even demeaning. But instead people took them just the other way.

So I started doing that myself. When I'd correct other people, I'd preface my corrections with a self-confession, or a comment about how often I'm wrong, although I think that I'm right this time.

Now, it's almost like people are lining up to be my friends. While I used to lose friends all the time because of my big mouth, now I seem to both attract and keep them. I've never had more friends in my life. And Billy has promoted me to head waiter, so I'm the boss of the other waiters, and I use his technique with them, too, and it's amazing how rarely I get in fights with people now.

It's so simple, but it is such a powerful technique. I wish I'd known about this in high school!

9

Relationship Success Stories

"Let me light my lamp,"
Says the star,
"And never debate
if it will help to remove the darkness."
                            —Rabidranath Tagore, *Fireflies* (1928)

■ We all experience love differently

How do you know if somebody loves you?

Most people think they know the answer to that question—and many are wrong.

The problem is twofold.

First, we can never really know what another person is thinking or feeling: we can only observe their behavior and draw inferences from that.

The second is that we judge others by our own standards. If I'm a person who feels loved when somebody hugs me and kisses me, I'm most likely going to try to show love to another person by hugging and kissing them. But what if they experience the feeling of being loved when somebody brings them an unexpected gift, and hugs or kisses are relatively meaningless to them?

This isn't an abstraction: it's a very real problem of communication, particularly for people with ADD, in relationships ranging from those with our spouses to those with our friends or children.

For example, after eight years of marriage, Bill and Sue were both concerned. Bill was worried that Sue didn't love him any more, even though she insisted she did. And Sue suspected that Bill had fallen out of love with her, even though he thought he was expressing his love for her on a daily basis.

The problem was that Bill felt loved when he received affection. A simple touch on the shoulder would give him a warm feeling inside: a hug or kiss would make his day. And so this is what he did to Sue every day.

But physical affection wasn't particularly important to Sue. These touches from Bill seemed gratuitous to her, and she thought he was just doing it because it made *him* feel good. To her, being loved meant that the other person went out of their way to make special time for you, to spend time talking, walking, and sharing. And Bill's attention span was so short that these kinds of things hadn't happened since they were courting and first-married, when he was still fascinated by the newness of their relationship.

The root of their different ways of experiencing love came from their experiences as children, and, for Bill at least, was also rooted in his ADD.

In Sue's family, her parents had made a ritual of family dinners, and the family would have long, involved discussions over the dinner table. That always made her feel loved: they listened to her, asked her questions and paid attention to her answers. Neither of her parents had Bill's short attention span, and the attention they gave her became the basis for her concept of love. They were also far more cerebral than affectionate.

Bill, on the other hand, grew up in a family where people would hug each other constantly. His parents never took him out or had "special time" for him, like Sue's did, but they constantly touched him, hugged him, and told him how much they loved him. At least one of Bill's parents, and possibly both, were ADD, and for them the idea of sitting over the table for hours was inconceivable: dinner was often an on-the-run or sit-in-front-of-the-TV affair. But people with short attention spans develop fast ways of showing love, and in Bill's family it was those brief touches and words of affirmation.

So, for Bill, the best way to show love was a hug. For Sue, love was best demonstrated by participating regularly in a long conversation.

Bill hadn't grown up feeling unloved because his family rarely had meals together, and Sue hadn't grown up feeling unloved because her parents rarely touched her. Both had taken the paradigms of their families and developed the assumption that that particular behavior was how "everybody" showed love.

But neither had ever told this to the other (probably neither realized it).

Bill's ADD made long conversations uncomfortable for him. He hated them, and bluntly said so whenever Sue suggested they sit at the dinner table for a long or formal meal, or sit afterwards and talk over coffee.

Sue interpreted this as Bill no longer loving her; after all, if he loved her, he'd want to talk for hours. And she was confused when Bill would tell her that she obviously didn't love him because it had been four days since she'd as much as put her hand on his. What on earth did that have to do with love?

Bill, on the other hand, was feeling that Sue didn't love him because she could go months without giving him even a single unsolicited hug. She, instead, was always wanting to "sit and talk for a while," which Bill found irritating. After all, if you loved somebody, didn't you touch them and tell them that you loved them? What did long talks about often-irrelevant matters have to do with love? If anything, it seemed to him that her demands for conversation were just a way of hassling him.

The beginning of the solution was relatively straightforward. Upon learning about different loving styles, each made the effort to honestly tell the other what made him or her feel loved. Then each made a commitment to follow through by giving the other what they wanted, and suspend for a while their monitoring of the other's behavior. The emphasis shifted from getting to giving, and each said "thank you" when they realized that the other was going out of his or her way to give touches or attention.

Bill, with his newfound awareness of his own ADD, made a special effort to push through his impatience and to spend time sitting and talking with Sue. At first, he had to take Ritalin to make it through, or drink a lot of coffee, or a few beers. Whenever they were in a room together, that was a reminder cue to Bill to give Sue a chance to initiate a conversation, or for him to start one, and to not leave until she signaled that it was over. Over a few months, he learned how to be a good listener and conversationalist. And for the first time in years, Sue felt like Bill really did love her.

For her part, Sue, realizing that Bill needed more affection than was normal for her, put an equal effort into trying to reach out to him. When they passed in the house, she'd touch him briefly. In the mornings and evenings when waking up or going to sleep, she'd make an effort to remember to kiss him or say good night. Whenever he was in the same room with her, that was a reminder cue to her to touch him at least once before they left the room. And for the first time in years, Bill now knew that Sue loved him.

And, of course, this goes way beyond just couples.

I was startled recently when I asked each of my children what made them feel loved. Our oldest said that she felt loved when she was hugged, or told "I love you." Our middle child said he felt loved when we took him to a restaurant without his siblings and bought him a meal. And our youngest said that she felt loved when we played games with her, helped her with her schoolwork, or took her to a movie with her friends.

I'd always assumed that when I told any one of them that I loved them that they'd then know that I loved them—but words like that were only meaningful to one of the three.

We all experience love differently, and what we want to get is very often quite different from what we should be giving to make those around us feel that we love or care about them.

The challenge for all of us is to pay attention closely to the signals others give about how they want to be loved, and then express our love to them in the way they will hear/see/feel it, no matter how odd or counterintuitive it may seem to us. The most difficult part of that for people with ADD is when their partner considers "paying attention" to be a sign of "love." This is common in our culture, particularly among Farmer types of people.

But self-knowledge is always half the battle. Making an effort to give our partners, friends, and family members expressions of love on *their* terms is one of the first and most effective ways of getting back love on our own terms.

■ Plan for variety in life and activities

A woman at a speech I gave in Columbus, Ohio, said this works for her:

I find that if I don't plan for variety in my social activities, then I get bored and restless with the day-to-day stuff. I either get grouchy, or else find myself jumping into doing things impulsively that aren't always so constructive.

Now when I see things in the paper that look interesting to me, like a new group playing in town, or an exhibit, or an upcoming lecture, I immediately call and book a reservation for myself and a friend. I try to pay for things over the phone in advance when I can: that way I'm committed, and have to attend.

I started doing this about four years ago, and I'm continually amazed by the variety of activities out there, even in a city as small as Columbus. I've learned so many interesting things, and met so many interesting people, as a result of doing this, that it's really helped me in many ways. The friends I've brought along with me like it, and it's often led to deeper relationships with them.

I know, from my patterns in the years before, that if I hadn't decided to start doing this (I actually started because of a suggestion in an Ann Landers column) I'd still be sitting in front of the TV at night. Or else I'd be going to bars, and complaining about how boring my life is or about the quality of the people I was meeting.

■ Create variety in your sex life

Several different people emailed me via CompuServe about the import-ance of building variety into their sex lives to keep things stimulating and interesting. Here are some of their suggestions/experiences:

• Do things in unconventional places. "My husband and I will occasionally make love in different rooms in the house. Last year we did it in the back seat of our car at the drive-in, something I haven't done since I was eighteen."

• Try different positions. "We got this book about different posi-tions, and tried out a bunch of them. Every few weeks we'll try some-thing different now, just to keep from getting into a rut (no pun intended)."

• Act out fantasies. Some of these stories were a bit strong for a general-interest book, but the title speaks for itself. Have an agreement in advance that neither of you will laugh at or ridicule the other's fantasies, and then share them with each other. Figure out ways to try acting them out.

• Take turns being responsible for initiating intimacy. "This may sound weird, but every Tuesday night my wife is responsible for initiat-ing intimacy, and every Friday night I am. What's useful about this is that, knowing it's my turn, I think throughout the day of how I can turn her on in a new way, or the best way, and I know that she's giving her night the same sort of thought. It's revitalized our sex life."

• Get instruction in technique. "We bought one of those How To Make Love' videos that *Playboy* magazine sells and watched it together. It's not the gross stuff that they sell in the dirty book stores, and it was an ice-breaker for both of us, even though we've been married for six years. Now we're both more willing to experiment and try new things, and watching the tape together got us talking about what works for each of us."

• Practice intimacy without making love. "We saw Dr. Ruth on TV and she suggested that a couple should try being affectionate for two weeks without making love at all, just to practice intimacy. We tried it, and it was really great. We rediscovered each other, and, when the two weeks were over, we had a really wild time."

■ Budget in communication time

From Steve in New York:

My wife has complained for years that I never listen to her. I never really knew what she was talking about, because it seemed to me that I listened to her just fine. But I finally understood that it wasn't that she wanted me to listen to her, but that she wanted me to listen to her for a long time. I was interested in getting to the meat of the discussion, resolving things, and then getting on with my life. She wanted to talk, without any specific goal in mind just for the conversation.

It took me the better part of twelve years to figure this out, and it wasn't until I started taking Ritalin, and could sit down with her for an hour at a time, that I realized what she meant.

So now we play backgammon. We have a board, and play a few games, and that's our time to talk. It keeps me interested, and gives her time to talk. We've been doing this for about six months now, and we're not only both getting pretty good at the game, our communication is better, too.

■ Choice of mate

From Sheila in Michigan:

The oddest advice I ever got from my mother was to study the parents of every boy I dated. She said that everybody eventually ends up being much like their parent of the same sex, and I thought she was nuts. But now, after being married for seventeen years, I can say that it's very often true.

My advice to people who have ADD is to look for a mate who's not ADD and can coach you through life, take care of the checkbook and other things. And check out their parents to see what life with him (or her) will be like ten or twenty years down the road.

■ Choose as a partner someone who offers you encouragement

Many people wrote or told me about the importance of finding a mate who was supportive and nurturing. Here's one story from a person who didn't want his name used:

Growing up with undiagnosed ADD, I had a bad time. School was hell, my parents were always on my case, I couldn't keep my room clean, and so much other stuff. Everybody blamed me for it all, and I ended up with a lousy self-image and very little self-confidence.

Then I met my current wife. She's not any happier than my mother was about how messy I am, but she doesn't criticize me for it. Instead, when I leave a mess, she won't serve me dinner until it's cleaned up. She doesn't get angry: she gets even, but not in an angry way. So I don't feel bad, and she has a clean bedroom.

But most important to me is how supportive she is. Some people are like this, I've discovered, and others are just the opposite. Every day my wife tells me something nice about myself. She'll compliment me on my clothes, or the way I look, or on something I said or how smart I am. She means it, too. She doesn't just make things up, or flatter me with generalities. It's always specific, something that I've done or how I look.

I guess you could say that she's got me house-trained. I don't mess in the house anymore (at least not too often), and I always feel welcome and loved. This has given me the inner strength to try for new jobs, move up the ladder, and really be successful in my work.

My wife has rebuilt me from the damage that was done by my childhood ADD, and I can't thank her enough.

■ Understand how you're drawn to "high stim" relationships

From Bryan in San Francisco:

I'm ADD and hyperactive. I was diagnosed with it when I was in school as a kid, and was on Ritalin from the time I was eleven until I turned sixteen. That was ten years ago.

I've always been drawn to explosive relationships. Not like abusive explosive, but really fast-moving, very intense relationships. What I've found, though, is that those kinds of relationships don't last.

I dated this guy a few times on and off over the years who was quite different from the usual person I'm attracted to. He was stable, had a job as an architect that he'd had since he graduated from college, and didn't like to hit the bars. He wouldn't have sex with me on our first few dates, so I dropped him, but we remained friends.

Now I've realized the value of people like that. When I read your book about Hunters and Farmers I realized that I was a Hunter, and all these years I'd been dating other Hunters. It was wild fun, but none of them lasted: we'd both get bored and the relationships always fell apart.

After I read the book, I thought that maybe I should try dating a Farmer, and that made me think of Keith. We went out and I told him all about ADD, and we rekindled our friendship. He's still the cautious type, which is important in this day and age, and at least I've managed to avoid the plague, if you know what I mean. He had me get tested, in fact, before he'd start the relationship with me.

So now we're living together, and have been for almost a year. We have fights sometimes, usually about how he wants things neat and clean and how I'm a slob, but I think those kinds of things are normal in a relationship. I'm seeing the value, for the first time, of finding a stable person to anchor me down. I always used to think people like Keith were just boring, and I'd put them down. Now I'm discovering, as I get to know him, that there's a lot of depth to his personality. I'm learning new things all the time. And he's become a hitching-post for me, a center I can spin around without getting lost or tangled.

■ Expect boredom in relationships, and plan for ways to transform it rather than fleeing the relationship

From Michael in Atlanta:

I've been married for twenty-six years now, and have been ADD all my life, although I only realized it two years ago. My success story is staying married.

In the first few years of our marriage, I had a few affairs. I was very distractible, and if somebody offered themselves, I'd jump at it.

Then I brought home a venereal disease to my wife, and we both had to go to the doctor to get penicillin shots, and the whole thing came out. She threatened to leave me, and I asked her to give me another chance.

Since then I haven't strayed. Sometimes I'll fantasize a lot about other women, but that's it. Instead, whenever I think about straying, I tell myself all the important things about my marriage and our kids, and then that night I go out of my way to really have a great evening with my wife.

I know it's possible to be ADD and to be faithful because I've done it. And as I get older, I can tell you it's worth the effort. I think it was Ben Franklin who said that a man's best three friends were an old dog, an old wife, and ready money. He was right.

10

Workplace Success Stories

The world is sown with good; but unless I turn my glad thoughts into practical living and till my own field, I cannot reap a kernel of the good.   —Helen Keller, *Optimism* (1903)

■ Make being organized interesting

This story is from Greg Vetter, the president of an organizational training and consulting firm in Atlanta. He tells how he discovered that being distractible and high-stim do not necessarily mean you can't get organized, and shares one of the techniques that he's taught to people ranging from entrepreneurs to presidents of Fortune 500 companies:

I've gotten to meet a lot of new people in my career. I changed jobs like some people change hair styles. The first job I had other than working for my family's business was mowing lawns. Then at seventeen I moved up to bigger and better things: I was working at the 7-11, but not for long.

I'll never forget, my sole purpose was to organize the store's cooler and candy section. Never mind that I was supposed to be checking customers out at the register. The owner's priorities and mine were worlds apart, so he asked me to organize elsewhere. Little did I know that later in my life I'd be organizing presidents of Fortune 500 companies. Obviously my boss didn't either, because he certainly never would have let me go. Who knows, if he hadn't fired me, I still might be working at a 7-11.

For as long as I can remember, I've needed things to be in an orderly, familiar way. If they weren't, I felt anxious and out of my element. When I would work on a charitable project I used to go crazy, because everything was so disorganized and so much time was being wasted. I found it very hard to be in a disorganized environment. If I didn't have all my ducks in a row, I got frustrated pretty quickly because it wasn't familiar to me and I felt out of control.

In college I majored in psychology; actually I double majored in it. During an Industrial Psychology class, we toured a John Deere factory to study how productive the factory and the workers were. I was hooked by this experience, and couldn't get enough. I wanted my career to involve something regarding how people worked, but I didn't know exactly what yet.

Fifteen years later, after working and struggling in corporate America and elsewhere, I decided to start my own business. It was a restaurant and catering company which I started with my partner, Bill. Putting it together was a ball, but after it was up and running I was bored. No challenge, nothing new to learn. Running that business did, however, drive me crazy, because it was one interruption after another and I could never get anything accomplished.

What I found in my career was that I got bored very easily if I was in any sort of routine. The constantly changing and exciting atmosphere was great, but routine wasn't. Half my jobs have been in management and starting things from scratch. Once they're up and running smoothly, though, I'd invariably become bored and lose interest in what I was doing.

Through the years I've always had the urge to create a better organizational system for myself, whether it was selling, running a restaurant, or supervising a sales district. Finally, in 1989, I decided to create my own organizational consulting business. Every job that I had had gave me another chance to perfect a system of how to work. I collected all my thoughts, experiences, and systems that I had developed and created "A Vetter Way To Master Your Paper And Priorities." I created a system to meet my own needs: one that would allow me to function and excel in getting things accomplished at work. Here's how it works:

Many of the people I've worked with find the most useful part of my system is the idea of a paper-free desk. Every loose piece of paper on your desk represents a decision not made. Think about when you sit down in front of your desk and there are stacks of paper and loose pieces of paper everywhere. If you feel constantly interrupted, it's probably due to that little voice in your head reminding you of all the things you still need to do. Each piece of paper is a distraction and an interruption. If you videotaped your head movements during the day, you'd find your head turning to the left, the right, the top of your desk, and so on and on, noticing all those pieces of paper and constantly distracting you from what you were attempting to do.

In the Vetter system, there should only be five things on your desk: An In Box on one side, and an Out Box on the other; your phone should be on your left if you're a righty and on your right if you're a lefty; your appointment book and computer complete the list. Everything else is filed away with a system in place on how to get your priorities done.

One of the most useful parts of the Vetter system is my five-step system to empty your In Box of papers and materials in five minutes or less.

Most of us do our work out of our In Boxes. As a result, they're almost never emptied, we never want to go through them, and the pile of stuff in them grows at an unexplainable rate.

So here's the five-step system that's perfect for ADD people:

1. *Stand up.* When we sit, we have a tendency to take longer with whatever we do, but when we stand we become energized.

2. *Ask yourself OATS.* There are only four places anything in your office can go. Out Box (out of your office), Action (things to do), Trash (anything you want to get rid of), and Support (things you refer to).

3. *Decide the category and the file.* Categories are groupings of similar or like things. Files are the individual components that make up a category. When you decide to keep something, it will go into either one of your Action or Support categories. It always works from general to specific, big to little. The sequence starts with category, then goes to sub-category, then file, then sub-file.

4. *Say it, hear it, see it, touch it, and, if you're weird, smell it.* The reason we forget where we put something is because we don't decide what to name it (categories and files) and because we don't reinforce where we will keep it. Use all your senses when you sort through your In Boxes. Say the category and file name out loud, see what it is (visualize it in your mind), touch it and sometimes even smell it. (Remember those perfumed letters you got years ago?)

5. *File it away.* Simply put your papers away. When you're finished with this process, you can work on getting things done *one at a time*. In the meantime, you have a paper-free desk with an empty In Box, you can find everything in five seconds or less, and you're in control.

Not a bad way to start out a day's work!

■ Use one of the commercial calendar notebook systems
Richard on CompuServe wrote:
I use a Franklin Planner and have found it very helpful. I work for

an engineering consulting firm and often have two or three projects going on at the same time.

I found it useful to create a prioritized task list of all of the outstanding items (no matter how small) and put them into the list.

First I write down everything I can think of that still needs to be done. Then I group them into A, B, and C priorities (high, medium, and low priority, respectively). Then within each group I put them in the approximate order of importance.

I don't number the items since I use a word processor to keep the list and I just rearrange the lines within the text should priorities shift/change. At the end of each item I put the initials, in parentheses, of the person(s) responsible for the item. This forces me to think about what tasks can be delegated to others.

I place an asterisk in front of items that are started but not yet finished. Sometimes this is because I am waiting for someone else to finish, or I need a piece of information.

I print out the list, fold it in half, and stick it in the pocket in the back of my Franklin planner (I use the 8.5" x 5.5" or "Classic" size).

If I think of something to add to the list while I am away from my computer, I just jot it down on the printed list. As items are finished I cross them off. Every couple of days I update and print out a new copy of the list.

Items from the list get added to the daily task list in the planner as required. This is really just an extension of the Master Task List idea that the Franklin planner already uses. Since people with ADD find it helpful to break a project down into a smaller series of steps, the Master Task List provided in the planner would fill up very quickly.

Although doing all this sounds cumbersome, it takes far longer to explain than to do. I've been using this idea for about six months and it has been very useful.

■ Build in as much external structure as possible

Bill found success in the Army:

This may sound odd, but I think that the military is one of the best places for people with ADD. The reason is that there are systems for everything, you always know what is expected of you, and, if your commanding officer is any good at all, you get instant feedback on whether you're doing things right or not.

Before I joined the Army, I was a wreck. In fact, I joined the Army because I was having such a hard time keeping a job, and a difficult time in general. I'd graduated from high school, but even that was difficult. Not because I'm dumb, because I'm not, but because I had a hard time staying interested and getting my homework done.

After I had about six jobs in my first year out of high school, my uncle, who's a Sergeant at Fort Benning, was visiting over at our house around Christmas time. We talked, and he told me that he thought that the Army would be perfect for me and that I should consider it as a career.

My first thought was that it would be just like school, that it would be awful. More rules, and more pig-headed people full of their own authority, just like so many of my teachers were. I told him that, and also that I'd just read about ADD and thought that I was an ADD person and thinking of finding a doctor to get me some Ritalin.

But he said the Army wasn't like high school at all, except maybe for the first few months, through basic training and settling into a job. He told me how he was on Ritalin in elementary school years ago in the early 1960's, and that if he could make it in the Army, anybody with ADD could.

So I joined up, figuring I had nothing to lose.

I'm now on my second tour of duty, and this has turned out to be a great place for me. In all the areas where I'm weak, the military has developed systems to compensate, or even to make me strong. And the areas where I'm strong are useful here.

I have noticed that a lot of the other guys here are ADD, too. I don't see it so much in the officers, although those who are drawn to combat operations are generally more ADD-ish than those who have the "professional" jobs. It's probably a great place for somebody with ADD who can make it through college, too, though. (Usually you have to graduate college to be an officer.)

I think that if they did a study, they'd find that the military is a huge secret pocket of ADD people, kind of hidden away from the rest of society. We really do well with the way things are run, and I recommend the Army to anybody just out of high school who is ADD and looking for a career with both variety and structure.

■ Prioritize: The ABC system for organizing the day

From Clyde in Tampa:

I'm in business for myself, and my best success story has been to use a legal pad. I started doing this at my first job out of college, at the suggestion of my boss, and have been using it ever since.

Every morning I sit down at my desk, take my yellow legal pad and tear off the top page. On the fresh page, I write today's date. Then I list on that page all the things that I need to get done. Most of these get copied from the previous day's list, which I just tore off the pad.

Then I go through the list and decide which items are the most important. I write an "A" next to those; they are the first things I do that day.

Usually I don't have time to get to any of the lower priority tasks, but when I do, I then re-prioritize the list. "B's" are the things that I do after the "A's," and "C's" are the things that are the lowest priority.

Things change every day, by the way. What was a B yesterday might be an A today. Or it might turn into a C. It all depends on how the day is going and what I'm getting done.

I also have my files set up that way. I have a drawer in my desk that's my "C" drawer, where I just throw things. Every few years I'll sort through it, and throw away most of the stuff in it.

The A items are in a file-folder holder on the top of my desk where I can see them, and B things go into my filing cabinets.

■ Visible filing systems

Many Hunters report that the problem with filing things is that they're then lost forever. "Out of sight, out of mind," is a saying that must have been first written by an ADD individual, because it's so true. Even the existence of file folders and filing systems is often forgotten, because the drawers are closed.

The founder and president of one of Germany's largest charities has a filing system which eliminates this problem. Behind his desk is a tubular metal system which contains about four dozen small wire baskets, each about two inches high, ten inches wide, and a foot or so deep. The front of each basket has a small paper tag on it, identifying its contents.

In addition to this "instant visibility" filing system, this gentleman uses transparent plastic folders, instead of the opaque manila file folders common here in the United States, to store information, papers, and other things. The most important of the data or papers is on top, and can be instantly seen through the cover of the folder, which instead of being open on three sides (like a manila file folder) is only open on the right side and the top. Things don't fall out, they're immediately recognizable, and the system works.

When I first saw his system, I assume it was something that he'd developed, as he's a rather Hunter-ish fellow himself. Living and working in Germany for a year, however, I saw similar systems in offices all over the country.

In some of the larger office-supply stores here in the United States you can now find these types of systems, and they may one day become the norm for Hunters in the business world.

■ Color-coding filing systems

Martha in Las Vegas uses colors to organize things:

I read somewhere that ADD people are often very creative and very visual. I know that I am. So when the office supply store started carrying colored file folders a few years ago, I thought that was a great idea and started using them.

I use the Pendaflex folders to hold general categories of things. Within those, I use colored file folders. I'm a secretary for a small business, so I've assigned colors to each of the people here, and that works for me because I may have several different people's expense reports in the expense report file, for example, and now it's easier to find them.

I imagine you could use any other sort of color-coding system, though, for whatever your situation was. Not only do the colors help keep things organized, but they also make my files more interesting to look at!

■ Having an executive assistant who runs your life

Greg is an attorney:

I owe the secret of my success to my paralegal and my secretary. They absolutely run my life here in the office.

I'm a great litigator. I can stand up in front of a courtroom and hold people spellbound. When I pounce on an inconsistency in a witness's testimony, the jury will sometimes move so much that you can hear their chairs squeaking.

But I'm totally disorganized, and I hate handling details. So my secretary keeps me organized, and is completely in charge of my schedule. She tells me what to do, where to go, and when.

My paralegal handles all the legal details. She writes the first drafts of just about everything, does all our contract work, and proofreads everything I do.

Between the three of us, we're making a very good living.

■ Consider unconventional careers: don't feel bound by others' or society's expectations

One of the great tragedies of ADD is the number of people who have plugged themselves into a Farmer's job when they're ideally suited for Hunter work. Paul discovered this mistake after reading a book about ADD, and made some changes in his life:

I'm a CPA. My father was a CPA and since I'm the oldest boy in the family he always wanted me to follow in his footsteps, so I did. I went to college to study accounting, got my degree, got my CPA, and then went to work for a large accounting firm in San Diego.

My father was proud of me, but for seven years my life was hell. I hate accounting! It's not the numbers that I dislike. I'm pretty good with those. I even get a buzz off working things out, particularly if I can save a client some money or if I discover something that others overlooked.

But that's a very small part of accounting. Most of it is drudge work. Filling out forms (mostly mandated by the government), double-checking other people's work, and keeping things organized. This is boring!

When I read Lynn Weiss's book about adult ADD, I realized that I'm not my father. He's not at all ADD, in fact he's the exact opposite. But my mother, I now see, is ADD, and I must have gotten it from her. So it makes no sense to be an accountant like my father, when I'm ADD like my mother who, before becoming a housewife, was an actress in local theater.

However there was this small matter of my having invested my entire life into becoming a CPA. I couldn't just chuck all that.

So I went to the head of our branch of the firm and told her I'd like a position that involved more variety. I didn't dare tell her that I had ADD, but did say that I was bored with what I was doing, and that I was ready to consider something different, even if it meant a pay cut.

She moved me into an account representative position, which is sales. I now go out to visit prospective clients and pitch our firm's services.

I'm having a great time in sales. And, even though the base pay is almost half of what I used to make, with commissions I'm now earning more than I was before.

■ Put most commonly-used and commonly-filed files physically near you

Angela on CompuServe suggests:

Most people think they have to have filing systems organized alphabetically. That's OK, but I suggest an important first step.

If you have a drawer in your desk that holds files, use that drawer *only* for those things that you need frequent access to. They can still be alphabetical, but only the papers that you most commonly have to handle.

In the filing cabinet that you have to walk to, put everything else.

This way, since your file drawer in your desk is so close, you're more likely to file papers when you have them on your desk, instead of tossing them in a "to be filed" pile that collects for six months before you do anything about it.

■ Create a "circle of light"

From a discussion on CompuServe:

Being an engineer, I work at a desk and spend most of my time at my computer.

The lighting in most offices is far too bright when you stare at a monitor all the time. To get around this, I started shutting off the lights in my office and using one of those extension lamps with an incandescent bulb.

This creates a circle of light. The stuff outside the circle is not well lit, and anything distracting outside this circle is easier to ignore.

■ Build sound barriers for yourself

Richard on CompuServe's ADD Forum has a high-tech way of eliminating distractions:

I started using a CD player and headphones at work. The headphones are the small, unobtrusive, in-the-ear type.

I play music that I like and know very well, stuff that I don't have to specifically concentrate upon.

■ Create visible, physical reminders

Richard shares an instant reminder strategy:

As I think of things that I want to take with me the next day, I pile then in front of the door. That way I physically cannot leave my home or office without seeing them and remembering to pick them up.

Similarly, when getting into the car I frequently have a pile of stuff in my hands that I need to set down in order to unlock and open the door. In the past, I would use the roof for this purpose. After several instances of forgetting to retrieve my stuff before driving off, however, I came up with a different approach.

Now I put the pile on the hood of the car on the driver's side, so that it will be right in front of me when I get into the car. Since it's in my line of vision, I don't forget about it. The old saying, "Out of sight, out of mind," applies to me, so my solution is to keep things in sight.

■ Create deadlines for *everything*

Greg in Long Island, NY, puts timelines on everything he does:

For me it's not enough just to have a to-do list. I have to have deadlines, because I know that I only do things when the deadline is drawing near.

So no matter what it is, even things in my personal life, I write them down in my calendar and use that date as a deadline.

This probably sounds silly, as though I'm trying to trick myself, but it works. When I talk to someone and we agree on a commitment, I either give myself a deadline (and tell the other person what it is), or give them a deadline for it.

I've seen so many things in life and in business just fall through the cracks because nobody put a deadline on them.

■ Break large jobs into small pieces

It took me almost a year to write this book, because I own three companies and I give about fifty speeches a year around the country.

Over and over again, when I'm giving talks about ADD, people ask me how I could ever get it together enough to write an entire book (this is actually the 14th book I've written, and the 4th I've had published).

The system I use is one I learned from Michael Kurland, one of the most brilliant writers and fine human beings I know (you can find his books in any bookstore). His idea is to break the big job of writing a book down into little pieces.

I work on my book for a few hours every morning, and then go to my other jobs for the rest of the day. Occasionally, I'll take a weekend day, or even a free weekday and write all day, but this is the exception. Writing for only 2-3 hours at a time is a strategy that many writers use, and it seems to work well.

The same strategy of breaking big jobs into little pieces can be applied to just about any other type of project. Start out by planning the project in outline, and assigning timelines to the parts you'll need to do. And then go about doing it, step by step.

Randy in Kentucky wrote:

For me, the key to getting things done is to know that if it will take more than an hour, I'll put it off forever. That's why the garage never gets cleaned, and why the big projects at work only get done at the last minute. By then, I can't put it off anymore, and I have no choice.

What I started doing a few years ago was to break jobs into pieces. My wife actually got me started on it with the garage. She suggested that I organize only the tool-bench one Saturday, so I went out and did that. The next weekend, she asked me to organize and clean out the boxes of old junk we've accumulated, from old Christmas tree trimmings to pictures of the kids. I did that. And the next weekend it was the lawn stuff.

By the end of six weeks, the garage looked great. She pointed out that she'd been looking for one-hour chunks to have me do, and suggested that I should learn how to do this for myself.

I follow this method now all the time, and it's really useful.

■ Choose work that's "purposeful."

Jim works as a child-care worker in a group home:

Like many ADD people, I sort of drifted through life for a number of years. I put my wife through college and she got her MSW, although I dropped out of school three times. I had a variety of jobs, from manager of a mall shoe-store to manager of a MacDonalds (their "university" is really interesting!).

Joan and I have always loved children, but she can't have any, which I think is one of the reasons why she went into social work in college. After she graduated, she suggested we get a job together in a home for kids.

We've been working here for three years now, and I think I've found my niche. I feel as though I'm doing something really good, that's going to benefit the lives of people. These kids need a lot of help, and most of them are ADD themselves, whether they know it or not. I can identify with them, and even teach them some of the things I've learned.

What's particularly important to me is that this is the first job I've ever had where I feel I'm really doing something valuable. Even when things are difficult (and these kids can be a royal pain in the neck—it's beyond anything that most people could even imagine), I remember the children who've left here and gone out in the world successfully. These kids would have to go back to terrible home situations if we weren't here, and it keeps me going on.

I stumbled into this sense of purpose because of my wife's love of social work, but I think that many of the other people here came to it intentionally. They decided that they wanted to do something useful in the world, and that working with children was it for them. I respect that, and wish I'd sat down in high school or after graduation and given serious thought to what I wanted to do. I think that a sense of purpose is a very important thing, particularly for those of us who so easily go adrift.

■ Determine your best work style and organize your office and/or work that way

Dorothy in South Dakota sees differences in ADD people's work styles:

My husband and I are both ADD and we're both on medication for it (he takes dexedrine and I take Ritalin). Though we're both diagnosed with ADD, we have totally different work styles.

He loves stimulation in his working environment. At his office he keeps the radio going all day. He shares a cubicle area with six other people, and he likes it when people walk by and talk with him: the interruptions don't seem to bother him.

I'm just the opposite. I sell insurance for a small independent agency, and I have to have my own private office. I keep the door closed so there are no distractions, and keep my office as clean and simple as possible. While my husband's office is a mess, mine's well-organized. He says that he requires the mess to keep track of the things he's working on; I know that I require orderliness or I go into a tailspin and can't get anything done. When there are too many things on my desk I feel paralyzed.

So either there are different types of ADD, or else there are different types of people that have ADD. Whatever it is, I don't think there's one peg you can put everybody into; we all have to figure out what's our own best work style, and then try to create that for ourselves.

■ Only do what you're good at, and don't feel guilty about not being able to do what you're bad at

Victoria tried "women's jobs" for years, then stopped feeling guilty and found her niche:

I'm in my late thirties and only found out about ADD in the past year, but of course I've had it all my life.

Once out of high school, I got the obligatory woman's jobs. I started out working as a clerk in a department store. That didn't pay very well.

I'd taken typing in high school and was pretty good at it, so I moved from the store to a job as receptionist for a building-supplies company.

From there, I had about ten more secretary-type jobs over the next ten years. Every time I changed positions, I rationalized it as an increase in pay, or that I needed to get away from some creepy person, usually one of the guys who was hitting on me. (In this day and age I could probably sue, but that wasn't the case years ago.) Now I know that I not only wasn't happy, but also bored by work that didn't suit me.

Two years ago, before I knew about my ADD, a friend of mine got me a job selling telephone systems. He was an installer for the company, a guy I'd dated a few times (we're now just friends). Every one of the other salespeople in the company was a man, as was every person with any authority. (They had a woman secretary, of course.)

But I got the job with them, and I'm now doing better than most of the men. They've hired another woman, I think because I changed their attitude about women.

The "close" here is that I've finally found my calling, and it's sales. All those years I felt guilty as hell for hating being a secretary or receptionist, but did it because I thought it was expected. I couldn't figure out how some women could stay with their jobs in some of the places I worked and continue doing the same thing for years, or even decades. I thought they were just as miserable as I was and just faking it about enjoying their work.

Now I know that I was the one faking it, and they probably enjoyed what they were doing, if they weren't ADD. Good patient Farmers make great secretaries. When I read your book *Focus Your Energy*, I realized that I was a Hunter, I saw instantly how much sense it made that I'd enjoy this job selling phone systems and why I'd hate being a secretary. Now I'm on the hunt every day!

■ Build "reflection time" into your day

Brian in Chicago has an interesting way to spend his lunch hour:

In my company we have an hour for lunch. Since I bring my lunch to work, it never takes me more than ten or fifteen minutes to eat it.

I use the rest of my lunch hour to daydream. I close my office door, sit back in my chair, and just reflect on things. I think about whatever I want to think about, and just relax.

What's amazing to me is how often at this time I remember things, or think of things that are really important. Without my reflection time, I probably would have missed them.

I think that most people, particularly those of us with ADD, hurry through their days at a frenetic pace and never take the time to stop and smell the flowers. Well, I don't have any flowers in my office, but the stopping and reflecting is very useful for me. It's my best success story.

■ Don't hesitate to ask people to repeat themselves when you "space out"

David, who works in a research lab, says that he developed the strategy that pilots and air traffic controllers use when they miss something. Often, if you listen to ATC radio transmissions, you'll hear pilots or AT controllers say, "Say that again...":

A real challenge for me all my life has been to develop the ability to concentrate on people who are talking to me.

(On a positive note, I surprise people when I handle more than one task with apparent ease. Only I know, however, how difficult it is for me to remember where I was five minutes earlier!)

Without a doubt, the hardest thing for me to do is to concentrate on someone's words in my busy setting. Because I listen to and notice everything around me, I miss what they're saying.

To deal with this, I've gotten in the habit of telling them, "I'm sorry, but I missed that." Or sometimes I'll say, "I'm sorry, I didn't hear that."

These short sentences are forever ingrained in my mind!

I used to just agree with people when they were talking to me and often I'd hear them ending with something like, "Right?" Of course, then I'd be embarrassed and just say, "Yeah, right."

After a few Big Mistakes in the lab because of this, though, I learned that it's better to be thought of as hard-of-hearing than to screw up research bloodwork. So now I *always* say, "I'm sorry, but I didn't hear you," or something similar.

■ Set specific career goals with deadlines

Jeff and Louise plan their lives:

Every year, on New Years Day, my wife and I sit down and write down our goals for the coming year. We record personal goals, goals for our kids, income goals, and career goals for both of us.

We also review our success in meeting the previous year's goals.

We've been doing this ever since we were married (it's something my wife got from her family: I'm too ADD to think up something this organized). What I've learned is that by setting goals, we're more likely to reach them. I didn't used to have goals in my life, and just kind of drifted from thing to thing. But once you identify a goal, and write it down, it seems that all of a sudden you start noticing things that will help you reach that goal.

My wife has our kids doing this, too, for their school year. They set their goals the week before school every year, and then review their goal sheet whenever the report cards come out.

■ **Expect a letdown after career highs. Carry on!**

John sells printing in Atlanta:

I've been selling printing for almost twenty years, and I live for the high of making a sale. There's nothing quite like it, particularly if it's a big account. My boss congratulates me, I brag about it to my wife, I go out and celebrate, and I see an increase in my paychecks. It's a feeling that I don't think people who've never done sales could understand, but maybe it's like the way people feel when they win at gambling.

The problem has always been, though, that the sales don't happen every day. Sometimes they don't happen every week, and once in a while they don't even happen every month (at least the big sales).

This used to really get me down. Sometimes I'd knock off work in the middle of the day and go to a movie or hit the bar for a drink. My boss thought I was making sales calls, but I was really getting depressed because I hadn't made a big sale. Of course, when you're in a bar or movie, you don't often meet many prospective customers.

But I did meet a guy in a bar about ten years ago who changed this all for me. He was a retired salesman for an aluminum siding company. He said that since he'd retired, he spent his afternoons in this little neighborhood tavern to avoid his wife.

He revealed to me what he called "The Law of Numbers."

"Sales is a numbers game," he said, pulling over a dry napkin. "If you talk to a hundred people, you'll find twenty suspects. Those are people you suspect might buy your product." He wrote down 100, and then put 20 below it. "Of those twenty suspects, when you go back and talk to them some more, you discover that only five of them are prospects. Those are the ones who have the money to buy, are thinking about re-siding their house, or are upset about their heating bills." He wrote down 5 below the 20. "Of those five prospects, you turn one into a customer." He wrote a 1 below the 5.

"So, you see," he summarized, "you've got to talk to one hundred people to make a sale. Whenever somebody turns you down, don't feel bad about it. Celebrate! That means that there's one fewer that you have to talk to before you hit your hundredth and find your customer."

I took his advice, and started telling myself that whenever I'd walk away from an unsuccessful sales call. It makes it easier to handle the rejection, and keeps me focused on my goal, which is my next sale. My next high.

■ Don't quit before you're finished

Another story from John, the printing salesman:

A few years ago our company brought this kid in from some consulting company to tell us how to sell. Of course, most of what he had to say was either BS or stuff we all already knew, but one thing that he said really hit me. According to statistics compiled by a national company (I think it was Dunn & Bradstreet), over 80 percent of all sales were made after the fifth sales call. But 80 percent of all salesmen give up after the third sales call.

When he said that, I realized that I was one of the 80 percent who give up. I always figured that if somebody didn't give me an order after three visits, they weren't worth wasting my time on.

But now I go the extra mile, and make two more calls. It's nearly doubled my sales.

I see this same thing in other areas. We used to have a stripper who'd always strip up negatives and then toss them off to have the plates burned. But he never double-checked them. He finally got fired because he didn't take the extra five minutes to double-check a half-hour job.

Going the extra mile is very important in business, whether you're in sales or any other field. And we impatient guys always want to quit while we're ahead, or get things over with quickly. I think we have to learn to stick to things until the end, and I know from experience that it's possible to do, once you understand why.

11

School Success Stories

*In the first place, God made idiots. This was for practice. Then he
made school boards.* — Mark Twain (1897)

■ Buy two of each textbook and make wallpaper

Bridgette, a psychiatrist, told me this story at an ADD Conference:

I'm so ADD—and hyperactive—that I can hardly sit still for five
minutes, yet I made it through medical school and am now a psychiatrist. Here's the strategy I developed for studying, particularly during the
tough years of medical school.

I'd buy two copies of each textbook. One copy I took to class, and
used the way people normally do; I'd plan to sell it back to the bookstore
at the end of the year.

The second copy, however, I had other plans for. At the end of each
day, I'd tear out of the second book the pages that had the information I
most needed to memorize. I'd highlight the important points. And then
I stuck them on my wall with thumbtacks or pins (I had a cork-board
wall over my bed).

Every time I walked by the wall, I'd read the highlighted stuff. Before
going to sleep, and upon first awakening, I'd read it again. These regular
reminders kept the information in my mind, and also forced it eventually from short-term memory into long-term memory.

This strategy is a little odd, but it certainly worked for me. Without
it, I never would have made it through medical school. And a couple of
my friends, who at first were making fun of me for doing it, started it
with their tougher classes.

Breaking homework into small pieces

From Jane, the mother of an ADD teenager in Philadelphia:

Our first breakthrough was getting a commitment from Jared to do his homework. It was something he'd never had to do before, because he was smart enough to get by in school just paying partial attention and then doing well on tests. But in the eighth grade homework was his downfall.

After he committed to doing the homework, he was really good about it for a while. Every day after school, he'd come home, sit down and spend an hour or so doing his work. But by the end of the first week he was hating it, looking for excuses to put it off, and pretty soon we were back to the same old routine. He was either not doing it at all, or else bingeing it at the last minute.

When we sat down and talked about it, Jared said that doing homework was actually physically painful to him. After about fifteen minutes, he'd start to get bored, and then it was really difficult for him to sit any longer without somebody forcing him to do it.

I wasn't about to play homework cop for the rest of my life, so I asked him if he found the first fifteen minutes difficult, and, to my surprise, he said no, that was easy. Then it got boring.

It turned out that it wasn't the work that he was doing that was hard or painful for him, it was how long it took him to do it. I guess he's part of the MTV generation or something, but we found that he has an attention span that lasts for about fifteen minutes for boring stuff like homework.

So we split his homework into fifteen-minute segments. He does one when he gets home from school, then one before dinner, then one after dinner, then one before bed. This adds up to an hour; he now gets his homework done (almost) every day and no longer complains about how hard or boring or painful it is.

Sitting at the front of the class

From a teacher in Atlanta:

One of the most successful things I've learned to do with ADD kids in my classes is to move to them to the front of the class. I mean physically, as in the front row.

This way they don't have other students around them that they can see and who distract them. That goes a long way for helping out kids with ADD; if they have distractions available, they're drawn to them like steel filings to a magnet.

By putting them in front of the room, I also can keep a better eye on the state of their attention. When they start to daydream or drift off, I walk near them to catch their eye. I try not to let the other kids know I'm doing this; I don't want them to think that I'm singling them out. But it works to catch them just when they begin to zone out, and bring them back to the task.

Finally, I've found that if I can get them involved in things going on in class, that's the very best. So I call on them a lot to talk in front of the class, and if I need somebody to clean the chalkboard or write things down, I'll most often call on one of my ADD kids. They need the stimulation, and they often are the most battered in the self-esteem department. These small jobs and accomplishments, which mean so little to the average student, are really important to them.

■ Look for small classes

Bill is a college student in Ohio:

I learned about ADD, and realized that I was Hunter (to use that metaphor), when I was a freshman in college. I tried Ritalin for a while, and it was useful—particularly when I had to cram for tests. But I've found another strategy that's even more useful: small classes.

I started out at a major university. Some of the classes had over 200 students in them, and I was totally unable to concentrate. There was the distraction of all the other people in the class, particularly the attractive girls. And, of course, with that many in a class, quite a few were ADD. Their eyes roamed around, catching mine, and it just all added up to a mess. In addition to that, I felt no connection whatsoever with the professors: they were physically far away, with no real opportunity for discussion. I couldn't do well in those large classes, and my grades suffered for it.

I met with my counselor and found that most of the large classes were the required basics: that's why there were so many people in them. And I could take some of those classes in the summer, or during the evening, or even at a local junior college, and not have to be in a huge auditorium.

So for the rest of my college career, I'm going to continue with the strategy I developed after meeting with my counselor. (It worked great last semester.) Before I sign up for a course, I find out roughly how many students are taking it or have taken it in the past, so I'll know if it's going to be a large or a small class. If it's a small class, then I sign up for it. If it's going to be a large class, I look for other options, or else limit myself to only one large class per term and that's the one that I take the Ritalin for.

A friend of mine who's also ADD took this even a step further: he transferred to a smaller college. I've thought about that, but this place is my dad's alma mater, and I get a tuition discount for that. I also have a small scholarship here, so I think I'm stuck with this university.

This strategy of looking for the smaller classes and knowing what works and doesn't work for me, though, has been a huge help in improving my grades to where I need them to be.

■ Find the best teachers and request their classes

Bill's a high school student in suburban Atlanta:

It's not much of a secret which teachers are interesting and which are boring. As a high-school junior, I have the privilege to select most of my classes in advance and I choose wisely.

When I was a freshman, a friend of mine who was a sophomore gave me some good advice.

"Forget about the class subjects," he said, "it's the teachers you need to focus on. A good teacher can make even a boring subject interesting, and a bad teacher can turn the most exciting subject into a painful experience."

So as I go through the school year, I keep an eye and ear out for who the best teachers are: they're the ones I'm going to try to get for the next year.

In one case, I even went to the teacher and told her that I'd heard so many great things about her that I wanted to take her course the following year. She was so flattered to hear this that she made sure I got her class. This year I'm in that class, and even though it's a subject that I might not have otherwise taken (French—and I thought I had no interest in languages!), I'm finding it fascinating. She really cares about French, she really cares about the students, and I'm learning.

So my advice to other students is what my friend gave me: check out the teachers first. If you're ADD, you need a teacher who can keep the class exciting and interesting, who cares about the subject, and who doesn't mind being interrupted with a question. Such teachers are rare in public schools, or at least in my experience, but they are out there, and they're worth the effort to find.

■ **Color-code things relating to classes, and to whether they need action or not.**

Sarah is a junior high school student and active on the ADD Forum on CompuServe:

We discovered my ADD when I hit junior high school. That was the first time I really had to study, to get organized, to keep track of my assignments and all that sort of thing.

At first I was clueless. I didn't have any systems, didn't know how to get organized, and just threw everything into my book bag. This was a disaster: it very quickly started to be as much of a mess as my purse was.

So my mom brought home from work some color-coded file folders. They're made out of the same material that normal manila file folders are, except each is a different color. You can buy them at any office store.

I keep the red one for homework. It doesn't matter which class it is; if it's something I have to do tonight or this weekend, it goes into the red folder. Then the green folder is for things that have to be turned in at school. That's where I move my homework when I finish it, and also where I put my lunch vouchers, notes that I have to take to school, and stuff like that.

The yellow folders are for all my individual classes: I write the name of the class on the tab, and this is where I keep notes, finished homework, and stuff like that.

And I use the blue folder for math. Because it's my hardest subject, I have it in a separate folder so it's always easy to find.

Finally, I have an orange folder for non-school stuff that I want to keep in one place with everything else. It'll have articles from the paper about a band that's coming to town, or notes to or from my friends, pictures, and stuff like that. It's replaced much of the mess that was in my purse.

With this color-coded system, I now get almost all of my homework done, and don't lose things. At home at night, I just pull out the red folder. If I need to refer to a previous test, I can find it in the yellow folders. And when I'm done with my homework, it goes into the green folder.

At school, when it's time to turn in things in each class, I just pull out the green folder. Since it never has more than a day or two's worth of stuff in it, I didn't think I needed to have a different current-homework folder for each class. I can always find what I need for each class in the green folder.

In fact, I've gotten in the habit of always checking my green folder when I first go into a class and sit down at my desk, and always checking my red folder just before class to be sure that I've put in there notes about homework that I need to do that night.

Maybe this wouldn't work for other people, but I like colors and it's worked great for me. I plan on using it all the way through college.

■ Create deadlines for everything

Janie's a high-school student who didn't want her address mentioned:

I have to have deadlines. I can't do anything without a deadline, I've discovered.

It used to be that I used other people's deadlines. If the teacher said the homework was due on Friday, and today was Tuesday, I'd wait until bedtime Thursday night to start it.

At least I kept track of the deadlines in my notebook, and usually got my homework done, but it was really draining me. Sometimes things took longer than I thought they would. Other times I discovered that I needed something to do the homework, a book or other material, and didn't have it with me. And it was too late to go find it!

So now I work on my own deadlines. If homework is due Friday, then I give myself a deadline of Thursday, which means I work on it Wednesday night. I know this sounds silly, like my dad who sets the clock in his bedroom fifteen minutes fast, but it works for me.

When I note that something is due on Friday, I actually write down Thursday, and then put (Fri) in parenthesis next to the word Thursday. I know that I'm fooling myself, but I keep in my mind a Thursday deadline, not Friday, and get the work done by Thursday.

I've also started doing this with things around the house that I normally never get around to, like organizing my room, or doing my chores. For two years my bookshelves in my bedroom were a disaster. So I gave myself a deadline of Saturday night to finish cleaning them out and organizing them. It worked, and on Sunday my mom came in, looked at them and was amazed.

The next deadline I've set for myself has to do with this guy, Justin. He's so cool, and I've been dreaming about him for over a year now. So I set a deadline of next Friday to walk up to him and tell him that I like his clothes or something like that, just to start a conversation. I'll let you know how it turns out.

(Two months later, Janie sent me an email on CompuServe to let me know that she and Justin were going to the movies that weekend: she'd met her deadline. Her new deadline is to be going steady with him by the end of the month!)

■ Highlight and mark up books

Bill is a high school student in New York City:

I learned this trick from my dad. When he was in school, back in the old days, the schools just gave you books, and you could keep them. Or maybe his parents had to buy them, he doesn't remember.

Anyway, what he did was use a highlighter pen on the pages to mark the things that were important. He said that the opening few paragraphs and the closing few paragraphs of each chapter usually had summaries of what would be important. Also, on each page you could usually find a few "nuggets" or things that needed to be highlighted. When you study, you just look at the highlighted stuff: it saves a lot of time and makes it much easier.

I highlight things during class as the teacher is lecturing, as well as when I'm studying.

In our school, you have to return the books at the end of the year, and you're not allowed to mark them up. But my dad really believed in this system, because it worked for him, and he's as ADD as I am. He said that paying for some extra schoolbooks was a heck of a lot cheaper than paying for a shrink or special ed or drugs, and he went into the school and told that to the principal and my counselor. They agreed that if this would keep me out of special ed, so I wouldn't need an IEP (Individualized Educational Plan), it would be a good thing even from their point of view. They let him buy a set of books for me that I could mark up and not have to turn in at the end of the year.

A couple of other students saw me doing that and made a stink about not being able to mark up their books. The school decided that anybody could buy the books if they wanted them, but would have to pay for them in advance like my dad did. Now there are about five kids in my physics class who use highlighters like I do. We're all ADD, and we're all doing much better.

■ Write summaries of what you've just read

Dan is a freshman at a southern university:

The way that my ADD kicks my butt is with my long-term memory. I can read something, know what I read and tell you all about it, and then the next day it's as if I never read it at all.

But I learned a strategy to get around this from a teacher I had for American Literature in high school. She required us to summarize everything we read, at the time we read it. We couldn't wait until later, and we couldn't use Cliff Notes. She wanted us to read it and write the summary for the particular pages in the book the same night. It was of if the summaries were only a sentence or two long, but it was proof for her that we'd actually read those pages.

For me, though, it turned out to be something much more important. I discovered that if I write down a summary of something I've just learned or read, I remember it better later. I don't even have to read my summary (although sometimes I do, and it's nice to have them available). The act of writing it down, for me, makes it stick in my head.

So now when I'm studying or in class, whenever I learn something new, I ask myself how I can summarize it in a few sentences, and then write it down.

It takes a little bit of time, and when I'm reading something long it takes a lot more time, but it's worth it. I don't forget things now. Somehow, that two-step process of thinking about something hard enough to figure out how to summarize it, and then writing it down, kicks it into the back of my head where I keep memories permanently.

■ Read the summaries before you read the chapters

In *The Gift of Learning**, Dr. Sandra Thorpe-Garrett points out that some people learn sequentially, from the details up to the finished concept, whereas others require an understanding of the overall concept before they can absorb the details.

In her tape series, she uses the example of an automobile engine. She'd have a much better understanding of a discussion of how an engine's individual parts work if she'd helped take apart a fully-operational one first.

Bill in Sandy Springs, Georgia, has a similar suggestion:

Whenever I do my homework, I always read the first few paragraphs and the last few paragraphs of a chapter before I try to dig into the chapter itself. Then I scan the pages, looking for illustrations or pictures with captions that help me better understand what the chapter's about. If there's a summary at the end of the chapter, I'll read that first, too.

*To order: (800) 678-2349.

Only after I've done these things will I read the actual chapter, straight through.

I got this technique from a tutor my mom hired for me in junior high, who said that he'd learned it in college. I'm in high school, and it works great for me. I used to have to read chapters sometimes two or three times to absorb the information in them. Now I just do this, and read them once. I have a better understanding of the contents than I ever had before, even when I was reading them several times.

■ Give yourself a reason to pay attention

Justin is a high school student in Atlanta:

I discovered something about the way that I pay attention in school when I had this really cool teacher, Gary, who taught me civics. Gary really cared about us kids, and he even liked to stay after class and talk with us about politics and things; he liked us and he loved the subject he was teaching. He also coached the drama club.

And I noticed that in Gary's classes, even when the material was boring, I worked harder to pay attention because I cared about what Gary thought of me. I wanted to make him happy and proud of me, because I liked and respected him.

This made me think about my other teachers. Most of them I didn't know at all. The kids would tell jokes about them, and we'd just try to get through the class, you know; they really didn't seem like people. They were just teachers.

So I thought, I wonder what would happen if I got to know some of my other teachers?

I started out with Mrs. Billingham, who teaches math, which is a subject I don't much like, and I never really liked her that much, either. But, of course, I never got to know her, and she looks sort of like a tank, if you know what I mean. Her giving me a D on my last semester didn't help, either.

But I tried to get to know her. I went up after class, asked for her help with some things, and asked about her life. I learned that she spent part of her childhood in China and that her parents were missionaries. She decided she wanted to become a teacher because they were. I was blown away. I asked her if I could come in early for a few weeks, maybe a half-hour before school started, so she could help me catch up. She got really enthusiastic about it, and we did it for two weeks.

Now I have a solid B in math, and it's not because I've become the teacher's pet or anything stupid like that, but it's because I've gotten to know her, and so now I care about her and what she thinks of me. So now when I drift off in her class, I catch myself and bring myself back.

It's amazing, you know, what you can do if you want to. And how hard it is to do things, like paying attention in class, when you don't give a damn.

■ Develop relationships with your teachers

Darren is a high school student in downtown Atlanta:

I suppose kids have known about this forever, but it was new to me. I say they've known about it forever, because the old joke about bringing an apple to the teacher is such a cliché. But, for me, it works.

I don't literally bring my teachers an apple. But the point is that I try to get to know them. If I'm confused about something, I'll ask if they can spend some time with me before or after class to work it out. And in that time, I'll look for opportunities to turn them, in my mind, from a teacher into a human being.

I've found that some of the best questions are: "How old were you when you decided you wanted to be a teacher?" or, "What subjects were hardest for you when you were a student, and how did you get through that?" I'll also look for things that can be conversation starters. One teacher was always wearing this little pin on his suit with an airplane on it. When I asked about it, he told me that he was a pilot and it was a membership pin in the AOPA, a pilot's organization. So I asked him how he got started in that, and that really got him excited and he spent a half-hour telling me about flying. So we became friends based on that. I thought it was interesting, and now I'm going to look for a chance to learn to fly when I get out of high school.

I know this sounds like I'm trying to manipulate people, and I admit that I started out with something like that in mind. My mom told me about this after she read Dale Carnegie's book, How To Win Friends And Influence *People.* But what I found out very early on was that if you ask people about themselves and they tell you things that are personal, you can't help but start to actually like them and to care about them.

That's the key to this as a school success strategy. It's not to try to manipulate teachers, or to become the teacher's pet, or even to hope that they'll treat me any better than anybody else or cut me some slack.

What happens is that when I get to know my teachers, I begin to think of them as people, rather than just as teachers. That makes me want to work harder for them, to do better in their classes. Which I do.

And I think they care more about me and work harder to make sure that I succeed.

Getting to know people is my success strategy. I imagine it'll work just as well when I go to college, and when I get a job. At least my mom says it will, and she was right with this one so far.

■ Double-check everything

Don's a high school student in Austin, Texas:

My dad's always saying that anything worth doing is worth doing right. For me, though, it was always that anything worth doing was worth doing as quickly as possible and getting it over with.

The problem with that, though, was that I'd make mistakes. On my homework, reports, projects, all sorts of stuff. Even when I'm supposed to be doing chores around the house.

So my dad made me start to double-check things. He told me how he did it as a habit, and about how it takes twenty-one days of daily practice for something to become a habit. He hassled me for three weeks about it.

It works. If I spent an hour with my homework, I used to just say, "Ok, that's done," and put it back in my book bag. Whatever I was doing, I always was impatient to just jump along to the next thing.

I'm still impatient, and always want to jump to the next thing. But I've developed this habit of taking an extra few minutes to double-check what I've done. It really only takes a few minutes. I don't mean that I re-do all the math problems. I just check to make sure that each one is done, and it correlates to the correct question, that sort of thing. Sometimes I'll do a spot-check and double-check a few of the questions, just to be sure I didn't get an entire row out of order or something.

The only way I could survive this was with the words my dad said. Not the, "Anything worth doing is worth doing right," which still sounds like a cliché to me, but when he said, "It only takes a minute or two to be sure you got it right."

So I tell myself it's only a minute or two of extra effort. Not a big deal. It's not going to be difficult or painful or boring. Just a minute or two.

It's amazing to me how many mistakes I catch now, and how this simple trick has kicked all my grades up.

Part Four

Reference Material for ADD Success

SECTION ONE

Various Therapeutic Approaches to ADD

■ 1. Pharmaceutical interventions

By far, the largest number of stories I received from people who responded to my inquiries on CompuServe and the Internet had to do with the success of using medications.

The most common medications for ADD/ADHD are the stimulant drugs: Ritalin (methylphenidate), Desoxyn (methamphetamine), dexedrine (in various forms and from various manufacturers), and Adderall (a composite of several amphetamine and dextroamphetamine salts). While Ritalin is the most commonly prescribed, this is probably because it's been used the longest for this condition. On the ADD Forum on CompuServe, at least once a week somebody pops up to talk about how one of the other drugs listed here was more effective for them (and others will say that they tried everything else and settled back with Ritalin).

Other drugs used for ADD include Cylert (a different type of stimulant), Norpramine and Prozac (two different types of antidepressants), and occasionally Monoamine Oxidase (MAO) inhibitor types of drugs.

It's important to note that no person is claiming that any of these drugs "cure" ADD or ADHD. They don't work like penicillin, which can actually kill off the germs that cause an infection, just as ADD is not a bacterially-caused disease. Instead, these drugs modify brain chemistry to change the way the brain works, and thus modify a person's behaviors and mental processes. In this manner, one could say that they're masking or treating the *symptoms* of ADD, rather than changing the underlying personality.

All of these drugs must be prescribed by a licensed M.D. or D.O.

Phil is a chiropractic neurologist who sent me the following story about his experience with Ritalin:

My success story concerns my relationship with my family.

For years my wife and child complained about the high degree of inappropriate anger I would express. We couldn't have a conversation without it leading into an argument.

In my post graduate studies I could not pay attention to lectures or read for more than five minutes without wandering off to something else.

And, as a professional I could not relate very well to my patients; they wouldn't follow my recommendations simply because they didn't feel a rapport me.

Finally, after twenty-one years of marriage, my wife told me she could take it no longer, and that if I didn't get some counseling she would divorce me. After much argument and soul-searching, I visited a psychologist who diagnosed me as ADD. I was referred to a psychiatrist for treatment.

The psychiatrist began me with Ritalin, 25 mg./day, and I immediately became a different person. No more anger!

I have only been angry with my family three times since treatment; my 15-year-old son actually seeks out my company and my 12-year-old daughter tells me her feelings.

Professionally, I find that I'm much more focused in my work and on my patients. As a result my practice has literally doubled in the past year.

Judy sent a narrative about how Ritalin helped her son:

I'll share with you a success story I've experienced with my son.

Although my son could read at age three, I held him back in kindergarten because he had trouble adjusting to school. The pressure on him to be in a school situation caused him to stutter. This lasted through first grade.

All throughout grammar school, we tried every method to help him concentrate and remember. The teachers had him tested in second grade because it was obvious he was not achieving his potential. Other teachers assumed he was lazy. They agreed to check his homework assignments, his desk was set up to exclude distractions of any kind, and he was seated in the front of the class.

However, one morning when he was in 6th grade, I was at my wit's end and on the verge of tears as I walked him to class: I realized that something else had to be done. He had forgotten ten things that week, including several tests and homeworks. I now also had a younger son, and felt I could no longer continue to check everything for my oldest boy.

The teacher could sense my frustration and the tears I was holding back, and she suggested that I let him take the drug Ritalin, which had been prescribed for him. She assured me it was in his best interest, and that she had seen many children benefit from it.

I finally accepted her advice, and started him on Ritalin. My son is not hyperactive, so unfortunately the decision was much harder to make.

I now feel it is something I should have done much earlier. His self-esteem skyrocketed; he was no longer criticized for forgetting things, no longer feeling guilty that it was somehow his fault that he had had these kinds of difficulties, but understanding it was just his ADD.

He joined the Academic Games team that year, and qualified for the National Olympics! My 14-year-old son has now been to three consecutive National Olympics, and very much enjoys representing his school. His SRA test scores increased, and he was identified by Duke University in their Talent Identification Program for 7th graders. As part of this program, he scored a twenty composite on the ACT test—a test given to graduating seniors. In his last two years of grammar school, he brought home the team trophy for 3rd place all-around in the country, as well as other team trophies. He is now in Jesuit High School, where last year he again brought home individual and team trophies as a representative of his school, and placed 4th out of 250 in the critical thinking game, Propaganda.

I feel sure that this would not have happened if he had not been put on this medicine. I have epilepsy, and I know I need medicine every day of my life in order to control the symptoms. I now feel that ADD is a similar physical problem, and he should not have been allowed to suffer just because the public's perception is that we want to medicate a lazy child for our own convenience. I only wish I had made this decision sooner. I now know we did the best thing for our son, and I feel comfortable knowing I've done what any good mother would do.

And, of course, many adults discover their own ADD when their children are diagnosed, as was the case with Stuart:

I was one of those people who figured out I may be ADD after my son was diagnosed. Ritalin helped him tremendously. When I learned what ADD was and what characteristics an ADD person lives with, I knew I should be tested.

I am in sales. More specifically, I am a financial planner for a large institution. My whole career had been inconsistent, in terms of having one good year and the next one mediocre. It reminded me of the frustration I had during my school years. I tried so awfully hard to be focused. The paperwork and organization of my operation was driving me crazy. I would spend whole weeks just trying to organize my desk with little or no success.

When I went on Ritalin in June, 1993, things began to change. I noticed some results almost immediately. In September, I hired a friend's mother to help me get the office organized. In October I decided to purchase a computer to get a handle on how I did my work and to help me complete projects. In January I hired a public relations person to secure exposure to new marketplaces. In March I hired a telemarketer to make appointments while I tended to sales and developing new markets.

I have made more money so far in 1994 than I have in thirteen of the fourteen years I have been in the business.

There are still some unresolved issues. I have only just begun to do the reading necessary to develop better means to deal with the problems of ADD. Ritalin alone is not the complete answer. I feel about 35 precent of the way there. There still is so much more to do.

▪ 2. Psychology therapies

Psychological therapies run the gamut from psychotherapy to Neuro-Linguistic Programming to tutoring to coaching. Because ADD is a core condition, rather than a neurotic response to something, the goal of most of these therapies is to either give the person insights and skills to make them more effective in the world, or else to help resolve the pain and difficulties that have accumulated through a lifetime of being a Hunter in a Farmer's world.

Phyllis in Santa Barbara had a good experience with her psychotherapist:
When I first learned about ADD, I freaked out. I saw a show on TV, I think it was 20/20, and started screaming at the screen that they were describing me. Fortunately, I was alone in my apartment at the time.

Which was part of my problem: I was alone in my apartment a lot of the time. After at least fifty boyfriends, and even an affair once with one of my professors (before I dropped out of college), I'd been through it all, and given up. My career was much like my personal life; I've had at least twenty jobs in the past sixteen years.

So when I saw that show on TV, I called my best friend, who sees a therapist she's always raving about. She gave me her therapist's name, and I called her and made an appointment for the next week.

It was the best thing I ever did.

The first thing that Faye (the therapist) did was listen to the story of my life. That took about two sessions, but she was a good listener. She told me everything that she knew about ADD, and said that there was a lot of debate in the field about what it was and where it came from. She gave me your book, and one called *Driven To Distraction*, and told me to read them both. She said that she thought Hunters and Farmers was probably not scientifically sound, but it was a nice model that could be useful in therapy, and that Drs. Hallowell and Ratey's book was an excellent description of ADD and more clinically sound.

On my third visit, after I'd read both books, she said that her work with me and my life would now be about the present and the future. I needed to develop some new skills to stop ruining my relationships and jobs. We went through some of the things I'd done in the past and pinpointed my destructive patterns; we worked every week on a different way to replace one of those patterns with something new.

I think it was after about two months that she gave me a third book to read: *Dale Carnegie's How To Win Friends And Influence People*. I thought she was joking when she handed it to me (I've seen the book for years but never read it; I figured it was just for losers). She said she wanted me to find two strategies in the book and put them into practice during the next two weeks (we were now seeing each other every two weeks), and keep a journal of what happened.

First of all, I'm convinced that Dale Carnegie himself was ADD. His book really struck a chord with me.

Second, I picked out one of his listening skills stragegies, and one of his "How to win others to your way of thinking" skills for my work for Faye. I decided to try them out on this guy at the junior college where I was taking a night course in fiction writing (one of my secret ambitions). Wow! The results were incredible.

I'd been wanting to have a relationship with him since the day I set eyes on him, but every time we talked, I always monopolized the conversation. All my life, in fact, I've monopolized the conversation. But I tried Carnegie's techniques with him, and the next thing I knew he was inviting me to a movie.

To make a long story short, Faye kept with me for about a year. She helped me understand myself, and to build some new skills that I didn't have before. She never belittled me or used psychobabble at me or tried to convince me that I was somehow damaged goods.

I'm living (and now married) proof that psychotherapy, with the right therapist, can work successfully for people with ADD.

SECTION TWO

Psychological Therapy References

National Coaching Network
Sue Sussman M.Ed. & Nancy Ratey Ed.M., co-founders
PO Box 353
Lafayette Hill, PA 19444

The National Coaching Network serves several functions:
1. Providing a national network and professional forum for people who do coaching for individuals with ADD.
2. Creating a database of coaches to match people who want coaches with people who provide coaching.
3. Providing education and training on coaching of ADD individuals.
4. Publishes a newsletter and other collateral materials.

■ 1. EEG Neurofeedback

EEG Neurofeedback is a very controversial treatment for ADD. Some advocates have made what are considered exaggerated claims of "cure" for ADD, and some clinics are not operated by licensed professionals. There is, however, a steadily growing body of research evidence which indicates that EEG Neurofeedback, when performed appropriately by trained clinicians, may be of some benefit to persons with ADD. Therefore, I'm including a few stories about it in this book (with the preceding caveat), and a short resource directory.

Nancy White, Ph.D, a clinical psychologist in Houston, shares her personal and professional experience with EEG Neurofeedback therapy:
As a psychologist and a marriage and family therapist, I frequently work with families struggling with ADD and ADHD children, particularly adolescents who are acting out destructively, taking large risks without considering consequences, and earning poor grades in school—if, indeed, they still are in school. A number have run away and even threatened suicide.

Because I was the professional, these people were coming to me for answers.

At the same time, however, I was the mother of four children (now all adults), three of whom were distinctly attention deficit or hyperactive (they called it minimal brain dysfunction or dyslexia back then). I worked with them as best I could, shuttling them back and forth to special training and therapies. But the fact was that I had no good answers for either my patients or my children, other than to use my conventional skills to help them cope.

I was frustrated, and felt helpless in the face of their pain and confusion.

For a long time I'd been intrigued by the mind/body/spirit connection, and I saw the brain as a facilitator of that connection. The best way I knew to communicate at all directly with the brain was by means of a new device, the computerized electroencephalograph (EEG), so I decided to get one, even though I was discouraged by many on the grounds that they were not very accurate, or that "no one was using such things these days." To my dismay, I found that there was no software to help me accomplish what I had in mind. Frustrated again, and almost ready to hang it up, I went on to other things.

Less than a year later, Drs. Peniston and Kulkosky published their landmark research on the use of EEG neurofeedback in the treatment of severe, chronic alcoholics. They had developed a protocol that used EEG feedback to help subjects attain—and maintain—a state of theta consciousness while they contemplated specific imagery and desired outcomes.

The results were impressive: 85 percent success rates with loss of craving, accompanied by unexpected, but quite definite and positive personality changes. Somewhat later these two researchers went on to publish similarly strong results from a study using EEG neurofeedback on veterans with post-traumatic-stress disorder. This protocol had helped the brain facilitate the mind/body/spirit connection to create positive, practical outcomes at a high level of significance.

Hope rekindled, I bought a new computerized EEG, this time with the software to support what I wanted to do. We were ecstatic with the results we were able to achieve with a range of diagnoses, documented by pre- and post-testing.

A year later, we discovered EEG neurofeedback software for addressing attention deficit disorder (ADD) and closed head injury. I wondered: did I now have the tools I longed for, so many years ago, but had despaired of ever finding?

Our first ADD patient was a precious seven-year-old girl whom I'll call Sarah. A bright child, Sarah had flunked first grade, and her mother was very distressed; the first grade had been a difficult year for the entire family.

Sarah's mother blamed the teachers, the curriculum, and made any excuse she could to rationalize the problem her daughter was having. Sarah herself, usually an outgoing child, was becoming irritable, shy, and withdrawn. There were instances of hitting, biting, and bed-wetting. She responded to medication, but lost her appetite and became quite thin.

When Sarah's grades began dropping again, her parents faced the decision of whether to increase the dosage of her medication or to try something else. They decided to give EEG neurofeedback a try, and brought Sarah to us.

After five months of EEG neurofeedback training, Sarah experienced a complete turnaround. Her handwriting, reading, and math skills all blossomed, and her personality regained some of her old charm and sparkle. Today, years later, Sarah does well in school and, her parents report, has made the honor roll several times.

Since Sarah, we have seen the scenario repeated countless times. Some children—and adults, as well—make stupendous strides, many others show significant improvement, and only a very few fail to respond to the process. We find that our success rate using this technology for ADD/ADHD is between 70 and 80 percent.

From my personal experience, I believe EEG neurofeedback is earning its place as a viable choice in the spectrum of treatments for ADD and ADHD. Large-scale research projects soon to be undertaken may validate the rapidly-accumulating nationwide clinical results for all to see.

Looking back to that time, years ago, when I and so many other parents with ADD children were groping for new answers, little did I knew what I would eventually come upon.

With this new tool, I no longer feel frustrated and helpless; instead, I look forward each day to the bright faces gaining hope from what we are now able to do.

Here are a few case histories provided by Seigfried Othmar, Ph.D., the director of EEG Spectrum, one of the oldest and most highly respected EEG Neurofeedback centers in the US:

Clifford Gorton (pseudonym) was a boy of ten when he came to us at EEG Spectrum in April of 1991. He had been diagnosed with ADHD and also Tourette's syndrome, and had been a participant in a research study on EEG biofeedback for Tourette's syndrome at the City of Hope in Duarte, California. When he came to us he was extremely immature. He was learning disabled, in special education classes, and his behavior was often aggressive and otherwise out of control. He motored through life like a toy truck without a remote control, oblivious to his impact on others.

The research study provided for forty training sessions of EEG biofeedback. He was also put on clonidine to help with the Tourette's syndrome. The mother found that when the training was stopped, her son lost some of the gains he had made. However, when more clonidine was administered to control Clifford's behavior, he would become somnolent. So it was decided to continue the EEG biofeedback training at a reduced level of one or two sessions per week. For some time thereafter, the biofeedback and the clonidine complemented each other. When the mother could only bring Clifford once a week, he would need two-thirds of a patch of clonidine. If he came twice a week, it was one-third of a patch.

Full of hope, the mother signed him up for summer camp. Once a week, she would take him out for his EEG training. At the end of the summer session, the camp counselors said that they had enjoyed having him, and would like to see him back the following year. This could have been written off as having been motivated by commercial interests. However, the mother saw the compliment as genuine. It was the first time in Clifford's life that anyone had ever said anything nice to her about her son.

Gradually, Clifford learned to retain the benefits of the training, and the clonidine was eliminated entirely. The mother also worked with Clifford with behavior mod techniques. In combination, Clifford thrived, and he was able to terminate the brainwave training. He flourished in Hebrew school, and was well-behaved in his bar mitzvah. Once, while dancing at his bar mitzvah, he started to get too excited. He caught himself and said to his mom: "I better stop because I am getting out of control." Months earlier, the parents could not imagine his behaving himself through such an occasion. When asked about what the biofeedback did for him, his mom says that "it gave him the information he needed to know what control feels like." Clifford has now incorporated all this in his life, and is very much in charge of himself.

Leroy Redman (pseudonym) was a very successful businessman, a building contractor, of about fifty years of age. He was very ADD. It was hard for him to work with distractions. He would jump from task to task. If he really tried to focus on something, he would get fatigued. He was also tense and irritable. He would get angry easily and had a low frustration tolerance. In consequence, he was hard on his employees.

By session six of the EEG training, Leroy reported feeling calmer. He said that he had just done what he felt was a week's worth of work in a day. "The chatter in my brain is gone." At session eleven he said he was "now able to read a newspaper article from start to finish without stopping."

After a total of twenty sessions, Leroy said that he was now able to process one thing at a time, and no longer jumping from task to task. He felt calmer and not as tense, because he wasn't carrying as many things in his head at once. His state of frenzy had disappeared, as he could recover better from distractions. He was less irritable. He felt happier, and was more patient with others. He enjoyed being able to read more easily.

Neville Albertson (pseudonym) came to EEG biofeedback as a successful independent businessman, age fifty-three, in insurance and financial planning. He had brought his son in to us for EEG training, and he realized that he himself could potentially benefit from the training as well. He knew himself to be impulsive, with difficulty handling stress, and occasional feelings of being out of control.

With the EEG training, he reported that he felt more creative and more productive. He developed a greater awareness of stress and of his reaction to it. With more training, he learned how to relax and keep focused. He reported being calmer, yet feeling more energetic. His sleep was improved.

The emerging awareness of his susceptibility to stress came about in an interesting way. Neville was fond of skeet shooting, where his perfectionist nature came to the fore. When he missed a skeet, he would become anxious about missing on subsequent pulls. That in turn worsened his performance. In consequence, he would either shoot with high accuracy or his performance would go into a tailspin. While sitting in the chair doing the EEG training, he would be confronted with the part of the EEG that reflected his anxiety. Whenever the brainwave on the screen reflecting anxiety came up in magnitude, he would try to get it down. Instead, it would increase! Here he had come face to face with his own performance anxiety. He gradually learned that could not simply wrestle this problem to the ground in his usual manner. It would only get worse—instantly. He had to back off and let the anxiety subside. Gradually, he learned how to manage these excursions. A new mode of control was required, which he eventually made his own.

After the training, he reported being much better able to handle the problems in his business. Months afterwards, the Northridge, California, quake hit his business, which put him under enormous stresses. He was surprised how well he handled those problems with equanimity. He hardly recognized himself. Before the EEG Neurofeedback, he would have just been overwhelmed by all the problems. After the training, he was able to pick up one problem at a time and deal with it, set it aside, and pick up another. He is convinced he could not have done that before the training.

Richard Corbin (pseudonym) is thirteen years old, and has ADD. He talks all the time. His spelling and handwriting are poor. He has difficulty learning math, and doesn't do well with word problems either. Richard's reading retention is poor, and he also has problems copying from the board. His grades are much poorer than his native intelligence would indicate. His teachers described him as having difficulty concentrating, and following through on instructions. Even if Richard listened, he sometimes failed to absorb the information. He was highly distractible, and did not seem to want to do the work. At home he would get stuck on one thing. He suffered from restless sleep.

With the EEG training, Richard's grades improved, and he also spent more time studying. His handwriting improved. He doesn't get upset too easily anymore. It was more apparent that Richard was a very bright boy. He reported that he felt more organized, and that his school work seemed easier. During the training Ryan reported that he felt more organized and that school work seemed easier. Later in the training Richard reported excitedly that he was reading a book and could not put it down. His mother had to tell him to stop and go to sleep at midnight.

Late in his training, Richard wrote: "When I get done with the thirty-minute training session I feel completely open to everything. My mind tenses up over the week until Saturday when I am renewed by the training to the point where I have no tension in my mind. I feel that my mind loses a little tension every week."

EEG Neurofeedback References

Southern California
EEG Spectrum (Home Office)
   Seigfried Othmer, Ph.D.; Susan
   F. Othmer, BCIAC, ACN, NRNP;
   Howard F. Detwiler, M.D.
   1600 Ventura Blvd., Suite 3
   Encino, CA 91436.
   (800) 789-3456; (818) 789-3456;
   Fax: 788-6137

EEG Spectrum
   Jeanette Deybrook R.N.
   16 South Oakland, Suite 208
   Pasadena, CA 91101
   (818) 577-2202

Los Angeles Healing Arts Center
   Caroline Grierson R.N.
   2211 Corinth Ave., Suite 204
   Los Angeles, CA 90064
   (310) 477-8151

Thomas Brod, M.D.
  12304 Santa Monica Blvd., #210
  Los Angeles, CA 90025
  (310) 207-3337

Biofeedback Institute of Los Angeles
  Victoria Ibric, M.D., Ph.D.,
  Marjorie Toomim, Ph.D.
  3710 South Robertson Blvd.,
  Suite 216
  Culver City, CA 90232
  (310) 841-4972 (800) 246-3526

Jan C. Horn, Ph.D.
  7177 Brockton Ave., Suite 447
  Riverside, CA 92513
  (909) 683-5810

Kandis Follin, M.A. Bethena
Nuzback, R.N.
  3200 Telegraph Rd., Suite 209
  Ventura, CA 93003
  (805) 650-0968

Kandis Follin, M.A.,
Darylene Williams, M.A.,
Sean Goldman, Ph.D.
  100 E. Thousand Oaks, Blvd.,
  Suite #180
  Thousand Oaks, CA 91360
  (805) 379-5151
  David Young, Ph.D.
  4482 Barranca Pkwy, Suite 131
  Irvine, CA 92714
  (714) 551-4272

Bret Mosher, OMD, Jodi Mosher
  5230 Carroll Cyn Rd., #214
  San Diego, CA 92103
  (619) 450-2999

Richard L. Zweig, Ph.D.
  333 N. Lantana
  Camarillo, CA 93010
  (805) 482-9601

Tony & Linda Hall
  2248 Glenn St.
  Los Osos, CA 93402
  (805) 528-4074

Olive Branch Counseling Center
  Ken Olson, Ph.D.,
  Sandra DeJarnett
  9033 West Baseline, Suite A
  Rancho Cucamonga, CA 91730
  (909) 989-9030

California Counselors
  M. Robert Morrison, Ph.D.
  327 Laurel Street
  San Diego, CA 92101
  (619) 544-0844 Fax: 544-0024

Associated Medical Psychotherapists
  Richard Ellsworth, Ph.D.,
  Barbara Linde
  1220 E. Avenue S, Suite A
  Palmdale, CA 93550
  (805) 265-8690

Learning and Growing
  Peter Ruthenbeck, Ph.D.
  1641 W. Imperial Hwy, Suite E
  La Habra, CA 90631
  (310) 691-5536

Nadeau Educational Services
  Ray Nadeau, Ph.D.
  11060 Artesia Blvd., Suite D
  Cerritos, CA 90701
  (800) 462-7323

Scott Kamback, Ph.D.
  1235 N. Harbor Blvd., Suite 100
  Fullerton, CA 92632
  (714) 447-4422

Cecile West, Ph.D.
  7373 N. First, Suite 106
  Fresno, CA 93720
  (209) 432-4051

Sharon Rae Deacon, Ph.D.
  3245 Verdugo Road
  Glendale, CA 91208
  (818 957-5166

Leslie Hendrickson
  317 E. Camino Real, Suite 201
  Encinitas, CA 92024
  (619) 220-2458

Northern California
EEG Spectrum
  425 Divisadero Street, Suite 302
  San Francisco, CA 94117
  (415) 621-4969

EEG Spectrum
  Julian Isaacs, Ph.D.,
  Pat Fields, Ph.D.
  21 Tamal Vista Blvd., Suite 205
  Corte Madera, CA 94925
  (415) 924-8435

Mark Steinberg, Ph.D.,
Cindy Pitcock
  74 Harold
  San Jose, CA 95117
  (408) 554-6008; Fax: 554-8548

Nancy B. Larsen
  915 San Ramon Valley Blvd.,
  Suite 160
  Danville, CA 94526
  (510) 831-9592

John Finnick, Ed. Psy.
  3000 N. Lake Blvd., Ste. 6
  Tahoe Vista, CA 96148
  (916) 546-1314

Michael Je'Naye, M.S.
  20128 Brougham
  Grass Valley, CA 95949
  (916) 346-6876, Fax:-7019

Arizona
Judith DeGrazia, Ph.D.
  10250 N. 92nd St., #303
  Scottsdale, AZ 85258
  (602) 860-9644

Arkansas
Arkansas Recovery Group
  Marianne Frans, M.A.
  840 N. College
  Fayetteville, AR 72701
  (501) 443-0378

Colorado
Michael Hoffmann, Stan Paprocki
  360 South Monroe Street, # 160
  Denver, CO 80209
  (303) 377-2631

Florida
George von Hilsheimer, Ph.D.
  175 Lookout Place #1
  Maitland, FL 32751
  (407) 644-6464 Fax: 660-2082

Georgia
David Bailey, Ph.D.
  200 E. Enota Drive NE
  Suite #400
  Gainesville, GA 30501
  (404) 534-3619

Hawaii
Amanda S. Armstrong, Ph.D.
  46-259 Kape'A Street
  Kaneoh'e, Hawaii 96744-3615
  Fax: (808) 247-7875

Illinois
Ann Richman, M.A.
  6305 N. Milwaukee Ave.
  Chicago, IL 60646
  (312) 774-0909

Joy Lunt, R.N.
  3444 Dundee Road
  Northbrook, IL 60062
  (708) 509-0010

Joseph O'Donnell, Ph.D.
  1443 W. Schaumburg Rd., #205
  Schaumburg, IL. 60194
  (708) 590-0939

Rockford Neurodiagnostics
Marabella Alhambra, M.D.
  4855 E. State St.
  Rockford, IL 61108
  (815) 394-0703

Kansas
Tim S. Sippola, Ph.D.
  702 Commercial Street, Suite #3B
  Emporia KS, 66801
  (316) 342-1998

Maine
David Margolis, Ph.D.
  38 Lafayette Street
  Yarmouth, ME 04096
  (207) 846-6200 X3

Peter Smith, Psy. D.
  24 West Cole Road, Box #5
  Biddeford ME 04005
  (207) 286-8700

Maryland
Michael Sitar, Ph.D.
  11303 Amherst Ave., Suite 1
  Wheaton, MD 20902-4600
  (301) 949-0045

Michigan
Ben Chapman, Ph.D.
  111 N. Main
  Crystal, MI 48818
  (517) 235-4940

Minnesota
A Chance to Grow
  Michelle Schutt, Bob &
  Kathy DeBoer
  3820 Emerson Ave.
  Minneapolis, MI 55412
  (612) 521-2266

Nebraska
Professional Counseling Associates
  Virginia White, Ph.D.
  Landmark Center, Suite 330
  2727 West Second Street
  Hastings, Nebraska 68901
  (402) 461-4917

New York/New Jersey
Les Fehmi, Ph.D.
 317 Mt. Lucas Road
 Princeton, N.J. 08057
 (609) 924-0782

Susan Shor, M.S.W.
 30 Lincoln Plaza, Suite 16-A
 New York, NY 10023
 (212) 265-1983

Michael B. Galante, M.D.
 31 Cragmere Road
 Suffern, NY 10901
 (914) 369-6900

Ohio
Glen P. Martin, L.P.C.
 251 Leatherman Rd.
 Wadsworth, OH 44281
 (216) 922-1183

Hal Schaus, Ph.D.
 1655 W. Market
 Akron, OH 44313
 (216) 836-2003

Center for Better Living
 Alan Bachers, Ph.D.
 Mark Brown, Ph.D.
 551 East Washington Street
 Chagrin Falls, OH 44022
 (216) 463-5553

Center for Better Living
 Alan Bachers, Ph.D., Mark
 Brown, Ph.D.
 170 S. Chillicothe Rd.
 Aurora, OH 44202
 (216) 562-9411

Oklahoma
Marion Sigurdson, Ph.D.
 4520 So. Harvard, #170
 Tulsa, OK 74135
 (918) 743-9355

Oregon
Matthew Fleischman, Ph.D.
 860 West Park, Suite 250
 Eugene, OR. 97401
 (503) 343-9221

Lila McQueen, Ph.D.,
Dean McQueen
 1195 Main Street
 Sweethome, OR 93780
 (503) 367-8220

Texas
Edward C. King, Jr., Ph.D.
 5929 Balcones Drive, Suite 305
 Austin, TX 78731
 (512) 459-0739

Jonathan Walker, M.D.,
Mike Dunagan,
 12870 Hillcrest Road, #201
 Dallas, TX 75230
 (214) 991-1153

Nancy White, Ph.D.
 4600 Post Oak Place, Suite 301
 Houston, TX 77027
 (713) 961-5243

Dallas Neurotherapy Associates
Ernie Bel, Ph.D.
 3000 N. Garfield, S. #272
 Midland, TX 79705
 (915) 682-1414

Neuro-Mastery, Inc.
John Holbert, Ph.D.
1100 Round Rock Ave., S. 111
Round Rock, TX 77027
(713) 961-5243

AM/PM Clinic
Gloria Noah,
303 Anderson, Suite D
College Station, TX 77840
(409) 696-3250

Utah
Steve Szykula, Ph.D.
1245 Brickyard Rd., Suite 595
Salt Lake City, UT 84106
(801) 483-1600

Virginia
The Oaks
A Center for Psychology, Health
Promotion, and Rehabilitation
Robert W. Hill, Ph.D.
P.O. Box 2077
Abingdon, VA 24212-2077
(703) 628-4707

Eduardo Castro, M.D.
3040 A-1 Berkmar Dr.
Charlottesville, VA 22901
(804) 978-3939

Kathy J. Forti, LPC
1544 Bay Point Dr.
Virginia Beach, VA 23454
(804) 481-3244

Washington
Evergreen Clinical Services, P.S.
Steve Rothman, Ph.D.
2025 112th Ave N.E., Suite 200
Bellevue, WA 98004
(206) 454-4266

Evergreen Clinical Services, P.S.
Barry A. Carlaw, Ph.D.
4606 Bridgeport Way West,
Suite B
Tacoma, WA 98466
(206) 564-8322

Wyoming
Wellness Clinic, St. John's Hospital
Michael Enright, Ph.D.,
Joanne Scott
555 E. Broadway
Jackson, WY
(307) 733-7771; Fax: 733-8276

SECTION THREE

Homeopathy and Alternative Approaches

■ 1. Homeopathy

Homeopathy is a medical system that was developed in the last century by a German physician, Samuel Hahnemann. He'd observed that quinine could help the symptoms of malaria in sick people, while an overdose of quinine in a healthy person would produce the symptoms of malaria. This led him to develop the homeopathic principle of "likes cure likes."

Over a period of several decades he and his colleagues gave large doses of hundreds of drugs and other substances to healthy medical school volunteers and observed the symptoms of near-toxic doses. They tried using those same substances, in lower doses, on people with diseases which produced similar symptoms to the poisoning.

During this time, Hahnemann noticed another curiosity: often when the dose of the drug was reduced, its effectiveness increased. This led him to try radical reductions in drug potencies, diluting drugs to thousandths, hundred-thousandths, or even millionths of their original strengths. Theorizing that the dilution allowed some "subtle essence" of the drug to be released into the dilutant (usually water, alcohol, or lactose), he further developed a method to bring out this subtle power of the drug, which he referred to as "potentizing the remedy." In the early days, this involved shaking the dilution 100 times, thumping it on the leather cover of a book with each shake. As time went on, the process was mechanized.

Practitioners of homeopathy (sometimes also spelled homoeopathy, the old-world usage) argue that their remedies work from the subtle to the coarse, from the energy-body or subtle body of the person, and flow from that into the physical body. A dead person, they point out, still has a physical body, but is totally lacking an energy body. It's this subtle, energy body which homeopathy treats, as that energy is the animating and correcting force that drives the physical body.

Because homeopathy doesn't recognize specific diseases, but rather looks at the person as a whole being expressing hundreds of symptoms and personality aspects, there is rarely any one remedy for any one condition. A good homeopathic physician may spend two to five hours taking a person's history. They ask questions leading back into the furthest realms of memory, looking for cardinal clues about which remedy is most appropriate for that individual person.

Once the history is taken, a single dose of a remedy is tried. Results are usually apparent (or not) within a few days, although occasionally it will take a month or more for change to appear. If there is no change, the history is re-taken, because apparently the wrong remedy was used and another is called for.

When change does happen with homeopathy, the results can be startling. In 1976 my wife and I were driving through Colorado to visit an old friend, Dr. Tim Binder. Tim had a thriving practice in Boulder (he's now the president of a college on the east coast), and used homeopathy along with other forms of medical practice. We had in the car with us our oldest (at that time our only) child, who was then about four years old, and for the past day or two she'd been complaining about a stomach ache, and seemed feverish. As we approached Boulder, she began to vomit in the back seat of the car.

I stopped at a pay phone to call Tim and tell him we'd be late because of Kindra's illness, and he suggested that we bring her by the office. An hour later, I carried a hot, lethargic, nauseated, moaning little girl into Tim's crowded waiting room. His nurse immediately took us back to his office.

He sat Kindra down in a child-sized chair and asked the three of us about two dozen questions. Some seemed rather unusual: "Has she recently wanted to be held a lot, or does she prefer not to be touched? Is her skin usually this red? Do you feel swollen inside or stretched out?" After about ten minutes of this, he went to a shelf, got down a bottle, and shook out a small pile of tiny white pills, each the size of a grain of sand. He asked Kindra to put them under her tongue, which she did.

Over the next ten minutes, as we sat there in Tim's office waiting while he attended to another patient, we watched a sudden and amazing transformation come over Kindra: her flushing went away, she sat up straight, she was no longer feverish, and she said that she felt great. The nausea was gone, as were all the other symptoms, by the time Tim returned.

When Louise commented on how amazed she was by the rapidity of the cure, Tim waved it away, saying that when the right remedy is chosen for an acute condition, it usually works quickly. Regardless of the bacteria, virus, or whatever other "cause" of the problem, when the body's own energies are properly stimulated it fights them off and rebalances itself rapidly.

During the year of 1986-1987, I worked in Germany with an organization which (among other things) runs a medical clinic in the town of Stadtsteinach. As is the case in most of Europe, homeopathy was used extensively in this clinic by its chief physician, Oswain Gierth, M.D. There, again, I saw hundreds of these types of "cures."

On the other hand, skeptics point out that a chemical analysis of high-potency homeopathic remedies will yield only the dilutant. How, they argue, can a drug work when none of the drug is present?

Homeopaths would answer that, as is the case with electricity (which we all can see the effects of but even Einstein couldn't explain) nobody knows for sure. It has to do with something subtle and, at this moment, relatively unmeasurable. Rupert Sheldrake in his books *The Presence of the Past* and *Morphic Resonance: Toward a New Science of Life*, is one of the most articulate presenters of what may turn out to be the mechanism at work with homeopathy (although Sheldrake never mentions homeopathy itself in his books), and it's a topic of growing interest among, oddly enough, theoretical physicists. Traditional scientists, however, who base everything on observable measurements and replicatable, consistent results, scoff at such imprecise responses. And so the debate goes on, while the British Royal Family will only allow homeopathy to be used on members of their household, Prince Charles and Queen Elizabeth outspokenly advocate it, and tens of millions of people around the world use it.

To close this summary of homeopathy, it's interesting to note that while traditional Western medicine usually uses "opposites" to cure (aspirin reduces fever, so you give it for fever, for example), there is one glaring exception: Ritalin. Using stimulant drugs to treat hyperactivity is, at its core, homeopathic in concept.

Steve and Amy posted this message on the Internet in a conversation about natural remedies for ADD:

If you are one of those "Ritalin-or-die" types who insists that traditional medical science has the only answer to ADD, then you will probably not believe what you are about to read. I know that I would have had difficulty with this a year ago, and I am still amazed by it. Let's face it, my wife and I are computer scientists. My father is a doctor. We are not likely candidates for believing in what some might view as magical cures.

To begin, my son was branded ADD last year and eased out of the preschool that he attended (he's now in Montessori, which is much better for him). His speech was significantly delayed, and consequently his social development and integration was mismatched to the school's style. My wife and I enrolled him in a program of speech therapy here in the Palo Alto area. He was making the usual progress for a few months.

One day, my wife read an article in *Mothering* magazine entitled "A Homeopathic Approach to Behavioral Problems" (by Judith Reichenberg-Ullman, *Mothering*, No. 75, Spring 1995, p. 97-101). The author is a homeopath and has observed that homeopathy has been very successful in treating ADD and other behavior problems. One quote from the article impressed us very much: "I have found that of all children treated with homeopathy for behavioral or learning difficulties, about 70 percent improve significantly and many, dramatically."

We were totally unfamiliar with homeopathy. Europeans and those in many other countries are more familiar with it; it's extremely popular in Germany, where it was originated. It was also practiced in the U.S. in the early 1900's, often by M.D.s. However, Americans lost faith in homeopathy a few decades ago when the AMA decided that it was worthless. Some people have speculated that it was the drug companies that got the AMA to make this statement (homeopathic remedies are natural substances, therefore not patentable, and are also very cheap). You can ignore this bit of conspiracy theory if you like, but the fact remains that Americans are pretty much the only ones with attitude problems towards homeopathy. In many countries, people try homeopathy as a first approach before turning towards other medical solutions. For example, the U.S.'s heavy reliance on antibiotics as the first response to just about anything is regarded as very strange by most Europeans.

The homeopath we found conducted a long interview with us and gave us a remedy for our son. Within a few days of beginning this treatment, our son was noticeably improved. I don't mean that only we noticed it: the speech therapist noticed it, too.

After six weeks on the remedy, he was totally transformed—without any side effects. All the people who know him well believe this to be nothing short of a miracle. He is now gabbing away, totally connected to this world and us, happy and relaxed.

The speech therapist became so intrigued that she is now recommending homeopathy to other clients. She is even considering a study, coordinated with the homeopath, so that more information can be obtained. While she does not believe that our son is "cured," she does feel that he will have little trouble in school and may never need Ritalin. Although he is still a bit hyper and is still behind in his speech, he is really a different kid. He plays naturally with his brother now; he's totally easy to manage and talk to. This transformation has literally changed our family interactions in a significant way.

What is the downside? Well, it might not work. But then, it can't hurt. Homeopathic remedies are so dilute that they aren't even really present on a molecular level. It is a so-called bioenergetic medicine, similar in philosophy to other traditional medicines like Chinese acupuncture. And each homeopathic remedy has an antidote in case undesirable side effects appear.

"Enough," you're saying, "tell me what the remedy is so that I can go out and buy some." It's not that simple. Each child has his or her own problems. The remedy that worked for our child will not necessarily work for yours, you must consult a homeopath, especially for something as complex as ADD. (You can, however, buy over-the-counter homeopathic remedies for colds and such at the health food store and in most drug stores.)

But for complex chronic problems, the most important part of homeopathy is to find a remedy that's the best match for the spectrum of features of a particular person, rather than just the presenting complaint. In our son's case, the homeopath got a great match right away, not in small part because we had analyzed our son's problems and features in great detail. In many cases, the homeopath might have to experiment for a while until they get the right remedy. Also, if your child is already taking Ritalin, the ADD will be harder to treat because other medications block the homeopathic effect.

Homeopathic References:

Judyth Reichenberg-Ullman, ND
  Homeopath, treats ADD
  The Northwest Center
  for Homeopathic Medicine
  131 3rd Avenue North
  Edmonds, WA 98020

Hahnemann Medical Clinic
  828 San Pablo Avenue
  Albany, CA 94706
  (510) 524-3117
  (Homeopaths on staff, pharmacy)

National Center for Homeopathy
  801 N. Fairfax St., Suite 306
  Alexandria, VA 22314
  (703) 548-7790

Homeopathic Educational Services
  2036 Blake Street
  Berkeley, CA 94794
  (510) 649-0294
  *(free catalog of books & remedies,
  sells USA directory of homeopaths)*

International Foundation for
  Homeopathy
  2366 Eastlake Ave. East, #329
  Seattle, WA 98102
  (206) 324-8230

Homeopathic Academy of
  Naturopathic Physicians
  PO Box 69565
  Portland, OR 97201

■ 2. Herbs and natural remedies

Tim swears by an herb called Ginkgo balboa, which comes from the Ginkgo tree; some studies have shown it to both slow aging and improve mental functioning:

On those days when I forget to take my Ginkgo, I know it. At first, I thought my friend who was all hot about Ginkgo was one of those algae people or something, somebody who'd jump onto any fad going by. But I guess he wasn't, because I can sit through meetings now that would have driven me nuts a year ago, and my mind just seems sharper. Sort of like how you felt when you were a little kid and you woke up on a sunny morning: fresh and bright.

Tom in Atlanta prefers to chew on licorice roots:

I learned about this back around 1975 when I took a class in herbal medicine. Licorice roots contain an alkaloid that's a very mild stimulant to the mind, without the jittery feeling that you get from coffee. (The licorice candy you buy in the store does not contain the active ingredient, glycyrrizin.)

I learned about these just a few years after I'd quit smoking, and so instead of capsules, I got some of the roots themselves. They're about the diameter of a cigarette, and you can break them into cigarette lengths and chew on them. They go slowly: a root the size of a cigarette will last a week or so.

But they're great for keeping that smooth wide-awake feeling going along. I recommend licorice!

■ 3. Nutrition & vitamins

Many claims have been made over the years for elimination or natural-foods diets as a panacea for ADD. Recently the following news release appeared in newspapers nationwide, along with a comment from a fellow who runs a food-allergy clinic and a note that he was available for TV and radio appearances:

FORT LAUDERDALE, Fla., March 9, 1995 /PRNewswire/– According to a recent study published in the "Annals of Allergy," 73 percent of children diagnosed with Attention Deficit Disorder improved significantly be eliminating common food allergens and chemical additives. Another study published in the "Lancet," found 80 percent of children with A.D.D. had a clear, distinct improvement in their concentration, emotions and behavior from identifying and eliminating allergic foods.

What's unfortunate, is that this news release failed to mention that the children in both of these studies had been referred to the clinics because of their allergies, not because of their ADD. When their allergies were treated with diet, it also helped their ADD, which makes a lot of sense. It's hard to concentrate when you're sneezing, scratching, itching, or breaking out in a rash. But it doesn't usually work the other way around—that non-allergic ADD children respond so well to diet. These allergic children represent a very, very small subset of the population.

As I mentioned in the preface to my first book, I knew Dr. Ben Feingold; the residential treatment facility for children of which I was executive director used a natural foods diet for our children (and still does). We saw this diet help many children, particularly with their general health, and a few even settled their hyperactivity down to the point where they didn't need medications. In the New City Public schools study (*International Journal of Biosocial Research*, vol (8)2:185-195, 1986), they found over a 10 percent improvement in test scores when food additives were eliminated from school food. But still, these children were very much in the minority. For most children, the experience is that diet is important and useful for general health, but it's not going to turn a Hunter into a Farmer any more than it's going to turn brown eyes blue.

Perhaps the most important distinction here is that between ADD and hyperactivity. While I've seen and known a number of children who became less hyperactive when taken off sugar and junk foods and put on a healthy diet, I've never seen a child move from being a Hunter to being a Farmer, as defined in this book. ADD doesn't go away, because it's a natural part of who we are. It's something we're born with, and, as noted earlier, in some situations it's as much an asset as a liability.

So, by all means, follow a healthy diet. Be alert to allergies to sugar, corn, wheat, and, particularly, milk. They're all out there in surprising numbers (particularly milk allergies among children with chronic ear infections). But don't think that diet will turn your Thomas Edison child (or adult) into a bookkeeper or homework hound.

Bill in Minneapolis found that the vitamin choline was useful in increasing his attention span (and he was one of several people—including two high-school students—who shared similar stories about this product):

I have a girlfriend who's a health-food nut, and when she learned that I was diagnosed with ADD and was thinking of seeing a doctor to get some Ritalin or medication, she talked me into trying choline instead.

Choline is apparently a vitamin that will actually pass through the blood/brain barrier (most won't), and is converted in the brain into one of the neurotransmitters (acetylcholine, as I recall), which the brain needs to work well. It has an effect on memory and concentration.

So she got me a big bottle of this stuff called Choline Cocktail, and I take a couple of spoonfuls of it every morning in a glass of water. I saw a very quick change in both how alert I am, how much staying power I have for mental tasks, and my ability to concentrate on things. Maybe it's just because I wanted it to work, or because my girlfriend got me on it, but I've been using it for quite some time and it really seems to make a difference.

Choline Cocktail is manufactured by Twinlabs, the big vitamin company. In addition to very large amounts of the B vitamin choline, it contains extract of Ginkgo, a number of vitamins (Bs, C, E, etc.), chromium, DMAE (2-dimethylaminoethanol), and an extract of the herb Guarana, which contains caffeine.

■ 4. Mind machines

A number of companies manufacture and sell machines which are essentially small computers that drive a pair of headphones and glasses. The computer generates a tone that beats at a particular frequency, and the glasses have little lights inside them that flicker in rhythm with the tone.

The theory of these light-and-sound devices is that if you subject the brain to strong enough stimulation of and at a particular frequency, you'll produce an entrainment response in the brain: it will start firing itself at that frequency.

The significance of this is rooted in the different brain frequencies: Delta (.5-3 Hz), Theta (4-7 Hz), Alpha (8-12 Hz), SMR (Sensory Motor Response) (13-17 Hz), Mid-Beta (18-24 Hz) and High-Beta (24-30 Hz). (Hz is short for Hertz, which means flashes, cycles, or pulses per second.) Delta is most often associated with deep sleep, Theta with daydreaming or dreamlike states, Alpha with blissful awareness (it's often referred to as the "meditation frequency"), SMR with watchful awareness, Mid-Beta with learning and thinking, and High-Beta with anxiety.

While there's considerable science to back up the notion that it's possible to create an entrainment response in the brain, at the moment there's little to back up the claims that this produces anything more lasting than an interesting light show in the mind or a few moments of profound relaxation. Promoters of these machines claim that they will help memory, improve learning ability, and break up stale or rigid brainwave patterns. Skeptics say that an evening at the disco will do the same: the bass beat and the lights often reflect specific brainwave frequencies, and can produce an entrainment response which may be part of the lure of the disco.

Nonetheless, many people are purchasing and using these machines, and some reported to me that they found them beneficial.*

At least two rock bands are building Alpha and Theta frequency beats into their music intentionally, in order to produce a state-of-consciousness shift in their listeners. The whole area of brainwave manipulation is poised to follow smart drugs as the next altered consciousness fad.

In the meantime, scientists are now conducting research into the actual effects of these devices. At Wright-Patterson Air Force Base in Ohio, researchers are hooking EEG tracking devices to the heads of jet fighter pilots, and monitoring their brainwaves. When they notice that the pilots are drifting off into Theta (in flying it's called air trance; in a classroom, it's called "spacing out"), they turn on a flickering fluorescent light in the cockpit, which flashes at a Beta (awakeness) frequency. According to early experiments, the brainwave entrainment produced by this light snaps the pilots back to a state of higher awareness.

In the course of this research, reported in the April, 1995 issue of *Popular Mechanics*, psychologist Grant McMillan said that he'd discovered that many of the pilots had learned to actually control their brainwave patterns. Taking a logical leap, McMillan hooked the pilots' EEG outputs to the roll controls of a flight simulator. He found that pilots could learn to bank the simulated plane to the left or right solely through their own brainwave activity. Needless to say, these early experimental results have both the military and the medical community very interested.

So, while the light-and-sound machines are still in the realm of offbeat science, probably in the next few years there will be the beginning of a consensus as to their efficacy, and specific applications that are grounded in competent research.

■ 5. Chiropractic

After having broken my back skydiving back in 1972, I've became a longtime fan of chiropractic. When the orthopedists said there was

*More information on these and similar devices can be found on the Mind/Body Sciences Forum (GO MIND) on CompuServe

nothing that could be done except surgery to eliminate years of chronic pain, a chiropractor by the name of Charles Droste produced what was, for me, miraculous results. Over the years since I first met Charlie, I've moved to several cities and two continents, but always managed to find a good local chiropractor.

Chiropractors can do marvelous things for back pain. Even the US government's own research recently reported that chiropractic was often more effective than surgery for certain types of back problems.

But Attention Deficit Disorder?

If the claim of chiropractic practitioners—that theirs is a technology that increases the flow of "life energy" through the body—is true, I suppose it's possible that chiropractic might have value for ADD. There have been several discussions recently on the Internet and CompuServe where people with no (apparent) ties to the chiropractic industry have said that visiting their chiropractor regularly was definitely helpful for some of their more troublesome ADD symptoms. And my own chiropractor here in Atlanta told me that she has a number of ADD-diagnosed children whom she sees and whose parents report that chiropractic helps.

On the spectrum of "science has found this useful for ADD," however, chiropractic ranks, at the moment, low. I could only find one study correlating chiropractic with childhood behavior, and it was, in my opinion, not specifically relevant to ADD and not wholly scientific. (It's in the bibliography, however.)

So, while chiropractic may be a useful and even important part of a person's regular health and fitness program, it's probably not a good choice as a first-line therapy for ADD.

■ 6. Meditation training

Learning to center your attention, focus your energies, and concentrate are all important and laudable goals for Hunter-personality people. And in those societies with a high percentage of Hunters among their population, we find specific religious and philosophic techniques have evolved to train people to do all these things.

As I've traveled around the country over the past few years, dozens of people have told me how practicing Transcendental Meditation (TM), reciting the rosary, or other forms of daily concentration and prayer have been useful to them. (Some of their stories are told earlier in this book.)

Several psychologists have told me that they strongly recommend to their patients either a course like TM, or books like *The Relaxation Response*, as part of an overall and comprehensive approach to building ADD-solution skills.

Maharishi International University in Fairfield, Iowa (on the Internet it's at: *gopher://info.miu.edu*) is probably the most well-known center for information on TM, and they have affiliated groups or instructors in virtually every major city of the world.

Similarly, the Catholic church provides, as part of its instruction in Catholicism, instruction in how to use a rosary to perform a meditative ritual. The idea of regular and repeated chanting can be found in many other religions as well, and most large cities have New Age-type centers where meditation is taught. Unity Churches are also a good resource for this.

SECTION FOUR

Career Counseling for People with Attention Deficit Disorder

or

What makes an occupation "ADD-Friendly"

by Sharon Levine, MA, CRC, CIRS, CCM

Sharon Levine is president of SML Rehabilitation Consultants, Inc., a firm in Fort Lee, New Jersey which offers vocational assessment and career counseling for adults and adolescents with ADD. As one of the country's leading experts on career counseling for persons with ADD, Sharon wrote the following and was kind enough to offer us the opportunity to publish it in this book. The copyright for this career information section remains with Sharon, and you can find her in the Fort Lee phone book if you'd like more information about her services or publications.

Career guidance with adults and teens with Attention Deficit Disorder requires looking at variables counselors working with non-ADD clients usually do not consider. Attention Deficit Disorder is not a career death sentence: If the process of making a career choice includes a knowledge of what makes a job ADD-Friendly as opposed to ADD-Hostile, a person with Attention Deficit Disorder can soar, and break the cycle of frustration in school and in the workplace.

After administering a battery of aptitude and interest assessments, a career counselor will advise a client where their skills and interests may best be applied. However, traditionally they do not take into account the effects of Attention Deficit Disorder in the process. They don't factor in a person with ADD's need for pressure, autonomy and variety in a job. Repetition, whether for a rocket scientist or a laborer, is a prescription for failure for people with ADD.

Autonomy is not the same thing as control, such as in supervisory or management jobs. Autonomy refers to the ability to be responsible for one's own work, working at one's own pace, without the constant scrutiny of others. Pressure or stress is the excitement which causes the adrenaline to flow.

ADD-Friendly jobs continually enable the worker to see the entire picture but only require attention to detail for short spurts of time. However, if a person with ADD is sufficiently stimulated he/she is usually able to attend to the details required. For example, the jobs of neurosurgeon, fighter pilot, and the construction worker who rivets and welds the top floors of skyscrapers are ADD-Friendly. They are dealing with high stress, life-or-death situations which enable them to attend to the details at hand for finite periods of time. They finish one assignment and go on to the next. Entrepreneurial types of work are very ADD-Friendly. They provide the adrenaline rush of starting and building a new business, the autonomy of working independently, the variety of numerous responsibilities, and the ability to repeat the process as new creative ideas arise.

However, we can't all be neurosurgeons, fighter pilots, skyscraper construction workers or entrepreneurs. How do the rest of us attain the stimulation, variety and autonomy in our lives to be successful on the job?

The United States Department of Labor lists all jobs according to their *Dictionary of Occupational Title* number. These break each job into its component parts, including intelligence, specific vocational preparation required, verbal and numerical aptitudes, physical requirements, and temperaments. Included in the temperaments are *varied, control,* and *stress.* These were the variables I initially used to analyze whether a particular type of job is ADD-Friendly.

However, what I discovered when I started this analysis was that the Department of Labor's statistics and information are not ADD-Friendly.

For example, they say supervisors have *variety* and *control* which would theoretically be positives for people with ADD. However, supervisors are required to pay attention to other people's details as well as their own, and this is ADD-Hostile. A person with ADD may be the company's star Field Engineer, but would find frustration being the supervisor. The promotion takes away the activity needed, and confines him/her to inside responsibilities for other people's work.

My research and experience shows that people with Attention Deficit Disorder require the stimulation of changing environments, multiple responsibilities, and/or independence in order to achieve job satisfaction and success. Therefore, in order to determine ADD-Friendly jobs, I had to do some fine-tuning of the descriptions provided by the Department of Labor.

I investigated the following job areas: Technical, Technological, Sales Representative, Manufacturing, Maintenance, Mechanical, Machinist, Laborer, Scientific, Medical, Legal, Military, Managerial, Entrepreneurial, Office, Nursing, Allied Health, Education, Construction, Aviation, Dentistry, Public Protection, Creative, Cooking, Transportation, Engineering, Insurance, Recreation, Computers, and Consulting.

My criteria for ADD-Friendly are: allows the worker to work autonomously; enables the worker to remain active rather than stay in one place all day; the duties are varied and the worker can use his creativity to obtain stimulation for the adrenaline to flow. Some jobs meet all criteria, whereas others only meet some of the criteria.

Here are some jobs in each of the categories I've identified as ADD-Friendly. Some jobs may contain elements of more than one category; only the jobs that are representative of appropriate occupations for people with Attention Deficit Disorder are listed.

TECHNICAL—ADD-Friendly Technical jobs enable the worker to go out into the field and install and repair high-tech equipment. The worker has autonomy and variety. In Sales Engineering positions, he/she is able to interact with others in their office as well as their client companies' offices and plants. Representative jobs include:
- Biomedical Equipment Technician
- Sound Effects Technician
- Sound Technician
- Avionics Technician
- Electronics Mechanic
- Field Engineer
- Sales Engineer
- Customer Equipment Engineer (telephone)

TECHNOLOGICAL—ADD-Friendly Technological jobs are similar to Technical jobs in that they offer autonomy and variety. They require similar skills to technicians, but are involved in some state-of-the-art technologies. The problem with ADD and Technological jobs is that the same job title can apply to different applications. For example, Electronics Technologist can apply to someone who repairs computers on site (generally good for ADD people), or it can apply to people who help design computers in a laboratory (sometimes not as good for ADD people). Representative technological occupations include:

- Computer Technician
- Electronics Engineering Technologist
- Field Service Engineer
- Electronics Technologist

SALES REPRESENTATIVE—People with ADD make excellent outside sales representatives. It provides autonomy, variety, and the adrenaline that comes from thinking on one's feet. Unfortunately, sales representatives require follow-up and attention to detail. Therefore, Sales Representative jobs become ADD-Friendly when accompanied by a sales support staff. Examples of appropriate sales representative positions are:

- Sales Representative, Medical and Dental Equipment and Supplies
- Sales Representative, Pharmaceuticals
- Sales Representative, Chemical Equipment
- Manufacturers Representative
- Sales Representative, Radio and TV Advertising Time
- Sales Engineers
- Computer Consultants

MAINTENANCE—While nine Maintenance jobs listed by the Department of Labor offer variety, only two offer some degree of autonomy. Only the Maintenance Mechanic and Electronics Mechanic offer a degree of autonomy and are therefore more ADD-Friendly than the others. Representative jobs include:

- Carpenter
- Electrician
- Automotive Maintenance Mechanic
- Maintenance Mechanic
- Electronics Mechanic

MANUFACTURING—Manufacturing jobs usually do not offer autonomy or variety, and therefore are generally not ADD-Friendly.

MACHINIST—Machinist jobs offer variety but often do not provide autonomy or adrenaline-producing stimulation. Examples of ADD-Friendly jobs are:
- Maintenance Machinist
- Marine Engine Machinist
- Automotive Machinist

MECHANICAL—ADD-Friendly Mechanical jobs enable the worker to work in the field to repair and rebuild machinery, and provide variety in job requirements. Automobile Mechanic is not off-site, but the workers are able to perform their job without supervision.
- Laundry Machine Mechanic
- Mechanical Field Engineer
- Electronics Technician
- Electronics Mechanic
- Automobile Mechanic

LABORER—Most labor positions are routine and not ADD-Friendly. Heavy Equipment Machinery Operators, however, can achieve the adrenaline and stimulation ADD people need if a person's interests are in this area. ADD-Friendly laborer jobs are those where there is high risk that others will not attempt. Jobs which keep the worker physically stimulated are more ADD-Friendly than sedentary assembly line jobs. Representative of these are:
- Skyscraper Welder-Fitters
- Construction Worker
- Landscape Laborer
- Construction or Leak Gang Laborer

SCIENTIFIC—By the nature of scientific work, most jobs are sedentary research oriented positions. Those that may be ADD Friendly are technological or technical in nature such as:
- Biomedical Equipment Technician
- Pollution Control Technician

MEDICAL—While most physicians deal with life-or-death situations at times, some specialties are more ADD-Friendly than others. A Radiologist may have autonomy and variety, but they rarely have patient contact unless they are working with certain cancer and diagnostic treatments. Anesthesiologists, on the other hand, have a great deal of stress as they hold a patient's life in their hands: each operation is a

separate and distinct event requiring constant attention. This is ADD-appropriate, but is not as completely ADD-Friendly as surgery, which has stress, activity, variety and constant activity for a finite period of time. Surgeons can see the whole picture, and hyper-focus on the details for the specific time they are in the operating room. Physician specialties which meet the needs of ADD include:
- Surgeon—General
- Neurosurgeon
- Obstetrician/Gynecologist
- Neurologist
- Anesthesiologist
- Oncologist
- Reconstructive Surgeon

ATTORNEYS—ADD-Friendly Lawyers are active and think on their feet: i.e. trial attorneys. Insurance or corporate law requires constant attention to detail—decidedly ADD-Hostile. ADD-Friendly law specialties include:
- Trial Attorney
- Litigator

MILITARY—The military offers high-stimulation experiences while providing structure to young people with ADD. They can come out of military service with skills in ADD-Friendly occupations, and having learned organizational skills lacking in many ADD people. These include:
- Pilot
- Fighter Pilot
- Submersible Pilot
- Proof Technician
- Aircraft Launch and Retrieval Technician
- Paratrooper

MANAGERIAL—Management is not ADD-Friendly. It requires inactivity, and attention to everyone else's details. Managers have control but are not autonomous.

ENTREPRENEUR—For those people with ADD who are fortunate enough to enter into an entrepreneurial endeavor, they have found one of the most ADD-Friendly outlets. They use creativity to conceive the concept. They develop the business by getting others to attend to those areas which are difficult for them. They are stimulated by the uncertainty of their efforts to work. When they are successful, they can oversee the growth or sell to an interested buyer and start the process all over again with a new idea. Their job has variety, stimulation and autonomy.

OFFICE WORKER—Clerical work does not offer autonomy or stimulation; however, some jobs do provide variety and the ability to work with the public. These jobs require organizational skills which many people with ADD find difficult to sustain. Secretarial and Administrative Assistant jobs are not ADD-Friendly because they require a person to organize their boss as well as themselves: a good Administrative Secretary is constantly detail-oriented. The following are some clerk jobs which are less ADD-Hostile than the average in this category:
- Animal Shelter Clerk
- Hotel Clerk
- Bowling Alley Desk Clerk
- Automobile Rental Clerk

NURSING—Registered Nurses have the adrenaline flow and autonomy. Some have variety. A Nurse Midwife has pressure, autonomy and variety. A Nurse Anesthetist has stress but no autonomy or variety. A Nurse Consultant has variety and autonomy. A Rehabilitation Nurse working in a Rehabilitation facility has never been appropriate for ADD, while a Rehabilitation Nurse Consultant working for insurance companies has a very ADD-Friendly job with autonomy and variety. However, this may be changing with the advent of managed care, since insurance companies are turning towards telephonic case management, which is often very ADD-Hostile. Some nursing specialties which meet the needs of people with ADD are:
- Private Duty Nurse
- Nurse Midwife
- Nurse Consultant
- Nurse Instructor
- Nurse Anesthetist

ALLIED HEALTH—This category refers to those jobs which support the health and medical field. They include therapists and technicians. Few provide the adrenaline and stimulation people with ADD need, but some afford variety and autonomy. The Emergency Medical Technician job provides all requirements for ADD-Friendly. Some others are:

- Home Health Technician
- Physical Therapist
- Occupational Therapist
- Ultrasound Technologist
- EEG Technologist
- Athletic Trainer

EDUCATION—Teaching can be very ADD-Friendly, as it requires being able to see the entire class while attending to the subject matter at hand. Secondary school teachers usually teach one subject throughout the day and do not have variety but they do have autonomy. Adventure Education offers physical challenges to both the class and the teacher. Physical Education teachers maintain physical activity throughout the day, which is ADD Friendly. Representative teaching positions are:

- Pre-School Teacher
- Elementary School Teacher
- Adventure Education
- Physical Education   .

CONSTRUCTION WORKER—While Construction does not offer much variety, it is more ADD-Friendly than other types of unskilled or semi-skilled labor as it provides the physical release and adrenaline that comes from performing dangerous activities.

AVIATION—Flying, whether commercial, private, or military, provide ADD-Friendly jobs for pilots and support personnel. Anytime a pilot is responsible for the lives of passengers and the safety of equipment, the stimulation which enables a person with ADD to focus is achieved and sustained. There is autonomy and in some cases variety. Appropriate aviation positions include:

- Highway Patrol Pilot
- Air Traffic Controller
- Commercial Pilot
- Pilot Instructor
- Avionics Technician

DENTISTRY—Dentistry is basically a repetitive mechanical profession. Oral Surgery offers the variety of tasks and the pressure of providing general anesthesia. It also provides autonomy. A maxillofacial specialist is involved with the reconstruction of the human face and head and provides stimulation and creativity not evidenced in general dentistry.

PUBLIC PROTECTION—Police Officers and Fire Fighters know that every time they go to work they may not return alive. These jobs offer a high degree of stimulation and physical activity. There is not variety on the job unless there is a crisis. The degree of autonomy is relative to the rank and the function of the officer. Detectives may operate independently, while other police officers may be directly supervised or in pairs.

CREATIVE—Jobs which enable a person to express creativity may be ADD-Friendly. Creative writers have autonomy while Copy Writers are limited in their freedom. Some ADD-Friendly creative jobs are:
- Screen Writer
- Stained Glass Artist
- Dance Therapist
- Actor
- Pastry Chef
- Musician

CHEF—Chefs and Cooks are under continuous pressure, have various responsibilities, and are creative. The more autonomous chefs are executive and sous chefs, but they have assumed supervisory roles. The managerial requirements make the higher-level jobs less ADD-Friendly, but the adrenaline flow may compensate for this. Representative occupations include:
- Pastry Chef
- Sous Chef
- Cook
- Chef De Froid

TRANSPORTATION—Truck drivers, while lacking variety, possess autonomy while on the road. Some drivers work with constant stress. Included among these are:
- Ambulance Driver
- Tractor Trailer Driver
- Powder Truck Driver
- Explosives Truck Driver
- Armored Car Guard/Driver
- Ship Pilot

ENGINEER—The Department of Labor describes engineers in terms of the professional engineer and in some cases people who operate heavy machinery. For these purposes, I analyzed professional and sales engineers. Research and Design Engineer jobs are ADD-Hostile as constant attention to details is a requirement. Sales and Field Engineers, regardless if they are chemical, nuclear, electronics, mechanical, etc., are ADD-Friendly as they provide variety and autonomy.

INSURANCE—Most insurance jobs are not ADD-Friendly. Claims Adjusters, Examiners, Clerks, Managers, etc., sit in cubicles and attend to details. Some adjusters have more autonomy and spend time in litigation in court. ADD-Friendly insurance jobs include.
• Sales Representatives
• Litigation Adjusters

RECREATION—People with ADD are successful when they are permitted to be physically active. Recreation and Fitness oriented jobs are ADD-Friendly. Appropriate jobs include:
• Dancing Instructor
• Fitness Trainer
• Professional Athlete
• Aerobics Instructor
• Exercise Physiologist

COMPUTERS—Programming presents a problem as it requires sequential thought processes which may be difficult for a person with ADD. However, difficulty does not mean the concept and skill cannot be learned well enough to perform the job adequately. Programming by itself is ADD-Hostile as it requires a person to sit in one place all day with little autonomy and no variety. However, knowing how to program can open the door to very ADD-Friendly occupations providing autonomy, stimulation, and variety, such as networking. Other appropriate jobs include:
• Computer Consultant
• Computer Networking
• Computer Technician
• Electronics Technician

CONSULTANT—People with ADD often confront a problem. Once they find a type of work they enjoy and become successful at, they reach a crossroads both financially and professionally. There is a ceiling for the salaries of technicians, professionals, sales representatives, engineers, etc., working for a company. The company wants to reward good work by promoting people and increasing their salaries. However, they are often taken out of an autonomous and varied environment and put in an office: an intended reward has a negative effect. The solution to this problem is to become a consultant, and contract services to many employers. Financial rewards as well as risks increase. Autonomy and variety return, and the stimulation of starting and building your own business makes consulting a prime example of an ADD-Friendly job. Examples of these are:

- Computer Consultant
- Financial Consultant
- Engineering Consultant
- Rehabilitation Consultant
- Nurse Consultant

SECTION FIVE

ADD Publications and Support Groups
U.S., Canadian, and International

■ 1. Publications

The ADDed Line
3790 Loch Highland Pkwy
Roswell, GA 30075
(800) 982-4028
The ADDed Line is a newsletter "For Hunters in This Farmer's World,"
edited and published by Thom Hartmann.

ADDult News
Mary Jane Johnson, Editor
2620 Ivy Place
Toledo, OH 43613
ADDult News is a newsletter for adults with ADD, and covers a broad
spectrum of ADD issues.

ADD Warehouse
(800) 233-9273
The *ADD Warehouse* is an retail mail-order resource with an extensive
selection of books and materials on ADD. Catalog available.

■ 2. Support Groups and Organizations:
  National and International

National Coaching Network
Sue Sussman M.Ed. & Nancy Ratey Ed.M., co-founders
PO Box 353
Lafayette Hill, PA 19444
The National Coaching Network serves several functions:
 1. Providing a national network and professional forum for people
who do coaching for individuals with ADD.
 2. Creating a database of coaches to match people who want coaches
with people who provide coaching.
 3. Providing education and training on coaching of ADD individuals.
 4. Publishes a newsletter and other collateral materials.

CHADD (Children and Adults with ADD)
499 N.W. 70th Ave, Suite 308
Plantation, FL 33317
(800) 233-4050
CHADD publishes a magazine and newsletter, puts on an annual conference, and has affiliated groups all across the United States and Canada. It's the primary, and probably the best, international resource for parents of children with ADD.

ADDA (National Attention Deficit Disorder Association)
P.O. Box 972
Mentor, OH 44061
(800) 487-2282
Mary Jane Johnson, President
CompuServe: 75200,1463
Internet mail: 75200.1463@compuserve.com
ADDA puts on an annual conference and sponsors local support groups around the United States. Their emphasis is primarily adult ADD, and their annual conference is spectacular.

The ADD Forum on CompuServe
(Online, GO ADD)
CompuServe Information Service
(800) 524-3388, Representative 464
The ADD Forum is available 24-hours a day, every day of the year, and provides discussion groups, conferences, and resource information libraries. Over 45,000 members in more than 30 nations regularly visit.

■ 3. U.S. ADD Support Groups for Adults

ALABAMA
 Birmingham
 John Larson
 (205) 823-5910

ALASKA
 Anchorage
 Anchorage CH.A.D.D.
 (907) 338-1491

ARIZONA
 Ahwatukee (Phoenix area)
 South Mountain CH.A.D.D.
 (602) 820-4435
 Jeri Goldstein, M.C., R.N.
 (602) 345-6622

 Bullhead City
 Northwestern Arizona
 CH.A.D.D.
 (602) 763-7346

Glendale (Phoenix area)
Attention Deficit Disorder Clinic
(602) 863-7950

Prescott
Families with Attention Deficit
Disorder.
(602) 636-5160

Scottsdale
Attention Deficit Disorder Clinic
(602) 423-7770

Tucson (Northeast)
Steven Ledingham
A.S.K. about ADD
(602) 749-5465 or 621-3149

Tucson
CH.A.D.D. of Tucson
(602) 797-2162
Della Mays, Adult Coordinator
(602) 887-0978

CALIFORNIA
Alameda County
CH.A.D.D. of Alameda County
(510) 581-9941

Arcadia (Pasadena area)
Melissa Thomasson, Ph.D.
(818) 301-7977

Contra Costa County
Pat and Monte Churchill
(510) 825-4938

Encinitas (north of San Diego)
Coastal North County CH.A.D.D.
(619) 259-5325

Laguna Beach
CH.A.D.D. of Laguna Beach
(714) 457-2125

Long Beach
Patreen Bower, M.S., M.F.C.C.
Sue Griffith, M.A., Psy. Asst.
(714) 953-8220

Mountain View
CH.A.D.D. of Mid-Peninsula
(415) 969-6233

Newport Beach
Joan Andrews, L.E.P.
(714) 476-0991

Roseville (Sacramento area)
CH.A.D.D. of Roseville & Greater
Sacramento
(916) 782-5661
Milton Lucius, Ph.D.
(916) 933-5217
John R. Capel, Ph.D.
(916) 488-5788

San Diego
Andrea Little
Roland Rotz, Ph.D.
Learning Development Services
(619) 276-6912

San Francisco
San Francisco/
N. Peninsula CH.A.D.D.
(415) 994-2438

San Jose
Karen Neale, M.A.
(408) 395-1348

San Rafael
MATRIX
(415) 499-3877
David Hayes, Adult Coordinator
(415) 435-0994

Simi Valley
CH.A.D.D. of the Conejo Valley
(805) 520-4943

Ukiah
Mendocino County/
Redwood Empire
CH.A.D.D.
(707) 462-1133

Wildomar
CH.A.D.D. of Temecula Valley
(909) 674-8052

CALIFORNIA
SPOUSE SUPPORT GROUPS
Arcadia (Pasadena area) Melissa
Thomasson, Ph.D.
(818) 301-7977

Contra Costa County
Monte Churchill
(510) 825-4938

Folsom (Sacramento area)
Milton Lucius, Ph.D.
(916) 933-5217

Simi Valley
CH.A.D.D. of the Conejo Valley
(805) 520-4943

COLORADO
Boulder
John Cizman
(303) 786-8112

Colorado Springs
CH.A.D.D. of Colorado Springs
(719) 597-9857

Denver
Don Lambert
(303) 424-5272

Denver (Metro North)
Harry Orr
(303) 458-5675
(303) 424-3116

Fort Collins
Maxine Jarvi
(303) 223-1338
(970) 223-1338 effective 4/2/95

Lakewood (Denver area)
Mile Hi CH.A.D.D.
(303) 936-7821

Littleton (Metro South Denver)
Dennis Smith
(303) 790-2354

*For additional listings in Colorado,
contact:*
Ralph Myers, Editor
ADD VANTAGE
(303) 287-6944

CONNECTICUT
Avon (Hartford area)
CH.A.D.D. of the
Farmington Valley
(203) 651-3880

East Hampton
CH.A.D.D. of East Hampton
Cathy Ziegler, Coordinator
(203) 267-6807
Liz Johnson, Co-coordinator
(203) 873-1733

Mansfield
Mansfield CH.A.D.D.
(203) 429-2582
Paul Kalajain, Adult Coordinator
(203) 487-1920

New Haven
CH.A.D.D. of New Haven
County
(203) 888-1434

New Milford (north of Danbury)
CH.A.D.D. of Candlewood Valley
(203) 350-9484

Rocky Hill
Joel Shusman
(203) 257-3221

Waterford
CH.A.D.D. of Southeastern
Connecticut
(203) 443-2500
(203) 444-0263

CONNECTICUT
SPOUSE SUPPORT GROUPS
Avon (Hartford area)
CH.A.D.D. of the
Farmington Valley
(203) 651-3880

DELAWARE
Wilmington
Lizbee Mahoney, Adult Coordinator
CH.A.D.D. of Brandywine Valley
(302) 478-8202

FLORIDA
Fort Walton Beach
Okaloosa County CH.A.D.D.
(904) 863-2459

Jacksonville
CH.A.D.D. of Duval
(904) 390-0866
Bethann P. Vetter, Adult Coordinator
(904) 731-7230

Orlando
CH.A.D.D. of Seminole County
(407) 324-1442

Pembroke Pines
CH.A.D.D. of South Broward & North
Dade Counties
(305) 680-0799

Plantation
CH.A.D.D. of West Broward
(305) 721-8793

Tampa
Hillsborough County CH.A.D.D.
(813) 852-8075

GEORGIA
Atlanta (Buckhead)
L.D. Adults of Georgia
(404) 514-8088

Decatur (Atlanta area)
Joan Teach, Ph.D.
(404) 378-6643

ILLINOIS
Bloomington
Ron Ropp, Rel.D.
(309) 829-0751

Chicago (Northwest Suburban)
CH.A.D.D. of Northwest
Suburban Chicago
(708) 303-1189

Chicago (South Suburban)
South Suburban
Chicago CH.A.D.D.
(708) 798-9331
Chicago (Southwest Suburban/
Will County)
ADAPPT
(708) 361-3387

Freeport
Freeport Area CH.A.D.D.
(815) 235-8019

Peoria
Deborah Dornaus
(309) 693-0038

Rockford
CH.A.D.D. of Rockford
(815) 968-5640
Gary Hubbard, M.S., L.M.F.T.
(815) 282-1800

*For additional listings in Illinois,
contact:*
Illinois State ADD Council
(708) 361-4878

INDIANA
Bloomington
Abilities Unlimited
(812) 332-1620

Fortville (Indianapolis Eastside)
ADDults of Central Indiana
(317) 649-2871

Greensburg
Tree City CH.A.D.D.
(812) 663-6877

Portage (Northwest Indiana)
David Shultz
(219) 232-6690
Teresa Gross
(219) 465-0447

Richmond
Rita Spoonamore
Adult Attention Deficit Disorder
Support
(317) 966-0221

IOWA
Iowa City
CH.A.D.D. of Iowa City
(319) 656-3043
Don Walker, Adult Coordinator
(319) 337-5201

KANSAS
Overland Park
Avner Stern, Ph.D.
(913) 469-6510

Prairie Village
ADD/ADHD Education &
Resource Association
(913) 362-6108

KANSAS
SPOUSE SUPPORT GROUPS
Prairie Village
ADD/ADHD Education &
Resource
Association
(913) 362-6108

KENTUCKY
Lexington
CH.A.D.D. of the Bluegrass

(606) 272-2166
Nancy Blakley, Adult Coordinator
(606) 223-3074

Paducah
CH.A.D.D. of Western Kentucky
(502) 488-2252

LOUISIANA
New Orleans (Northern area)
River Parish CH.A.D.D.
(504) 467-4983

MAINE
Scarborough
Lindy Botto
(207) 883-2528

MARYLAND
Bel Air
CH.A.D.D. of Harford
(410) 569-3532

Frederick
Frederick County CH.A.D.D.
(301) 898-3912

Rockville
CH.A.D.D. of
Montgomery County
(301) 869-3628
Kathleen G. Nadeau, Ph.D.
(301) 718-8114

MARYLAND
SPOUSE SUPPORT GROUPS
Rockville
CH.A.D.D. of
Montgomery County
(301) 869-3628
Kathleen G. Nadeau, Ph.D.
(301) 718-8114

MASSACHUSETTS
Danvers (north of Boston)
Getchen M. May, M.A.
Living with ADD/LD
(508) 526-4927

Greenfield
CH.A.D.D. of Western
Massachusetts
(413) 665-2108
(413) 648-9801
Lori Roy, Adult Coordinator
(413) 773-5545

Lynn
North Shore Adults and
Children with ADD
(617) 599-6818
Linda Harrison
(508) 777-4077

Plymouth
Linda Greenwood
(508) 747-2179

Weston (Boston area)
John Patrick Moir
(603) 881-5540

MICHIGAN
Ann Arbor
Jim Reisinger
ADDult Information
Exchange Network
(313) 426-1659

Clinton Township/Pontiac/
 Royal Oak/Troy
Kathleen Van Howe
Adult ADD Awareness
(810) 939-1112

Cadillac
North Central Michigan
CH.A.D.D.
(616) 779-0482
Adult Coordinator
(616) 775-3754

Chesterfield (Macomb County)
Chesterfield CH.A.D.D.
(810) 949-7890

Gross Pointe
Gerhard W. Heinen
(313) 886-8907

Lansing
Sue Wallace
(517) 627-3387
Jennifer Bramer, Ph.D., L.P.C.
Lansing Community College
Counseling Services Department
(517) 483-1184

Novi
Fred Michaelson
(810) 348-2656

MINNESOTA
Minneapolis
William Ronan, LICSW
(612) 933-3460

St. Louis Park
(Minneapolis area)
Twin Cities CH.A.D.D.
(612) 922-5761

Southfield
Chuck Pearson
Adult ADD Lib
(810) 540-6335

MISSOURI
Kansas City
(see Overland Park and Prairie
Village, Kansas listings)

St. Louis
Barb Rosenfeld, Adult
Coordinator
Attention Deficit Disorder
Association of Missouri
(314) 963-4655

St. Louis area
DePaul Health Center/
Adults with ADD Support Group
(314) 344-7224

MISSOURI SPOUSE SUPPORT GROUPS

Kansas City
(see Prairie, Kansas listing)

MONTANA
Great Falls
Dennis Patton
(406) 454-1964
David Walker
(406) 727-2137

Havre
Cherie Miller
New World
(406) 265-1871

Kalispell
Flathead Valley CH.A.D.D.
(406) 257-5450

NEW HAMPSHIRE
Concord
Sarah Brophy, Ph.D.
(603) 226-6121

Nashua
John Patrick Moir
(603) 881-5540

Portsmouth
Seacoast CH.A.D.D.
(603) 430-8787

NEW JERSEY
Fair Haven
Robert LoPresti, Ph.D.
Adult ADD Self Help
Support Group
(908) 842-4553

Washington Township
(Gloucester County)
CH.A.D.D. of Washington
Township
(609) 582-5717

NEW JERSEY SPOUSE SUPPORT GROUPS
Fair Haven
Robert LoPresti, Ph.D.
Adult ADD Self Help
Support Group
(908) 842-4553

NEW MEXICO
Albuquerque
Attention Deficit Disorder Clinic
(505) 243-9600

Las Cruces
Dona Ana County CH.A.D.D.
(505) 523-5076
Adult Coordinator
(505) 523-8770

NEW YORK
Buffalo area
CH.A.D.D. of Western New York
(716) 626-4581

Hautpauge (Eastern Long Island)
CH.A.D.D. of Suffolk County
(516) 751-6989

Long Island
Joan B. Ells
(516) 244-3665

Manhattan
Barbara Andersen
(914) 476-0965

Queens
Forest Hills/Flushing CH.A.D.D.
(718) 969-0549

Rochester
Greater Rochester Attention Deficit
Disorder Association (GRADDA)
(716) 251-2322

Utica
CH.A.D.D. of Mohawk Valley
(315) 724-4233

White Plains
CH.A.D.D. of
Westchester County
(914) 278-3020
Susan G. Salit, M.S.W.,
Adult Coordinator
(914) 472-2935
Charlotte Tomaino, Ph.D.
(914) 949-4055

NEW YORK
SPOUSE SUPPORT GROUPS
Rochester
Greater Rochester Attention
Deficit Disorder
Association (GRADDA)
(716) 251-2322

NORTH CAROLINA
Charlotte
CH.A.D.D. of
Mecklenburg County
(704) 551-9120

OHIO
Eaton area
(see Richmond, Indiana listing)

Toledo
Jan Menzie
(419) 841-6603

Xenia
A.S.K. about ADD
Bettylou Huber
(513) 862-4573
Madge Jones
(513) 897-4380

OKLAHOMA
Oklahoma City
CH.A.D.D. of Central Oklahoma
(405) 722-1233

Tulsa
Shelley Curtiss
(918) 622-1370

Juan Wilson
(918) 486-5035

OKLAHOMA
SPOUSE SUPPORT GROUPS
Tulsa
Cathy Holmes
(918) 369-5750

OREGON
Portland (Northwest)
ADDVENTURES Support Group
(503) 452-5666

Portland (Northeast)
Metro-Portland CH.A.D.D.
(503) 294-9504

The Dalles
Mike Newman
(503) 296-4408

PENNSYLVANIA
Bethlehem
CH.A.D.D. of Lehigh Valley
(610) 258-9615

Bryn Mawr (West of Philadelphia)
Parents Supporting Parents
Main Line CH.A.D.D.
(610) 626-2998

Harrisburg
CH.A.D.D. of the Capital Area
(717) 766-8084

Lancaster
Lancaster County CH.A.D.D.
(717) 626-0745

Lancaster
Judy Mansfield
(717) 656-9515

Malvern
Jerry McCrone
(610) 647-8807

Philadelphia
Susan Sussman, M.Ed.
(610) 825-8572

Pittsburgh
Southwest Pennsylvania
CH.A.D.D.
Network Adult ADD
Support Group
(412) 531-4554

PENNSYLVANIA
SPOUSE SUPPORT GROUPS
Lancaster
Judy Mansfield
(717) 656-9515

RHODE ISLAND
Providence
Austin Donnelly
Rhode Island ADDult
Support Group
(401) 463-8778

SOUTH CAROLINA
Columbia
The Mental Health Association in
Mid-Carolina
(803) 733-5425

Seneca
CH.A.D.D. of Upstate South Carolina
(803) 882-8370

Spartanburg
CH.A.D.D. of Spartanburg
(803) 587-8756

TENNESSEE
Knoxville
CH.A.D.D. of Greater East Tennessee
(615) 681-1174

Nashville
ADD'sUP
(615) 292-5947

TEXAS
Austin
L.D.A. of Austin
(512) 477-5516
Jo Anne Nicholson, Adult Coordinator
(512) 892-3736

Denton
North Texas CH.A.D.D.
(817) 383-5795

Houston (Southwest)
Karen Kasper
Houston Adult ADD
Support Group
(713) 353-3898

For additional listings in Texas, contact:
Attention Deficit Disorders
Association—Southern Region
(713) 955-3720

UTAH
Salt Lake City
Joyce Otterstrom
L.D.A. of Utah
(801) 355-2881

VIRGINIA
Arlington
Maggie Baker, Adult Coordinator
CH.A.D.D. of Arlington/Alexandria/Falls Church
(703) 979-0820

Bon Aire (Richmond area)
CH.A.D.D. of Central Virginia
(804) 672-1308

Fairfax County
Susan Biggs, Ed.D.
(703) 642-6697

Glen Allen
CH.A.D.D. of Central Virginia
(804) 672-1308

Newport News
Jody Lochmiller-Jones
Adult Attention Deficit &
Related Disorders Outreach
(804) 930-1931

Peninsula Attention Deficit
Disorder
Association (PADDA),
Adult Chapter
(804) 874-2343

WASHINGTON
Bellingham
Lisa F. Poast
Adult ADD Association
(360) 647-6681

Kennewick
Kathy VanDyke
(509) 586-4257

Olympia
Attention Deficit Disorder Clinic
(360) 754-4801

Seattle
W. J. McNabb, Ph.D.
(206) 609-3470

Tacoma
ADDult Support of Washington
Cynthia Hammer
(206) 752-0801 (evenings)
Brian Howell
(206) 759-2914 (days)

Vancouver
Columbia River CH.A.D.D.
(360) 750-6387

WASHINGTON
SPOUSE SUPPORT GROUPS
Bellingham
Adult ADD Association
(360) 647-6681
Linda Hallmark, M.S.
(360) 715-0341

Olympia
Pat and Helena Nagle
Attention Deficit Disorder Clinic
(360) 754-4801

WISCONSIN
Milwaukee (Northeast)
Robert Lintereur
(414) 242-5387
Bob Fuller
(414) 377-6900

Milwaukee (Southeast)
CH.A.D.D. of Southeast Wisconsin
(414) 223-8310
Bob Roman, Adult Coordinator
(414) 291-7058 ext. 6797

Waukesha (Milwaukee area)
Paul Rembas
Adult ADHD Support Group
(414) 542-6694

WISCONSIN
SPOUSE SUPPORT GROUPS
Waukesha (Milwaukee area)
Amy Schley, Ph.D.
(414) 542-6694

■ 4. Canadian
Support Groups

Campbell River, British Columbia
Loring Kuhn, Adult Coordinator
CH.A.D.D. Canada
of Campbell River
(604) 923-7405

New Westminster,
British Columbia
Claudette Kovacs
ADDSA (Attention Deficit
Disorder
Support Association)
(604) 524-9183

Marielle Gauvin,
Adult Coordinator
(604) 524-0763

Bedford, Nova Scotia
Lida Currie
Attention Deficit Association of
Nova Scotia
(902) 835-2343

Ottawa, Ontario CH.A.D.D.
Canada of the National
Capital Region
(613) 722-8482

For additional listings of Canadian Support Groups, contact:
Mark Turcotte
CH.A.D.D. Canada
(613) 231-7646

The Adult ADD Association thanks the authors of Answers to Distraction, Ned Hallowell. MD *and John Ratey, MD for making possible this updated listing through their financial support, and to thank those individuals who so generously give of their time as volunteers to the many adults with ADD seeking referral and support.*

Changes and/or additions to this list may be sent to:
Lisa F. Poast
Adult ADD Association
1225 E. Sunset Drive, Suite 640
Bellingham, WA 98226-3526
(360) 647-6681

■ 5. A List of International ADD Support Groups

Thanks to Janie Bowman, on CompuServe at 72662,3716, for compiling and maintaining this list.

Learning Disabilities Association
of Canada
323 Chapel Street
Ottawa, Ontario
KIN 7Z2
President: Linda Jeppesen
Phone: (613) 238-5721
Fax: (613) 235-5391

For a listing of Provincial Learning Disabilities Association headquarters and LDA Ontario chapters, please download LDACAN.TXT.

LADDERS
Stan Mould,
95 Church Rd.,
Bradmore, Wolverhampton
WV3 7EW,
United Kingdom.

ADD-ADHD Family
Support Group
Mrs. G. Mead, President
1a, High Street
Dilton Marsh,
Westbury,
Wilts. BA13 4DL
Tel: 0373 826045
or
Mr. B. Tuffill
93 Avon Road,
Devizes,
Wilts, SN10 1PT
Tel: 0380 726710

Hyperactivity/Attention Deficit
Association (N.S.W.)
29 Bertram Street
Chatswood 2067
Australia

Hyperactive Children's Support
Group
Sally Bunday
71 Whyke Lane

Chichester, West Sussex
England PO19 2LD
Phone: International plus 44 for
UK then 903-725-182
(*Sysop Note: This group may lean
toward natural remedies*)

Stephanie Mahony
25, Lawnswood Park
Stillorgan
Co. Dublin
Phone: 2889766
Hyperactive Childrens Support
 Group—Ireland

■ 6. UK ADD-knowledgable physician list

This is a list of doctors in the UK who are known to understand and treat ADD, although your GP or Child & Adolescent Family Guidance Clinic may know of someone in your locality.

This list was compiled for the ADD forum on CompuServe by John Landells 75151,2423.

DR. P.V.F. Cosgrove, MB MRC
Psych. DPM.
Consultant Child & Adolescent
Psychiatrist.
Heath House Priory Hospital,
Heath House Lane,
Off Bell Hill,
Bristol. BS16 1EQ
Tel: 0272 525255
Fax : 0272 525552

Professor P. Hill,
Professor of Child & Adolescent
Psychiatry,
St. George's Hospital
Medical School,
Dept. of Mental Health Sciences,

Jenner Wing,
Cranmer Terrace,
Tooting,
London SW17 ORE
Tel: 081-672 9944 ext. 55531/2

Doctor Turk
Department of Child Psychiatry,
Lanesborough Wing,
St. George's Hospital,
Blackshaw Road,
Tooting,
London SW17 0QT

Doctor G.D. Kewley, MB
 BS MRCP FRACP DCH.
Consultant Paediatrician.
Learning Assesment Centre,
The Ashdown Hospital,
Burrell Road,
Haywards Heath,
West Sussex RH16 1UD
Tel: 0444 456999 ext 207

Doctor T. Hutchins
Consultant Community
 Paediatrician,
Child Health Department,
Newbridge Hill,
Bath BA1 3QE
Tel: 0225 313640

Professor J.R. Sibert, MD FRCP
DCH.
Professor of Community
Child Health.
University of Wales College
of Medicine,
University Dept. of Child Health,
Llandough Special Children's
 Centre,
Penlan Road,
Panarth CF64 2XX
Tel: 0222 712805/704542

Doctor A.J. Franklin, FRCP, DCH.
Consultant Paediatrician,
St. John's Hospital,
Wood Street,
Chelmsford,
Essex CM2 9BG
Tel: 0245 513261

Doctor R. Bailey,
Clinical Psychologists,
Milton Keynes General Hospital,
Standing Way,
Eaglestone,
Milton Keynes MK6 5LD
Tel: 0908 660033

Doctor J. Parker,
Senior Registrar,
Child & Family Psychiatry,
Royal United Hospital,
Combe Park,
Bath BA1 3NG
Tel: 0225 825075
 (0225 428311 ext 5075)

Acknowledgments

The biggest thank-you in the preparation of this book goes to the thousands of people who, over the past years, have shared their stories with me. You'll meet them throughout the book; without them this book never would have happened. To each of you who took the time to write, call, fax, or email me, thank you!

Sharon Levine deserves special acknowledgement for offering her guide to ADD-friendly occupations which appears in this book, as does Lisa Poast for compiling much of the list of Adult ADD support groups in the resource section.

Additional thanks go to those people who have offered me ideas, encouragement, inspiration (sometimes unknowingly), reference, and support (particularly with the ADD Forum on CompuServe). They include (but are not limited to): Alan Zametkin, Alfred Allen, Alysia Wurst, Anita Diamant, B.J. Yahr, Barry Berkov, Bill & Vicki Howard, Bill Watterson, Bob Brooks, Bob Koski, Brad Doss, Brad Walrod, Carl & Jean Hartmann, Carla Nelson, Carol LaRusso, Charlie Winton, Colleen Alexander-Roberts, Dale Hammerschmidt, Daniel Amen, Dave deBronkart, David Mullinax, David Vining, Deborah Carlen, Dennis Campbell, Dirk Huttenbach, Don Arnoldy, Don Haughey, Dorothy Smith, Doug Alexander, Ed Brewer, Ed Lindsey, Edward Hallowell, Elisa Davis, Elna Hensley, Frederick Earl, G.W. Hall, Gary Grooms, George Lynn, Gerhard Lipfert, Glenda Serpa, Gottfried Müller, Greg Vetter, Greg Winterhalter, Hal Meyer, Harlan Lampert, Harvey Parker, Howard Morris, Hugh Echols, Hunter S. Thompson, J., J.B. Whitwell, Jack Rieley, Jane Shumway, Janie, Clint, and Cj Bowman, Jay Fikes, Jeff Justice, Jerry Schneiderman, Jill Neimark, Jim Butler, Jim Hart, Jim Salvas, Jim Tucker, Joel Lubar, John & Nancy Ratey, John & Nancy Roy, John Knapp, John Landells, John Paddock, John Shumate, Karen Sanders, Kate Kelly, Kathleen Nadeau, Kathy Gerber, Kitty Petty, Lee Underwood, Linda Rawson, Linda Robertson, Louis Cady, Louise Hartmann, Louise Richards, Lynn Weiss, Mark Snyder, Mark Stein, Marty Stein, Mary Fowler, Mary Jane Johnson,

Michael Armstrong, Michael Cain, Michael Hutchison, Michael Kurland, Michael Popkin, Monica Sharp, Morgan Adcock, Nancy White, Owen Lipstein, Pablo Villegas, Pam Jacobs, Paul Elliott, Pete & Pam Wright, Phil Kavenaugh, Phil Torrance, Richard Andrews, Richard Rauh, Rick & Wanda Bogin, Rick Van Arnam, Rob Kall, Rob Mainor, Robert LoPresti, Roger Freeman, Rose Zagaja, Russell Wade, Sam Olens, Scott & Julie Cress, Scott Berg, Sherry Griswold, Siegfried & Susan Othmer, Skye Lininger, Stephen Bluestein, Stephen Katz, Steve Foust, Susan Barrows, Susan Baum, Susan Burgess, Susan Jacobs, Susan Reich, Tammie Norton, Tim & Deborah Underwood, Tom Allen, Tom Gumpel, Tom Rodgers, Tondra Morley, Veronica Deane, Wendy Hoechstetter, Will Krynen, Wilson & Charlene Harrell.

SECTION SIX
Bibliography

Albus, J. S. 1971. A theory of cerebellar function. Math. Biosci. 10:25-61

Alexander CN, Langer EJ, Davies JL, Chandler HM, Newman RI. Transcendental meditation, mindfulness, and longevity: an experimental study with the elderly. J Pers Soc Psychol. 1989; 57: 957, Table 3.

Alexander, C. N., and Langer, E. J., eds., Higher stages of human development: Perspectives on adult growth. New York: Oxford University Press, 1990.

Alexander, C. N.; Rainforth, M. V.; and Gelderloos, P. Transcendental Meditation, self actualization, and psychological health: A conceptual overview and statistical meta-analysis.Journal of Social Behavior and Personality 6(5), 189-247, 1991.

Allen, Tom (1994?). "Psychoneurotherapy: Is it the future?" In Kamiya, Joe & Schwartz, G. (In preparation)

Amaral, D. G. 1987. Memory: anatomical organization of candidate brain regions. See Plum 1987, pp. 211-94

American Psychiatric Association. "Tic Disorders." *Treatments of Psychiatric Disorders*, vol. 1. Washington, DC: American Psychiatric Association, 1989.

American Psychiatric Association. *Diagnostic and Statistical Manual of Mental Disorders*. 3rd ed. Washington, D.C.: American Psychiatric Association, 1987.

Anderson, J. C., et al. "DSM-III Disorders in Preadolescent Children. Prevalence in a Large Sample from the General Population." *Archives of General Psychiatry*, 44 (1987), 69-76.

Applegate, C. D., Frysinger, R. C., Kapp, B. S., Gallagher, M. 1982. Multiple unit activity recorded from the amygdala central nucleus during Pavlovian heart rate conditioning in the rabbit. Brain Res. 238:457-62

Applegate, C. D., Kapp, B. S., Underwood, M., McNall, C. L. 1983. Autonomic and somatomotor effects of amygdala central nucleus stimulation in awake rabbits. Physiol Behav. 31:353-60

Aron, A., and Aron, E. N., The Transcendental Meditation program's effect on addictive behavior. Addictive Behaviors 5: 3-12, 1980.

Aron, A.; Orme-Johnson, D.; and Brubaker, P. The Transcendental Meditation program in the college curriculum: A 4-year longitudinal study of effects on cognitive and affective functioning. College Student Journal 15(2): 140-146, 1981.

Aron, E. N., and Aron, A. The patterns of reduction of drug and alcohol use among Transcendental Meditation participants. Bulletin of the Society of Psychologists in Addictive Behaviors 2(1): 28-33, 1983.

Aron, E. N., and Aron, A. Transcendental Meditation program and marital adjustment. Psychological Reports 51: 887-890, 1982.

Assimakis, P. D. Change in the quality of life in Canada: intervention studies of the effect of the Transcendental Meditation and TM-Sidhi program. Psychological Reports (in press).

Badawi, K.; Wallace, R. K.; Orme-Johnson, D.; and Rouzer, A. M. Electrophysiologic characteristics of respiratory suspension periods occurring during the practice of the Transcendental Meditation program. Psychosomatic Medicine 46(3): 267-276, 1984.

Bakin, J. S., Weinberger, N. M. 1990. Classical conditioning induces CS-specific receptive field plasticity in the auditory cortex of guinea pig. Brain Res. 536:271-86

Barkley, R. A. "The Social Behavior of Hyperactive Children: Developmental Changes, Drug Effects, and Situational Variation." *Childhood Disorders: Behavioral-developmental Approaches.* Edited by R.J. McMahon and R.D. Peters. New York: Brunner/Mazel, 1985.

Barkley, R. A., *et al.* "Development of a Multimethod Clinical Protocol for Assessing Stimulant Drug Response in Children with Attention Deficit Disorder." *Journal of Clinical Child Psychology,* 17 (1988), 14-24.

Barkley, R. A., *Hyperactive Children: A Handbook for Diagnosis and Treatment.* New York: Guilford, 1981.

Benedetti, F., Montarolo, P. G., Rabacchi, S. 1984. Inferior olive lesion induces longlasting functional modification in the Purkinje cells. Exp. Brain Res. 55:368-71

Berger, T. W., Berry, S. D., Thompson, R. F. 1986. Role of the hippocampus in classical conditioning of aversive and appetitive behaviors. In The Hippocampus, ed. R. L. Isaacson, K. H. Pribram, pp. 203-29. New York: Plenum

Berger, T. W., Orr, W. B. 1983. Hippocampectomy selectively disrupts discrimination reversal conditioning of the rabbit nictitating membrane response. Behav. Brain Res. 8:49-68

Bermudez-Rattoni, F., Introini-Collison, I. B., McGaugh, J. L. 1991. Reversible inactivation of the insular cortex by tetrodotoxin produces retrograde and anterograde amnesia for inhibitory avoidance and spatial learning. Proc. Natl. Acad Sci. 88:5379-82

Berntson, G. G., Micco, D. J. 1976. Organization of brain stem behavioral systems. Brain Res. BUIL 1:471-83

Berntson, G. G., Torello, M. W. 1982. The paleocerebellum and the integration of behavioral function. Physiol Psych. 10:2-12

Berthier, N. E., Moore, J. W. 1986. Cerebellar Purkinje cell activity related to the classically conditioned nictitating membrane response. Exp. Brain Res. 63:341-50

Berthier, N. E., Moore, J. W. 1990. Activity of deep cerebellar nuclear cells during classical conditioning of nictitating membrane extension in rabbits. Exp. Brain Res. 83:44-54

Binney, Judith: Maori Oral Narratives, Pakeha Written Texts: Two Forms of Telling History, New Zealand Journal of History 21, 1 (1987): 16-28

Black, A. H., Prokasy, W. F., eds. 1972. Classical Conditioning. Vol. 2. Current Research and Theory. New York: Appleton-Century-Crofts Blanchard,

D. C., Blanchard, R. J. 1972. Innate and conditioned reactions to threat in rats with amygdaloid lesions. J. Comp. Physiol. Psychol. 81:281-90

Blackmore S. Is meditation good for you? New Scientist. 1991;131:30-33.

Bleick, C. R., and Abrams, A.I . The Transcendental Meditation program and criminal recidivism in California. Journal of Criminal Justice 15: 211-230, 1987.

Bloedel, J. R., Bracha, V., Kelly, T. M., Wu, J. Z. 1991. Substrates for motor learning: does the cerebellum do it all? Ann. N.Y. Acad. Sci. 627:305-18

Bolles, R. C., Fanselow, M. S. 1980. A perceptual-defensive-recuperative model of fear and pain. Behav. Brain Sci. 3:291-323

Bowen, Catherine Drinker. *The Most Dangerous Man in America: Scenes from the Life of Benjamin Franklin.* Boston: Little, Brown & Company, 1974.

Bracha, V., Wu, J. Z., Cartwright, M., Bloedel, J. R. 1990. Selective effects of lidocaine microinjections into the region of the spinal trigeminal nucleus on the conditioned and unconditioned responses of the rabbit nictitating membrane reflex. Soc. Neurosci. Abstr. 16:474

Bresnahan, J. C., Meyer, P. M., Baldwin, R. B., Meyer, D. R. 1976. Avoidance behavior in rats with lesions in the septum, fornix longus, and amygdala. Physiol Psychol 4:333-40

Brigo B, Serpelloni G. Homoeopathic treatment of migraines: a randomized double-blind controlled study of sixty cases. Berlin [G]ournal of Research in Homoeopathy 1991;1:98-106.

Bronowski, J. The Ascent of Man. Little, Brown, & Company, 1973.

Brooks, J. S., and Scarano, T. Transcendental Meditation in the treatment of post- Vietnam adjustment. Journal of Counseling and Development 64, 212-215, 1985.

Brown, Ronald T., et al. "Effects of Methylphenidate on Cardiovascular Responses in Attention Deficit Hyperactivity Disordered Adolescents." *Journal of Adolescent Health Care*, 10 (1989), 179-183.

Buckley, W. F., Jr. *Overdrive: A Personal Documentary.* New York: Doubleday & Company, 1983.

Buckman R, Sabbagh K. Magic or medicine? London: Macmillan, 1993.

Burdett, Osbert. *The Two Carlyles.* 1930 repr. 1980.

Cahill, L., McGaugh, J. L. 1990. Amygdaloid complex lesions differentially affect retention of tasks using appetitive and aversive reinforcement. Behav. Neurosci. 104:532-43

Campbell, Ian. *Thomas Carlyle.* 1975.

Campeau, S., Davis, M. 1991. Lesions of the auditory thalamus block acquisition and expression of aversive conditioning to an auditory but not a visual stimulus measured with the fear potentiated startle paradigm. Soc. Neurosci. Abstr. 17:658

Campeau, S., Miserendino, M. J. D., Davis, M. 1992. Intra-amygdala infusion of the Nmethyl-D-aspartate receptor antagonist AP5 blocks retention but not expression of fearpotentiated startle to an auditory conditioned stimulus. Behav. Neurosci. In press

Carter, J.L. & Russell, H.L. (1985). "Use of EMG biofeedback procedures with learning disabled children in a clinical setting." Journal of Learning Disabilities, 18(4), 213-216.

Carter, J.L., & Russell, H.L. (1981). "Changes in verbal performance IQ discrepancy scores after left hemisphere EEG frequency control training—a pilot report." American Journal of Clinical Biofeedback, 4(1), 66-67.

Cegavske, C. F., Patterson, M. M., Thompson, R. F. 1979. Neuronal unit activity in the abducens nucleus during classical conditioning of the nictitating membrane response in the rabbit, Oryctolagus cuniculus. J. Comp. Physiol. Psychol. 93:595-609

Chambers, K. C. 1990. A neural model for conditioned taste aversions. Annu. Rev. Neurosci. 13:373-85

Chang-tai, Hung: Going to the People: Chinese Intellectuals and Folk Literature, 1918-1937 (Cambridge: Harvard Asian Studies Series 1985), 10-12

Chapman, P. F. 1988. An analysis of the critical neural circuits for the conditioned eyeblink response in the rabbit. PhD dissertation, Stanford University, Stanford, Calif.

Chapman, P. F., Kairiss, E. W., Keenan, C. L., Brown, T. H. 1990a. Long-term synaptic potentiation in the amygdala. Synapse 6:271-78

Chapman, P. F., Steinmetz, J. E., Sears, L. L., Thompson, R. F. 1990b. Effects of lidocaine injection in the interpositus nucleus and red nucleus on conditioned behavioral and neuronal responses. Brain Res. 537:140-56

Chapman, P. F., Steinmetz, J. E., Thompson, R. F. 1988. Classical conditioning does not occur when direct stimulation of the red nucleus or cerebellar nuclei is the unconditioned stimulus. Brain Res. 442:97-104

Chopra D. Perfect Health. New York, NY: Harmony Books; 1990.

Clark, G. A., McCormick, D. A., Lavond, D. G., Thompson, R. F. 1984. Effects of lesions of cerebellar nuclei on conditioned behavioral arid hippocampal neuronal responses. Brain Res. 291:125-36

Clark, R. E., Brown, D. J., Thompson, R. F., Lavond, D. G. 1990. Reacquisition of classical conditioning after removal of cerebellar cortex in Dutch Belted rabbits. Neurosci. Abstr. 16:271

Clark, R. E., Lavond, D. G. 1992. Reversible lesions of the red nucleus during acquisition and retention of a classically conditioned behavior in rabbits. Soc. Neurosci. Abstr. In press

Clark, R. E., Zhang, A. A., Lavond, D. G. 1991. Cooling red nucleus or interpositus nucleus during acquisition of a classically conditioned eyeblink response in the rabbit. Int. NIBS Conf. Synaptic Plasticity, Nov. 5, 1991, Los Angeles

Clubbe, John, ed. Froude's Life of Carlyle, 1979.

Clugnet, M. C., LeDoux, J. E. 1990. Synaptic plasticity in fear conditioning circuits: induction of LTP in the lateral nucleus of the amygdala by stimulation of the medial geniculate body. J. Neurosci. 10:2818-24

Cohen, David William: The Undefining of Oral Tradition, Ethnohistory 36, 1 (winter 1989): 9-18; Vansina, Oral Tradition, 107-8

Cohn, R., & Nardin, J. (1958). "The correlation of bilateral occipital slow activity in the human EEG with certain disorders of behavior." American Journal of Psychiatry, 115, 44-54.

Comings, D. E., and Comings, B. G. "Tourette's Syndrome and Attention Deficit Disorder with Hyperactivity: Are They Genetically Related?" *Journal of the American Academy of Child Psychiatry*, 23 (1984), 138-146.

Comings, D. E., *et al.* "The Dopamine D2 Receptor Locus as a Modifying Gene in Enuropsychiatric Disorders." *Journal of the American Medical Association*, 266 (1991), 1793-1800.

Cranson, R, W.; Orme-Johnson, D.; Dillbeck, M. C.; Jones, C. H.; Alexander, C. N; and Gackenbach, J. Transcendental Meditation and improved performance on intelligence-related measures: A longitudinal study. Personality and Individual Differences 12: 1105-1116, 1991.

Cronin, William: A Place for Stories: Nature, History, and Narrative, Journal of American History 78, 4 (March 1992): 1347-76.

Cruikshank, Julie: Getting the Words Right: Perspectives on Naming and Places in Athapaskan Oral History, Arctic Anthropology 27, 1 (1990): 52-65.

Davis, M. 1990. Pharmacological and anatomical analysis of fear conditioning. In Neurobiology of Drug Abuse: Learning and Memory, ed. L. Erinoff, pp. 126-62. Rockville, MD: National Institute on Drug Abuse

DeMallie, Raymond: "These Have No Ears": Narrative and the Ethnohistorical Method; Ethnohistory 40, 4 (fall 1993): 515-38

Desmond, J. E., Moore, J. W. 1983. A supratrigeminal region implicated in the classically conditioned nictitating membrane response. Brain Res. BUIL 10:765-73

Diamond, D. M., Weinberger, N. M. 1984. Physiological plasticity of single neurons in auditory cortex of the cat during acquisition of the pupillary conditioned response: 11. Secondary field (AII). Behav. Neurosci. 98:189-210

Diamond, D. M., Weinberger, N. M. 1986. Classical conditioning rapidly induces specific changes in frequency receptive fields of single neurons in secondary and ventral ectosylvian auditory cortical fields. Brain Res. 372:357-60

Dillbeck MC. Test of a field theory of consciousness and social change: time series analysis of participation in the TM-Sidhi program and reduction of violent death in the US. Soc Indicators Res. 1990; 22:399-418.

Dillbeck, M. C. Meditation and flexibility of visual perception and verbal problem- solving. Memory and Cognition 10(3): 207-215, 1982.

Dillbeck, M. C. Test of a field theory of consciousness and social change: Time series analysis of participation in the TM-Sidhi program and reduction of violent death in the U.S. Social Indicators Research 22: 399- 418, 1990.

Dillbeck, M. C., and Abrams, A. I. The application of the Transcendental Meditation program to correction. International Journal of Comparative and Applied Criminal Justice 11(1): 111-132, 1987.

Dillbeck, M. C., and Araas-Vesely, S. Participation in the Transcendental Meditation program and frontal EEG coherence during concept learning. International Journal of Neuroscience 29: 45-55, 1986.

Dillbeck, M. C., and Bronson, E. C. Short-term longitudinal effects of the Transcendental Meditation technique on EEG power and coherence. International Journal of Neuroscience 14: 147-151, 1981.

Dillbeck, M. C., and Orme-Johnson, D. W. Physiological differences between Transcendental Meditation and rest. American Psychologist 42: 879-881, 1987.

Dillbeck, M. C.; Assimakis, P. D.; Raimondi, D.; Orme-Johnson, D. W.; and Rowe, R. Longitudinal effects of the Transcendental Meditation and TM-Sidhi program on cognitive ability and cognitive style. Perceptual and Motor Skills 62: 731-738, 1986.

Dillbeck, M. C.; Banus, C. B.; Polanzi, C.; and Landrith III, G. S. Test of a field model of consciousness and social change: The Transcendental Meditation and TM-Sidhi program and decreased urban crime. The Journal of Mind and Behavior 9(4): 457-486, 1988.

Dillbeck, M. C.; Cavanaugh, K. L.; Glenn, T.; Orme-Johnson, D. W.; and Mittlefehldt, V. Consciousness as a field: the Transcendental Meditation and TM-Sidhi program and changes in social indicators. The Journal of Mind and Behavior 8(1): 67-104, 1987.

Dillbeck, M. C.; Landrith III, G.; and Orme-Johnson, D. W. The Transcendental Meditation program and crime rate change in a sample of forty-eight cities. Findings previously published in Journal of Crime and Justice 4: 25-45, 1981.

Dillbeck, M. C.; Orme-Johnson, D. W.; and Wallace, R. K. Frontal EEG coherence, H-reflex recovery, concept learning, and the TM-Sidhi program. International Journal of Neuroscience 15: 151-157, 1981.

Disterhoft, J. F., Coulter, D. A., Alkon, D. L. 1986. Conditioning-specific membrane changes of rabbit hippocampal neurons measured in vitro. Proc. Natl. Acad. Sci. 83:2733-37

Disterhoft, J. F., Kwan, H. H., Lo, W. D. 1977. Nictitating membrane conditioning to tone in the immobilized albino rabbit. Brain Res. 137:127-44

Disterhoft, J. F., Quinn, K. J., Weiss, C., Shipley, M. T. 1985. Accessory abducens nucleus and conditioned eye retraction/nictitating membrane extension in rabbit. J. Neurosci. 5:941-50

Donegan, N. H., Gluck, M. A., Thompson, R. F. 1989. Integrating behavioral and biological models of classical conditioning. See Hawkins & Bower 1989, pp. 109-56 Dow, R. S., Moruzzi, G. 1958. The Physiology and Pathology of the Cerebellum. Minneapolis: Univ. Minn. Press

Doyle, Sir Arthur Conan. "The Sign of the Four." Lippincott's Monthly Magazine, London, 1890.

Eccles, J. C., Ito, M., Szentagothai, J. 1967. The Cerebellum as a Neuronal Machine. New York: Springer-Verlag Edeline, J. M., Weinberger, N. M. 1991. Subcortical adaptive filtering in the auditory system: associative receptive field plasticity in the dorsal medial geniculate body. Behav. Neurosci. 105:154-75

Einstein, Albert. Out of My Later Years. New York: Bonanza, 1956, 1990.

Enser, D. 1976. A study of classical nictitating membrane conditioning in neodecorticate, hemidecorticate and thalamic rabbits. PhD thesis, Univ. Iowa, Iowa City

Evans, R. W., Clay, T. H., and Gualtieri, C. T. "Carbamazepine in Pediatric Psychiatry." *Journal of the American Academy of Child Psychiatry*, 26 (1987), 2-8.

Fanselow, M. S., Kim, J. J., Landeira-Fernandez, J. 1991. Anatomically selective blockade of Pavlovian fear conditioning by application of an NMDA antagonist to the amygdala and periaqueductal gray. Soc. Neurosci. Abstr. 17:659

Farb, C. F., LeDoux, J. E., Milner, T. A. 1989. Glutamate is present in medial geniculate body neurons that project to lateral amygdala and in lateral amygdala presynaptic terminals. Soc. Neurosci. Abstr. 15:890

Farwell, Byron. *Burton: A Biography of Sir Richard Francis Burton*. London: Penguin, 1990.

Feingold, Benjamin. *Why Your Child is Hyperactive*. New York: Random House, 1975.

Ferley JP, Zmirou D, D'Admehar D, Balducci D. A controlled evaluation of a homoeopathic preparation in the treatment of influenza-like symptoms. Br [G] Clin Pharmacol 1989;27:329-35.

Fisher P, Greenwood A, Huskisson EC, Tuner P, Belon P. Effect of homoeopathic treatment on fibrositis (primary fibromyalgia). BM[G] 1989;299:365-6.

Fogelson, Raymond, The Ethnohistory of Events and Non-events, Ethnohistory 36, 2 (spring 1989): 133-47

Foy, M. R., Steinmetz, J. E., Thompson, R. F. 1984. Single unit analysis of cerebellum during classically conditioned eyelid response. Soc. Neurosci. Abstr. 10:122

Francis, J., Hernandez, L. L., Powell, D. A. 1981. Lateral hypothalamic lesions: effects on Pavlovian cardiac and eyeblink conditioning in the rabbit. Brain Res. BULL 6:155-63

Freud, S. Massenpsychologie und Ich-Analyse. Internationaler Psychoanalytischer Verlag, Leipzig, 1921.

Freud, S. Eine Kindhieitserinnerung des Leonardo da Vinci, Gesammelte Schriften, 9:371, Vienna, 1924

Friedman, Jonathan: The Past in the Future: History and the Politics of Identity, American Anthropologist 94, 4 (Dec. 1992): 837-59.

Gallagher, M., Kapp, B. S. 1978. Manipulation of opiate activity in the amygdala alters memory processes. Life Sci. 23:1973-78

Gallagher, M., Kapp, B. S., McNall, C. L., Pascoe, J. P. 1981. Opiate effects in the amygdala central nucleus alters rabbit heart rate conditioning. Pharm. Biochem. Behav. 14:497-505

Garber, et al. If Your Child is Hyperactive, Inattentive, Impulsive, Distractible...New York: Villard Books, 1990.

Gasser, T., Verleger, R., Bacher, P., & Stokes, N. (1988). "Development of the EEG in school-age children and adolescents; analysis of band power." Electroencephalography and Clinical Neurophysiology, 69, 91-99.

Gelderloos, P.; Lockie, R. J.; and Chuttoorgoon, S. Field independence of students at Maharishi School of the Age of Enlightenment and a Montessori school. Perceptual and Motor Skills 65: 613-614, 1987.

Gelderloos, P.; Walton, K. G.; Orme-Johnson, D. W.; and Alexander, C. Effectiveness of the Transcendental Meditation program in preventing and treating substance misuse: A review. International Journal of the Addictions 26: 293-325, 1991.

Gentile, C. G., Jarrell, T. W., Teich, A. H., McCabe, P. M., Schneiderman, N. 1986. The role of amygdaloid central nucleus in differential Pavlovian conditioning of bradycardia in rabbits. Behav. Brain Res. 20:263-76

Giesen, J.M., Center, D.B., and Leach, R.A.: An Evaluation of Chiropractic Manipulation as a Treatment of Hyperactivity in Children. Journal of Manipulation and Psysiological Therapeutics, October 1989; 12:353-363.

Gittelman-Klein, R. "Pharmacotherapy of Childhood Hyperactivity: An Update." Psychopharmacology: The Third Generation of Progress. Edited by H. Y. Meltzer. New York: Raven, 1987.

Glaser, J. L.; Brind, J. L.; Eisner, M. J.; Dillbeck, M. C.; Vogelman, J. H.; and Wallace, R. K. Elevated serum dehydroepiandrosterone sulfate levels in older practitioners of the Transcendental Meditation and TM-Sidhi programs. AGE 10(4): 160, 1987.

Gold, P. E., Hankins, L., Edwards, R. M., Chester, J., McGaugh, J. L. 1975. Memory interference and facilitation with posttrial amygdala stimulation: effect on memory varies with footshock level. Brain Res. 86:509-13

Gormezano, I. 1972. Investigations of defense and reward conditioning in the rabbit. See Black & Prokasy 1972, pp. 151-81

Gormezano, I., Kehoe, E. J., Marshall, B. S. 1983. Twenty years of classical conditioning research with the rabbit. In Progress in Psychobiology and Physiological Psychology, ed. J. M. Sprague, A. N. Epstein, pp. 198-275. New York: Academic

Goyette, C. H., Conners, C. K., and Ulrich, R.F. "Normative Data on Revised Conners Parent and Teacher Rating Scales." Journal of Abnormal Child Psychology, 6 (1978), 221-36.

Greenhill, Laurence, et al. "Prolactin: Growth Hormone and Growth Responses in Boys with Attention Deficit Disorder and Hyperactivity Treated with Methylphenidate." Journal of the American Academy of Child Psychiatry, 23 (1984), 58-67.

Grossman, S. P., Grossman, L., Walsh, L. 1975. Functional organization of the rat amygdala with respect to avoidance behavior. J. Comp. Physiol, Psychol. 88:829-50

Hallowell, E., Ratey, J.: Driven To Distraction (Pantheon, New York, 1993)

Hallowell, E., Ratey, J.: Answers To Distraction (Pantheon, New York, 1994)

Harlow, H. F., Davis, R. T., Settlage, P. H., Meyer, D. R. 1952. Analysis of frontal and posterior association syndrome in braindamaged monkeys. J. Comp. Physiol. Psychol. 45:419-29

Harvey, J. A., Gormezano, I., Cool-Hauser, V. A. 1985. Relationship between heterosynaptic reflex facilitation and acquisition of the nictitating membrane response in control and scopolamine-injected rabbits. J. Neurosci. 5:596-602

Harvey, J. A., Yeo, C. H., Welsh, J. P., Romano, A. G. 1990. Recoverable and non-recoverable deficits in conditioned responses (CRs) after cerebellar cortical lesions. Soc. Neurosci. Abstr. 16:268 Hawkins, R. D., Bower, G. H., eds. 1989. The Psychology of Learning and Motivation. New York: Academic

Harwood, Frances: Myth, Memory and Oral Tradition: Cicero in the Trobriands, American Anthropologist 78, 4 (Dec. 1976): 783-96;

Hayes, Peter L. Ernest Hemingway. New York: Continuum, 1990.

Helmstetter, F. J., Leaton, R. N., Fanselow, M. S., Calcagnetti, D. J. 1988. The amygdala is involved in the expression of conditioned analgesia. Soc. Neurosci. Absir. 14:1227

Henker, B., and Whalen, C.K. "The Changing Faces of Hyperactivity: Retrospect and Prospect." Hyperactive Children: The Social Ecology of Identification and Treatment. Edited by B. A. Henker and C. K. Whalen. New York: Academic, 1980.

Hitchcock, J. M., Davis, M. 1986. Lesions of the amygdala, but not of the cerebellum or red nucleus, block conditioned fear as measured with the potentiated startle paradigm. Behav. Neurosci. 100: 11-22

Hitchcock, J. M., Davis, M. 1987. Fear-potentiated startle using an auditory conditioned stimulus: effect of lesions of the amygdala. Physiol. Behav. 39:403-8

Hitchcock, J. M., Sananes, C. B., Davis, M. 1989. Sensitization of the startle reflex by footshock: blockade by lesions of the central nucleus of the amygdala or its efferent pathway to the brainstem. Behav. Neurosci. 103:509-18

Isaacson, R. L. 1974. The Limbic System. New York: Plenum. 3rd ed. Ito, M. 1970. Neurophysiological aspects of the cerebellar motor control system. Int. J. Neurol. 7:162-76

Ito, M. 1980. The Cerebellum and Neural Control. New York: Raven Iwata, J., Chida, K., LeDoux, J. E. 1987. Cardiovascular responses elicited by stimulation of neurons in the central amygdaloid nucleus in awake but not anesthetized rats resemble conditioned cardiovascular responses. Brain Res. 418:183-88

Ivkovich, D., Lavond, D. G., Logan, C. G., Thompson, R. F. 1990. Measurements of reflexive intensifies over the course of classical conditioning. Soc. Neurosci. Abstr. 16:271

Ivkovich, D., Logan, C. G. Thompson, R. F. 1991. Accessory abducens lesions produce perfonnance deficits without permanently affecting conditioned responses. Soc. Neurosci. Abstr. 16:271

Ivry, R. B., Baldo, J. V. 1992. Is the cerebellum involved in learning and cognition? Curr. Opin. Neurobiol. 2:212-16 Kandel, E. R. 1976. Cellular Basis of Behavior. San Francisco: Freeman

Iwata, J., LeDoux, J. E., Meeley, M. P., Arneric, S., Reis, D. J. 1986a. Intrinsic neurons in the amygdaloid field projected to by the medial geniculate body mediate emotional responses conditioned to acoustic stimuli. Brain Res. 383:195-214

Iwata, J., LeDoux, J. E., Reis, D. J. 1986b. Destruction of intrinsic neurons in the lateral hypothalamus disrupts cardiovascular but not behavioral conditioned emotional responses. Brain Res. 368:161-66

Jasper, H.H., Solomon, P., & Bradley, C. (1938). "Electroencephalographic analysis of behavior problems in children." American Journal of Psychiatry, 95, 641-658.

Josephson, Matthew. Edison: A Biography. New York: John Wiley & Sons, 1959, 1992.

Kaffman M. The use of transcendental meditation to promote social progress in Israel. Cultic Stud J. 1986;3:138.

Kaminer, Wendy: I'm Dysfunctional, You're Dysfunctional: The Recovery Movement and Other Self-Help Fashions. Vintage Books, NY, 1993.

Kan, See Sergei: Shamanism and Christianity: Modern Day Tlingit Elders Look at the Past; Ethnohistory 38, 4 (fall 1991): 363-87.

Kandler, K., Herbert, H. 1991. Auditory projections from the cochlear nucleus to pontine and mesencephalic reticular nuclei in the rat. Brain Res. 562:230-42

Kapp, B. S., Frysinger, R., Gallagher, M., Haselton, J. 1979. Amygdala central nucleus lesions: effects on heart rate conditioning in the rabbit. Physiol. Behav. 23:1109-17

Kelly, K., Ramundo, P.: You mean I'm not Lazy, Stupid or Crazy?, Tyrell & Jerem Press, Cincinnatti (1993)

Kelly, Kevin L., et al. "Attention Deficit Disorder and Methylphenidate: A Multistep Analysis of Dose-Response Effects on Children's Cardiovascular Functioning." International Clinical Psychopharmacology, 3 (1988), 167-181.

Kelly, T. M, Zuo, C. C., Bloedel, J. R. 1990. Classical conditioning of the eyeblink reflex the decerebrate-decerebellate rabbit. Behav. Brain Res. 38:7-18

Kesterson J, Clinch NF. Metabolic rate, respiratory exchange ratio, and apneas during meditation. Am J Physiol. March 1989:R635, 636-637.

Kim, J. J., DeCola, J. P., Landeira-Fernandez, J., Fanselow, M. S. 1991. N-methyl-D-as-partate receptor antagonist APV blocks acquisition but not expression of fear conditioning. Behav. Neurosci. 105:126-33

Kim, J. J., Fanselow, M. S. 1992. Modality-specific retrograde amnesia of fear. Science 256:675-77 Krupa, D. J., Weiss, C., Thompson, R. F. 1991. Air puff evoked Purkinje cell complex spike activity is diminished during conditioned responses in eyeblink conditioned rabbits. Soc. Neurosci. Abstr. 17:322

Kinsbourne, M., and Caplan, P. J., Children's Learning and Attention Problems. Boston, MA: Little, Brown and Company, 1979.

Kinsbourne, M., and Caplan, P. J. "Overfocusing: An Apparent Subtype of Attention Deficit-hyperactivity Disorder." Pediatric Neurology: Behavior and Cognition of the Child with Brain Dysfunction. Edited by N. Amir, I. Rapin, and D. Branski. Basel: Karger, 1991.

Kinsbourne, M., and Caplan, P. J. "Overfocusing: Attending to a Different Drummer." Chadder, 1992.

Kleijnen J, Knipschild P, Ter Reit G. Clinical trials of homoeopathy. BM[G] 1991;303:316-23.

Klein, Rachel G., *et al.* "Methylphenidate and Growth in Hyperactive Children. A Controlled Withdrawal Study." *Archives of General Psychiatry*, 45 (1988), 1127-30.

Knott, J.R., Platt, E. B., Ashby, M.C., & Gottlieb, J.S. (1953). "A familial evaluation of the electroencephalogram of patients with primary behavior disorder and psychopathic personality." Electroencephalography and Clinical Neurophysiology, 5, 363-370.

Kuczenski, R., *et al.* "Effects of Amphetamine, Methylphenidate and Apomorphine on Regional Brain Serotonin and 5-Hydroxyindole Acetic Acid." *Psychopharmacology*, 93 (1987), 329-335.

Kunert, W.: Functional Disorders of Internal Organs Due to Vertebral Lesions. CIBA Symposium 13(3): 85-96, 1965.

Lashley, K. S. 1950. In search of the engram. Soc. Exp. Biol. Symp. 4:454-82

Lavond, D. G., Hembree, T. L., Thompson, R. F. 1985. Effect of kainic acid lesions of the cerebellar interpositus nucleus on eyelid conditioning in the rabbit. Brain Res. 326:179-82

Lavond, D. G., Kanzawa, S. A., Esquenazi, V., Clark, R. E., Zhang, A. A. 1990. Effects of cooling interpositus during acquisition of classical conditioning. Soc. Neurosci. Abstr. 16:270

Lavond, D. G., Lincoln, J. S., McCormick, D. A., Thompson, R. F. 1984a. Effect of bilateral lesions of the dentate and interpositus cerebellar nuclei on conditioning of heartrate and nictitating membrane/eyelid responses in the rabbit. Brain Res. 305:323-30

Lavond, D. G., McCormick, D. A., Thompson, R. F. 1984b. A nonrecoverable learning deficit. Physiol Psychol 12:103-10

Lavond, D. G., Steimnetz, J. E. 1989. Acquisition of classical conditioning without cerebellar cortex. Behav. Brain Res. 33:113-64

Lavond, D. G., Steimnetz, J. E., Yokaitis, M. H., Thompson, R. F. 1987. Reacquisition of classical conditioning after removal of cerebellar cortex. Exp. Brain Res. 67:569-93

LeDoux, J. E. 1987. Emotion. See Plum 1987, pp. 419-59

LeDoux, J. E., Farb, C., Ruggiero, D. A. 1990. Topographic organization of neurons in the acoustic thalamus that project to the amygdala. J. Neurosci. 10:1043-54

LeDoux, J. E., Iwata, J., Cicchetti, P., Reis, D. J. 1988. Different projections of the central amygdaloid nucleus mediate autonomic and behavioral coffelates of conditioned fear. J. Neurosci. 8:2517-29

LeDoux, J. E., Iwata, J., Pearl, D., Reis, D. J. 1986. Disruption of auditory but not visual learning by destruction of intrinsic neurons in the rat medial geniculate body. Brain Res. 371:395-99

LeDoux, J. E., Sakaguchi, A., Reis, D. J. 1984. Subcortical efferent projections of the medial geniculate nucleus mediate emotional responses conditioned to acoustic stimuli. J. Neurosci. 4:683-98

Lee, Richard: Art, Science or Politics, American Anthropologist 94, 1 (March 1992): 31-54

Leiner, H. C., Leiner, A. L., Dow, R. S. 1986. Does the cerebellum contribute to mental skills? Behav. Neurosci. 100:443-54 Lewis, J. L., LoTurco, J. J., Solomon, P. R. 1987. Lesions of the middle cerebellar peduncle disrupt acquisition and retention of the rabbit's classically conditioned nictitating membrane response. Behav. Neurosci. 101:151-57

Lewith G. Every doctor a walking placebo. Complementary Medicine Research 1987;2:11-8.

Liang, K. C. 1991. Pretest intra-amygdala injection of lidocaine or glutamate antagonists impairs retention performance in an inhibitory avoidance task. Soc. Neurosci. Abstr. 17:486

Liang, K. C., Juler, R., McGaugh, J. L. 1986. Modulating effects of posttraining epinephrine on memory: involvement of the amygdala noradrenergic system. Brain Res. 368:125-33

Liang, K. C., McGaugh, J. L., Martinez, J. L., Jensen, R. A. Jr., Vasquez, B. J., Messing, R. B. 1982. Post-training atnygdaloid lesions impair retention of an inhibitory avoidance response. Behav. Brain Res. 4:237-49

Lincoln, J. S., McCormick, D. A., Thompson, R. F. 1982. lpsilateral cerebellar lesions prevent learning of the classically conditioned nictitating membrane/eyelid response. Brain Res. 242:190-93

Linke, Uli: Anthropology, Folklore and the Government of Modern Life, Comparative Studies in Society and History 32 (1990): 117-48.

Logan, C. G. 1991. Cerebellar cortical involvement in excitatory and inhibitory classical conditioning. PhD dissertation, Stanford Univ., Stanford, Calif.

Logan, C. G., Lavond, D. G., Thompson, R. F. 1989. The effects of combined lesions of cerebellar cortical areas on acquisition of the rabbit conditioned nictitating membrane response. Soc. Neurosci. Abstr. 15:640 Marr, D. 1969. A theory of cerebellar cortex. J. Physiol. (London) 202:437-70

Lorayne, H., and Lucas, J. The Memory Book, New York: Ballantine, 1986.

Lubar, J.F., & Deering, W.M. (1981). "Behavioral Approaches to Neurology. New York, Academic Press.

Lubar, J.F., & Shouse, M.N. (1976) "Use of biofeedback in the treatment of seizure disorders and hyperactivity." Advances in Clinical Child Psychology, 1, 203-265.

Lubar, J.F., & Shouse, M.N. (1976). "EEG and behavioral changes in a hyperactive child concurrent with training of the sensorimotor rhythm (SMR). A preliminary report." Biofeedback and Self-Regulation, 1, 293-306.

Lubar, J.F., (1991). "Discourse on the Development of EEG Diagnostics and Biofeedback for Attention-Deficit/Hyperactivity Disorders." Biofeedback and Self-Regulation, 16,3, (201-225)

Lubar, J.F., Bianchini, B.A., Calhoun, W. H., Lambert, W. E., Brody, M.A., & Shabsin, H.S. (1985). "Spectral analysis of EEG differences between children with and without learning disabilities". Journal of Learning Disabilities, 18, 403-408.

Lubar, J.F., Mann, C.A., Gross, D.M., & Shively, M.S. (1991). "Differences between normal, learning disabled, and gifted children based upon an auditory evoked potential task." Journal of Psychophysiology, 4, 470-481.

Lubar, J.O, & Lubar, J.F., (1984). "Electroencephalographic biofeedback of SMR and beta for treatment of attention deficit disorders in a clinical setting." Biofeedback and Self- Regulation, 9(1), 1-23.

Lubar, J.O., (1989). Electroencephalographic biofeedback and neurologic applications. In J.V. Basmagian (Ed.) Biofeedback, Principals and Practice for Clinicians, (pp. 67-90), Williams and Wilkins, Baltimore.

Malinowski, Bronislaw: Argonauts of the Western Pacific (London: Routledge 1922); Myth in Primitive Psychology (New York: Norton 1926)

Mann, C.A., Lubar, J.R., Zimmerman, A.W., Miller, C.A., & Muenchen, R.A. (1990). "Quantitative analysis of EEG in boy with attention-deficit/hyperactivity disorder (ADHD): A controlled study with clinical implication." Pediatric Neurology (in press).

Maslow, A. Personality and Motivation. HarperCollins, New York, 1954, 1987

Mauk, M. D., Steinmetz, J. E., Thompson, R. F. 1986. Classical conditioning using stimulation of the inferior olive as the unconditioned stimulus. Proc. Natl. Acad. Sci. 83:5349-53

Mauk, M. D., Thompson, R. F. 1987. Retention of classically conditioned eyelid responses following acute decerebration. Brain Res. 493:89-95

McCormick, D. A. 1983. Cerebellum: essential involvement in a simple learned response. PhD dissertation, Stanford Univ., Stanford, Calif.

McCormick, D. A., Lavond, D. G., Clark, G. A., Kettner, R. E., Rising, C. E., Thompson, R. F. 1981. The engram found? Role of the cerebellum in classical conditioning of nictitating membrane and eyelid responses. Bull. Psychon. Soc. 18:103-5

McCormick, D. A., Steimnetz, J. E., Thompson, R. F. 1985. Lesions of the inferior olivary complex cause extinction of the classically conditioned eyeblink response. Brain Res. 359:120-30

McCormick, D. A., Thompson, R. F. 1984. Cerebellum: essential involvement in the classically conditioned eyelid response. Science 223:296-99

McDonough, J. H. Jr., Kesner, R. P. 1971. Amnesia produced by brief electrical stimulation of amygdala or dorsal hippocampus in cats. J. Comp. Physiol. Psychol 77:171-78

McGaugh, J. L. 1989. Involvement of hormonal and neuromodulatory systems in the regulation of memory storage. Annu. Rev. Neurosci. 12:255-87

McGaugh, J. L., Introini-Collison, I. B., Nagahara, A. H. 1988. Memory-enhancing effects of posttraining naloxone: involvement of beta-noradrenergic influences in the amygdaloid complex. Brain Res. 446:37-49

McGuinnes, Diane. When Children Don't Learn. New York: Basic Books, 1985.

McGuinness, Diane. "Attention Deficit Disorder, the Emperor's Clothes, Animal Pharm, and Other Fiction." The Limits of Biological Treatment for Psychological Distress. Edited by S. Fisher and R. Greenberg. New York: Erlbaum, 1989.

Mendelsohn, Robert S., M.D. *How to Raise a Healthy Child...in Spite of Your Doctor.* Chicago: Contemporary Books, 1984.

Methylphenidate Effects on Ultimate Height. *Archives of General Psychiatry*, 45 (1988), 1131-34.

Miserendino, M. J. D., Sananes, C. B., Melia, K. R., Davis, M. 1990. Blocking of acquisition but not expression of conditioned fear-potentiated startle by NMDA antagonists in the amygdala. Nature 345:716-18

Molino, A. 1975. Sparing of function after infant lesions of selected limbic structures in the rat. J. Comp. Physiol. Psychol. 89:868-81

Moss, Robert A., and Dunlap, Helen H. *Why Johnny Can't Concentrate.* New York: Bantam Books, 1990.

Moyer, J. R., Deyo, R. A., Disterhoft, J. F. 1990. Hippocampectomy disrupts trace eye-blink conditioning in rabbits. Behav. Neurosci. 104:243-52

Murray, John B. "Psychophysiological Effects of Methylphenidate (Ritalin)." *Psychological Reports*, 61 (1987), 315-336.

Nagel, J. A., Kemble, E. D. 1976. Effects of amygdaloid lesions on the performance of rats in four passive avoidance tasks. Physiol. Behav. 17:245-50

National Research Council Report on Meditation. In the Mind's Eye: Enhancing Human Performance. Washington, DC: National Academy Press; 1991.

Nelson, B. J., Mugnoini, E. 1989. Origins of GABAergic inputs to the inferior olive. In The Olivocerebellar System in Motor Control, ed. P. Strata, pp. 86-107. New York: Springer-Verlag

Nidich, S. I.; Ryncarz, R. A.; Abrams, A. I.; Orme-Johnson, D. W.; and Wallace, R. K. Kohlbergian cosmic perspective responses, EEG coherence, and the Transcendental Meditation and TM-Sidhi program. Journal of Moral Education 12(3): 166-173, 1983.

Nordholm, A. F., Lavond, D. G., Thompson, R. F. 1991. Are eyeblink responses to tone in the decerebrate, decerebellate rabbit conditioned responses? Behav. Brain Res. 44:27-34

Nordholm, A. F., Thompson, J. K., Standley, S., Tocco, G., Dersarkissian, C., Thompson, R. F. 1992. Lidocaine infusion in a critical region of cerebellum completely prevents learning of the conditioned eyeblink response. Soc. Neurosci. Abstr. In press

Norman, R. J., Buchwald, J. S., Villablanca, J. R. 1977. Classical conditioning with auditory discriniination of the eyeblink in decerebrate cats. Science 196:551-52

Nowak, A. J., Gormezano, I. 1988. Reflex facilitation (RF) and classical conditioning of the rabbit's nictitating membrane response (NMR) to electrical stimutation of brainstem structures as an unconditioned stimulus (UCS). Soc. Neurosci. Abstr. 14:3

O'Halloran, J. P.; Jevning, R.; Wilson, A. F.; Skowsky, R.; Walsh, R. N.; and Alexander, C. Hormonal control in a state of decreased activation: Potentiation of arginine vasopressin secretion. Physiology and Behavior 35: 591-595, 1985.

Oakley, D. A., Russell, I. S. 1972. Neocortical lesions and classical conditioning. Physiol. Behav. 8:915-26 Oakley, D. A., Russell, 1. S. 1977. Subcortical storage of Pavlovian conditioning in the rabbit. Physiol. Behav. 18:931-37

Obeyesekere, Gananath: The Apotheosis of Captain Cook: European Myth-making in the Pacific (Princeton: Princeton University Press 1992);

Orme-Johnson D. Medical care utilization and the transc and statistical meta-analysis. J Soc Behav Pers. 1991; 6: 189-247.

Orme-Johnson DW, Alexander CN, Davies JL, Chandler HM, Larrimore WE. International peace project in the Middle East: the effects of the Maharishi technology of the unified field. J Conflict Resolution. 1988; 32: 776-812.

Orme-Johnson, D. W. Autonomic stability and Transcendental Meditation. Psychosomatic Medicine 35: 341-349, 1973.

Orme-Johnson, D. W. Medical care utilization and the Transcendental Meditation program. Psychosomatic Medicine 49(1): 493-507, 1987.

Orme-Johnson, D. W., and Farrow, J. T., eds. Scientific research on the Transcendental Meditation program: Collected papers, Vol. 1. Rheinweiler, W. Germany: Maharishi European Research University Press, 1977.

Orme-Johnson, D. W., and Gelderloos, P. Topographic EEG brain mapping during "Yogic Flying." International Journal of Neuroscience 38: 427-434, 1988.

Orme-Johnson, D. W., and Haynes, C. T. EEG phase coherence, pure consciousness, creativity, and TM-Sidhi experiences. International Journal of Neuroscience 13: 211-217, 1981.

Orme-Johnson, D. W.; Alexander, C. N.; Davies, J. L.; Chandler, H. M.; and Larimore, W. E. International peace project in the Middle East: The effect of the Maharishi Technology of the Unified Field. Journal of Conflict Resolution 32(4): 776-812, 1988.

Ornstein, Robert. The Roots of the Self: Unraveling the Mystery of Who We Are. HarperCollins Publishers, NY, 1993.

Othmer, S., Othmer, S.F., & Marks, C.S. (1991) "EEG biofeedback training for attention deficit disorder, specific learning disabilities, and associated conduct problems." EEG Spectrum, Inc., 16100 Ventura Blvd., Suite 10, Encino, CA 91316.

Pagden, Anthony: European Encounters with the New World: From Renaissance to Romanticism (New Haven and London: Yale University Press 1993).

Parent, M. B., Tomaz, C., McGaugh, J. L. 1992. Increased training in an aversively motivated task attenuates the memory impairing effects of posttraining NMDA-induced amygdala lesions. Behav. Neurosci. In press

Pascoe, J. P., Kapp, B. S. 1985a. Electrophysiological characteristics of amygdaloid central nucleus neurons in the awake rabbit. Brain Res. Bull. 14:331-38

Pascoe, J. P., Kapp, B. S. 1985b. Electrophysiological characteristics of amygdaloid central nucleus neurons during Pavlovian fear conditioning in the rabbit. Behav. Brain Res. 16:117-33

Pavy, R., & Metcalf, J. (1965). "The abnormal EEG in childhood communication and behavior abnormalities." Electroencephalography and Clinical Neurophysiology, 19, 414.

Peet, J.B.: Chiropractic Pediatric & Prenatal Reference Manual. The Baby Adjusters, Inc. 1992

Perrett, S. P., Ruiz, B. P., Mauk, M. D. 1991. Cerebellar cortex ablation disrupts extinction of conditioned eyelid responses. Soc. Neurosci. Abstr. 17:870

Peters, T., and Waterman, R. *In Search of Excellence.* New York: Harper & Row 1982.

Phillips, R. G., LeDoux, J. E. 1992. Differential contribution of amygdala and hippocampus to cued and contextual fear conditioning. Behav. Neurosci. 106:274-85

Picton, T.W., & Hillyard, S.A. (1974). "Human auditory evoked potential: Effects of attention." Electroencephalography and Clinical Neurophysiology, 36, 191-199.

Plum, F., ed. 1987. Handbook of Physiology, Vol. 5, Higher Functions of the Brain. Baltimore: Williams and Wilkins

Powell, D. A., Lipkin, M., Milligan, W. L. 1974. Concormitant changes in classically conditioned heart rate and corneoretinal potential discrimination in the rabbit Oryctolagus cuniculus). Learn. Motiv. 5:532-47 Prokasy, W. F. 1972. Developments with the two-phase model applied to human eyelid conditioning. See Black & Prokasy 1972, pp. 119-47 Rescorla, R. A., Solomon, R. L. 1967. Two-process learning theory: relationships between Pavlovian conditioning and instrumental learning. Psychol. Rev. 74:151-82

Rapaport, J. L., et al. "Dextroamphetamine: Its Cognitave and Behavioral Effects in Normal and Hyperactive Boys and Normal Men." *Archives of General Psychiatry,* 37 (1980), 933-43.

Rapport, M. D., et al. "Attention Deficit Disorder and Methylphenidate: A Multilevel Analysis of Dose-response Effects on Children's Impulsivity Across Settings." *Journal of the American Academy of Child Psychiatry,* 27 (1988), 60-69.

Reichenberg-Ullman, J., Mothering, no. 75, Spring 1995, pp.97-101

Reilly DT, Taylor MA, Campbell J, Beatie N, McSharry C, Aitchison T, et al. Is homoeopathy a placebo response? A controlled trial of homoeopathic immunotherapy (HIT) in atopic asthma. Complementary Therapies in Medicine 1993;1(suppl 1):24-5.

Reilly DT, Taylor MA, McSharry C, Aitchison T. Is homoeopathy a placebo response? Controlled trial of homoeopathic potency with pollen and hayfever as a model. Lancet 1986;ii:881-6.

Report commissioned by the German Ministry of Youth, Family, and Health. The Various Implications Arising From the Practice of Transcendtal meditation. Citation: The Edell Health Letter, March 1992 v11 n3 p3(1)

Rescoria, R. A., Wagner, A. R. 1972. A theory of Pavlovian conditioning: variations in the effectiveness of reinforcement and nonreinforcement. See Black & Prokasy 1972, pp. 64-99.

Restak, Richard. Receptors. Bantam Books, NY, 1993.

Riordan, Ann F.: Original Ecologists? The Relationship between Yup'ik Eskimos and Animals, in Ann Fienup Riordan, ed., Eskimo Essays (New Brunswick and London: Rutgers University Press 1990), 167-91.

Robinson, David L. (1989). "The neurophysiological basis of high IQ". International Journal of Neuroscience, 46, 209-234.

Rodman, Margaret: Empowering Place: Multilocality and Multivocality, American Anthropologist 94, 3 (Sept. 1992): 640-56.

Roizen, N., Blondis, T., Irwin, M., Stein, M: Adaptive Functioning in Children with Attention-Deficit Hyperactivity Disorder, Arch Pediatr Adolesc Med 148:1137-1141 (Nov 1994).

Romanski, L. M., LeDoux, J. E. 1991, Equipotentiality of thalmo-amygdala and thalmo-cortico-amygdala circuits in auditory fear conditioning. Soc. Neurosci. Abstr. 17:658

Rosaldo, Renato: Doing Oral History, Social Analysis 4 (1980): 89-99

Rosaldo, Renato: Ilongot Headhunting, 1883-1974 (Stanford: Standord University Press 1980)

Rosen, J. B., Davis, M. 1988. Enhancement of acoustic startle by electrical stimulation of the amygdala. Behav. Neurosci. 102:195-202

Rosen, J. B., Davis, M. 1990. Enhancement of electrically elicited startle by amygdaloid stimulation. Physiol. Behav. 48:343-49

Rosen, J. B., Hitchcock, J. M., Miserendino, M. J. D., Davis, M. 1989. Lesions of the perirhinal cortex block fear-potentiated startle. Soc. Neurosci. Abstr. 15:305

Rosen, J. B., Hitchcock, J. M., Sananes, C. B., Miserendino, M. J. D., Davis, M. 1991. A direct projection from the central nucleus of the amygdala to the acoustic startle pathway: anterograde and retrograde tracing studies. Behav. Neurosci. 105:817-25

Rosenfield, M. E., Dovydaitis, A., Moore, J. W. 1985. Brachium conjuntivum and rubrobulbar tract: brain stem projections of red nucieus essential for conditioned nictitating membrane response. Physiol. Behav. 34:751-59

Rosenfield, M. E., Moore, J. W. 1983. Red nucleus lesions disrupt the classically conditioned nictitating membrane response in the rabbit. Behav. Brain Res. 10:393-98

Safer, Daniel J., et al. "A Survey of Medication Treatment for Hyperactive/Inattentive Students." Journal of the American Medical Association, 260 (1988), 2256-2258.

Satterfield, et al. "Growth of Hyperactive Children Treated with Methylphenidate." Archives of General Psychiatry, 36 (1979), 212-217.

Satterfield, H.H., Lesser, L.I., Saul, R.E., & Cantwell, D.P. (1973). "EEG aspects in the diagnosis and treatment of minimal brain dysfunction." Annals of New York Academy of Science, 205, 274-282.

Satterfield, J. H., Satterfield, B. T., and Schell, A. M. "Therapeutic Interventions to Prevent Delinquency in Hyperactive Boys." Journal of the American Academy of Child Psychiatry, 26 (1987), 56-64.

Satterfield, J.H., & Dawson, J.E. (1971). "Electrodermal correlates of hyperactivity in children." Psychophysiology, 8, 191-197.

Scarnati, Richard. "An Outline of Hazardous Side Effects of Ritalin (Methylphenidate)." The International Journal of Addictions, 21 (1986), 837-841.

Schmaltz, L. W., Theios, J. 1972. Acquisition and extinction of a classically conditioned response in hippocampectoniized rabbits (Oryctolagus cuniculus). J. Comp. Physiol. Psychol. 79:328-33

Schneider, R. H.; Alexander, C. N.; Staggers, F.; Sheppard, W.; Gaylord, C.; Gelderloos, P.; Smith, S.; Kondwani, K.; Rainforth, M. V., and Cooper, R. Stress management in elderly blacks with hypertension. Proceedings of the 2nd International Conference on Race, Ethnicity, and Health: Challenges in Diabetes and Hypertension, Salvador, Brazil, July 1991.

Schneiderman, N., Fuentes, I., Gormezano, I. 1962. Acquisition and extinction of the classically conditioned eyelid response in the albino rabbit. Science 136:650-52

Schneiderman, N., Smith, M. C., Smith, A. C., Gormezano, I. 1966. Heart rate classical conditioning in rabbits. Psychon. Sci. 6:241-42 Schwaber, J. S., Kapp, B. S., Higgins, G. A, Rapp, P. R. 1982. Amygdaloid and basal forebrain direct connections with the nucleus of the solitary tract and the dorsal motor nucleus. J. Neurosci. 2:1424-38

Sears, L. L., Steinmetz, J. E. 1991. Dorsal accessory inferior olive activity diminishes during acquisition of the rabbit classically conditioned eyelid response. Brain Res. 545:114-22

Selden, N. R. W., Everitt, B. J., Jarrard, L. E., Robbins, T. W. 1991. Complementary roles for the amygdala and hippocampus in aversive conditioning to explicit and contextual cues. Neuroscience 42:335-50

Shaffer, D., et al. "Neurological Soft Signs: Their Relationship to Psychiatric Disorder and Intelligence in Childhood and Adolescence." Archives of General Psychiatry, 42 (1985), 342-51.

Shambes, G. M., Gibson, J. M., Welker, W. 1978. Fractured somatotopy in granule cell tactile areas of rat cerebellar hemispheres revealed by micromapping. Brain Behav. Evol 15:94-140

Sharma HM, Triguna BD, Chopra D. Maharishi Ayur-Veda: modern insights into ancient medicine. JAMA. 1991;265:2633-2634, 2637.

Sharma, Rajiv P., et al. "Pharmacological Effects of Methylphenidate on Plasma Homovanillic Acid and Growth Hormone." Psychiatry Research, 32 (1990), 9-17.

Sheppard, W. D. Pretrial EEG coherence as a predictor of semantic processing effects in a lexical decision test. Dissertation Abstracts International 49(9): B3610, 1988.

Shouse, M.N., & Lubar, J.F. (1979). "Operant conditioning of EEG rhythms and ritalin in the treatment of hyperkinesis." Biofeedback and Self Regulation, 4, 299-312.

Smith JC. Psychotherapeutic effects of transcendental meditation with controls for expectation of relief and daily sitting. J Consult Clin Psychol. 1976;44:6 Resolution. 1988;32:776-812.

Sokol, Mae S., et al. "Attention Deficit Disorder with Hyperactivity and the Dopamine Hypothesis: Case Presentations with Theoretical Background." American Academy of Child and Adolescent Psychiatry, (1987), 428-433.

Solomon, P. R., Lewis, J. L., LoTurco, J. J., Steinmetz, J. E., Thompson, R. F. 1986a. The role of the middle cerebellar peduncle in acquisition and retention of the rabbit's classically conditioned nictitating membrane response. Bull. Psychon. Soc. 24:75-78

Solomon, P. R., Vander Schaff, E. F., Thompson, R. F., Weisz, D. G. 1986b. Hippocampus and trace conditioning of the rabbit's classically conditioned nictitating membrane response. Behav. Neurosci. 100:729-44

Steinmetz, J. E. 1990. Neuronal activity in the rabbit interpositus nucleus during classical NM-conditioning with pontine-nucleusstimulation CS. Psychol. Sci. 1:378-82

Steinmetz, J. E., Lavond, D. G., lvkovich, D., Logan, C. G., Thompson, R. F. 1992. Disruption of classical eyelid conditioning after cerebellar lesions: Damage to a memory trace system or a simple performance deficit? J. Neurosci. In press

Steinmetz, J. E., Lavond, D. G., Thompson, R. F. 1985. Classical conditioning of the rabbit eyelid response with mossy fiber stimulation as the conditioned stimulus. Bull. Psychon. Soc. 23:245-48

Steinmetz, J. E., Lavond, D. G., Thompson, R. F. 1989. Classical conditioning in rabbits using pontine nucieus stimulation as a conditioned stimulus and inferior olive stimulation as an unconditioned stimulus. Synapse 3:225-33

Steinmetz, J. E., Logan, C. G., Rosen, D. J., Thompson, J. K., Lavond, D. G., Thompson, R. F. 1987. Initial localization of the acoustic conditioned stimulus projection system to the cerebellum essential for classical eyelid conditioning. Proc. Natl. Acad. Sci. 84:3531-35

Steinmetz, J. E., Sengelaub, D. R. 1988. Direct projections from the lateral pontine nucleus to the anterior interpositus nucleus: a potential CS pathway for classical conditioning. Soc. Neurosci. Abstr. 14:782

Steinmetz, J. E., Steinmetz, S. S. 1991. Rabbit classically conditioned eyelid responses fail to reappear after interpositus lesions and extended postlesion training. Soc. Neurosci. Abstr. 17:323

Sterman, M.B. & Friar, L. (1972). "Suppression of seizures in an epileptic following sensorimotor EEG feedback training." Electroencephalography, Clinical Neurophysiology, 33, 89-95.

Sterman, M.B., MacDonald, L.R., & Stone, R. K., (1974). "Biofeedback training of the sensorimotor EEG rhythm in man: Effect on epilepsy." Epilepsia, 15, 395-416.

Sternberg, Robert J., and Lubart, Todd L. "Creating Creative Minds." *Phi Delta Kappa*, April, 1991, pp. 608-614.

Stewart, A. "Severe Perinatal Hazards." *Developmental Neuropsychiatry.* Edited by M. Rutter. New York: Guilford, 1983.

Still, G.F. (1902). "Some abnormal psychological conditions in children." Lancet, 1(2), 1008-1012.

Strauss, C. C., et al. "Overanxious Disorder: An Examination of Developmental Differences." *Journal of Abnormal Child Psychology*, 16 (1988), 433-43.

Supple, W. F., Archer, L., Kapp, B. S. 1989. Lesions of the cerebellar vermis severely impair acquisition of Pavlovian conditioned bradycardic responses in the rabbit. Soc. Neurosci. Abstr. 15:640

Supple, W. F., Leaton, R. N. 1990. Lesions of the cerebellar vermis and cerebellar hemispheres: effects on heart rate conditioning in rats. Behav. Neurosci. 104:934-47

Swanson, J. M., and Kinsboume, M. "The Cognitive Effects of Stimulant Drugs on Hyperactive Children." *Attention and Cognitive Development*. Edited by G. A. Hale and M. Lewis. New York: Plenum, 1979.

Tansey, M.A. (1984). "EEG sensorimotor rhythm biofeedback training: Some effects on the neurologic precursors of learning disabilities." International Journal of Psychophysiology, 1, 163-177.

Tansey, M.A. (1985a). "Brainwave signatures—An index reflective of the brain's functional neuroanatomy: Further findings on the effect of EEG sensorimotor rhythm biofeedback training on the neurologic precursors of learning disabilities." International Journal of Psychophysiology, 3, 85-89.

Tansey, M.A. (1985b). "The response of a case of petit mal epilepsy to EEG sensorimotor rhythm biofeedback training." International Journal of Psychophysiology, 3, 81-84.

Tansey, M.A. (1986). "A simple and a complex tic (Giles de la Tourette's Syndrome): Their response to EEG sensorimotor rhythm biofeedback training."

Tansey, M.A. (1990). "Righting the rhythms of reason: EEG biofeedback training as a therapeutic modality in a clinical office setting." Medical Psychotherapy, 3, 57-68.

Tansey, M.A., & Bruner, Richard L. (1983). "EMG and EEG biofeedback training in the treatment of a 10-year old hyperactive boy with a developmental reading disorder." Biofeedback and Self-Regulation, 8 25-37.

Taylor, E., *et al.* "Which Boys Respond to Stimulant Medication? A Controlled Trial of Methylphenidate in Boys with Disruptive Behaviour." *Psychology Med*, 17 (1987), 121-43.

Teuber, H. L. 1955. Physiological psychology. Annu. Rev. Psychol 6:267-96

Teyler, T. J., Discenna, P. 1987. Long-term potentiation. Annu. Rev. Neurosci. 10:131-61

Thach, W. T., Goodkin, H. P., Keating, J. G. 1992. The cerebellum and the adaptive coordination of movement. Annu. Rev. Neurosci. 15:403-42

Thompson, J. K., Lavond, D. G., Thompson, R. F. 1986. Preliminary evidence for a projection from the cochlear nucleus to the pontine nuclear region. Soc. Neurosci. Abstr. 12:754

Thompson, J. K., Spangler, W. J., Thompson, R. F. 1991. Differential projections of pontine nuclei to interpositus nucleus and lobule HVI. Soc. Neurosci. Abstr. 17:871

Thompson, J. K., Thompson, R. F., Weiss, C., Lavond, D. G. 1988. Pontine projections of cochlear nuclei using anterogade HRP or PHA-L. Soc. Neurosci. Abstr. 14:782

Thompson, R. F. 1986. The neurobiology of learning and memory. Science 233:941-47

Thompson, R. F. 1992. Memory. Curr. Opin. Neurobiol. 2:203-8 Thompson, R. F. 1990. Neural mechanisms of classical conditioning in mammals. Philos. Trans. R. Soc. London Ser. B 329:161-70

Thompson, R. F., Berger, T. W., Cegavske, C. F., Patterson, M. M., Roemer, R. A., et al 1976. The search for the engram. Am. Psychol. 31:209-27

Thompson, R. F., Steinmetz, J. E., Chapman, P. F. 1987. Appropriate lesions of the interpositus nucleus completely and permanently abolish the conditioned eyelid/NM response in the rabbit. Soc. Neurosci. Abstr. 13:801

Tocco, G., Devgan, K. K., Hauge, S. A., Weiss, C., Baudry, M., Thompson, R. F. 1991, Classical conditioning selectively increases AMPA/Quisqualate receptor binding in rabbit hippocampus. Brain Res. 559:331-36

TRAVIS, F. Creative thinking and the Transcendental Meditation technique. A version printed in The Journal of Creative Behavior 13(3): 169-180, 1979. WALLACE, R. K.; DILLBECK, M.; JACOBE, E.; and HARRINGTON, B. The effects of the Transcendental Meditation and TM-Sidhi program on the aging process. International Journal of Neuroscience 16: 53-58, 1982.

Tsukahara, N. 1981. Synaptic plasticity in the mammalian central nervous system. Annu. Rev. Neurosci. 4:351-79

Tsukahara, N. 1982. Classical conditioning mediated by the red nucleus in the cat. See Woody 1982, pp. 223-31

Tuohy, Sue: Cultural Metaphors and Reasoning: Folklore Scholarship and Ideology in Contemporary China, Asian Folklore Studies 50 (1991): 189-220

Turner, B. H., Zimmer, J. 1984. The architecture and some of the interconnections of the rat's amygdala and lateral periallocortex. J. Comp. Neurol. 227:540-57

Turner, Terence: Ethno-Ethnohistory: Myth and History in Native South American Representations of Contact with Western Society, in Hill, Jonathan D., ed., Rethinking History and Myth: Indigenous South American Perspectives on the Past (Urbana: University of Illinois Press 1988), 235-81.

Ullmann, R. K., and Sleator, E. K. "Responders, Nonresponders, and Placebo Responders Among Children with Attention Deficit Disorder." Clinical Pediatrics, 25 (1986), 594-99.

US Congress. Senate. Examination Into the Causes of Hyperactive Children and the Methods Used for Treating These Young Children. Joint Hearing before a Subcommittee on Health of the Committee on Labor and Public Welfare and the Subcommittee on Administrative Practice and Procedure of the Committee on the Judiciary of the United States Senate, 94th Cong., 1st sess., September 11, 1975. US Government Printing Office.

Usher, Peter: Northern Development, Impact Assessment and Social Chance; Noel Dyck and James B. Waldram, eds., Anthropology, Public Policy and Native Peoples in Canada (Montreal and Kingston: McGill-Queen's University Press 1993), 98-130.

Voneida, T., Christie, D., Boganski, R,, Chopko, B. 1990. Changes in instrumentally and classically conditioned limbflexion responses following inferior olivary lesions and olivocerebellar tractotomy in the cat. J. Neurosci. 10:3583-93

Wagner, A. R. 1981. SOP: a model of automatic memory processing in animal behavior. In Information Processing in Animals: Memory Mechanisms, ed. N. E. Spear, R. R. Miller, pp. 5-47. Hillsdale, NJ: Lawrence Erlbaum

Wagner, A. R., Brandon, S. E. 1989. Evolution of a structured connectionist model of Pavlovian conditioning (AESOP). In Contemporary Learning Theories: Pavlovian Conditioning and the Status of Traditional Learning Theory, ed. S. B. Klein, R. R. Mowrer, pp. 149-90. Hilisdale, NJ: Lawrence Erlbaum

Wagner, A. R., Donegan, N. H. 1989. Some relationships between a computational model (SOP) and a neural circuit for Pavlovian (rabbit eyeblink) conditioning.

Wallace, R.K.; Orme-Johnson, D.W.; and Dillbeck, M.C., eds. Scientific Research on Maharishi's Transcendental Meditation program: Collected papers, Vol. 5. Fairfield, Iowa: Maharishi International University Press, in press.

Walton, E.V.: Chiropractic Effectiveness with Emotional Learning and Behavioral Impairments. International Review of Chiropractic; 29:2, 21-22; September, 1975.

Watson, P. J. 1978. Nonmotor functions of the cerebellum. Psychol Bull 85:944-67

Weinberger, N. M. 1982. Sensory plasticity and learning: the magnocellular medial geniculate nucleus of the auditory system. See Woody 1982, pp. 697-710

Weinberger, N. M., Hopkins, W., Diamond, D. M. 1984. Physiological plasticity of single neurons in auditory cortex of the cat during acquisition of the pupillary conditioned response: I. Primary field (AI). Behav. Neurosci. 98:171-88

Weingarten, H., White, N. 1978. Exploration evoked by electrical stimulation of the amygdala in rats. Physiol. Psychol. 6:229-35

Weish, J. P. 1986. The effect of nucleus interpositus lesions on retention of the rabbit's classically conditioned nictitating membrane response. MS thesis, Univ. Iowa, Iowa City

Weiss, G., and Hechtman, L. T. Hyperactive Children Grown Up: Empirical Findings and Theoretical Considerations. New York: Guilford, 1986.

Weiss, Lynn. Attention Deficit Disorder in Adults. Dallas: Taylor Publishing, 1992.

Weisz, D. J., Loturco, J. J. 1988. Reflex facilitation of the nictitating membrane response remains after cerebellar lesions. Behav. Neurosci. 103:203-9

Weizman, Ronit, et al. "Effects of Acute and Chronic Methylphenidate Administration of B-Endorphin, Growth Hormone Prolactin and Cortisol in Children with Attention Deficit Disorder and Hyperactivity." Life Sciences, 40 (1987), 2247-2252.

Welsh, J. P., Harvey, J. A. 1989a. Cerebellar lesions and the nictitating membrane reflex: performance deficits of the conditioned and unconditioned response. J. Neurosci. 9:299-311

Welsh, J. P., Harvey, J. A. 1989b. Intra-cerebellar lidocaine: dissociation of learning from performance. Soc. Neurosci. Abstr. 15:639

Wender, P. H. Minimal Brain Dysfunction in Children. New York: Wiley, 1971.

West M, ed. The Psychology of Meditation. London, England: Oxford University Press; 1987.

Whalen, C. K., et al. "A Social Ecology of Hyperactive Boys: Medication Effects in Structured Classroom Environments." Journal Appl Behav Anal, 12 (1979), 65-81.

White, Geoffrey: Identity through History: Living Stories in a Solomon Islands Society (New York: Cambridge University Press 1991).

Wilson, John. Thomas Carlyle: The Iconoclast of Modern Shams. 1973.

Winn, Marie. The Plug-In Drug. New York: Bantam, 1978.

Wolf: Eric R.: Europe and the People without History (Berkeley: University of California Press 1982).

Wolkenberg, F. "Out of a Darkness." The New York Times Magazine, October 11, 1987.

Woodruff-Pak, D. S., Lavond, D. G., Thompson, R. F. 1985. Trace conditioning: abolished by cerebellar nuclear lesions but not lateral cerebellar cortex aspirations. Brain Res. 348:249-60

Woody, C. D., ed. 1982. Conditioning: Representation of Involved Neural Functions. New York: Plenum Woody, C. D. 1986. Understanding the cellular basis of memory and learning. Annu. Rev. Psychol. 37:433-93

Woody, C. D., Gruen, E., Birt, D. 1991. Changes in membrane currents during Pavlovian conditioning of single cortical neurons. Brain Res. 539:76-84

Woody, C. D., Knispel, J. D., Crow, T. J., Black-Cleworth, P. A. 1976. Activity and excitability to electrical current of cortical auditory receptive field neurons of awake cats as affected by stimulus association. J. Neurophysiol. 39:1045-61

Woody, C. D., Yarowsky, P., Owens, J., Black-Cleworth, P., Crow, T. 1974. Effect of lesions of coronal motor areas on acquisition of conditioned eye blink in the cat. J. Neurophysiol. 37:385-94

Yeo, C. H. 1991. Cerebellum and classical conditioning of motor responses. Ann. NY Acad. Sci. 627:292-305

Yeo, C. H., Hardiman, M. J., Glickstein, M. 1984. Discrete lesions of the cerebellar cortex abolish the classically conditioned nictitating membrane response of the rabbit. Behav. Brain Res. 13:261-66

Yeo, C. H., Hardiman, M. J., Glickstein, M. 1985a. Classical conditioning of the nictitating membrane response of the rabbit. I. Lesions of the cerebellar nuclei. Exp. Brain Res. 60:87-98

Yeo, C. H., Hardiman, M. J., Glickstein, M. 1985b. Classical conditioning of the nictitating membrane response of the rabbit. II. Lesions of the cerebellar cortex. Exp. Brain Res. 60:99-113

Yeo, C. H., Hardiman, M. J., Glickstein, M. 1986. Classical conditioning of the nictitating membrane response of the rabbit. IV. Lesions of the inferior olive. Exp. Brain Res. 63:81-92

Yeo, C. H., Hardiman, M. J., Glickstein, M., Russell, I. S. 1982. Lesions of cerebellar nuclei abolish the classically conditioned nictitating membrane response. Soc. Neurosci. Abstr. 8:22

Zametkin, A.J., Nordahl, T.E., Gross, M., King, A.C., Semple, W.E., Rumsey,

J., Hamburger, S., & Cohen, R.S. (1990). "Cerebral glucose metabolism in adults with hyperactivity of childhood onset." New England Journal of Medicine, 323, 1361-1366.

Zhang, A. A., Clark, R. E., Lavond, D. G. 1990. Cooling cerebellar HVI lobule does not abolish conditioned responses. Soc. Neurosci. Abstr. 16:270

Zhang, A. A., Lavond, D. G, 1991. Effects of reversible lesion of reticular or facial neurons during eyeblink conditioning. Soc. Neurosci. Abstr. 17:869

Zhang, J. X., Harper, R. M., Ni, H. 1986. Cryogenic blockade of the central nucleus of the amygdala attenuates aversively conditioned blood pressure and respiratory responses. Brain Res. 386:136-45

Recommended reading

In intentionally random order, this list is a collection of books the author finds to be of particular value and relevance to the issues surrounding ADD in adults. All are available or orderable through any local bookstore.

- *Driven To Distraction* by Edward Hallowell, M.D. and John Ratey, M.D.

- *Dixie City Jam* by James Lee Burke

- *You Mean I'm Not Lazy, Stupid or Crazy?* by Kate Kelly and Peggy Ramundo

- *The Roots of the Self* by Robert Ornstein, Ph.D.

- *I'm Dysfunctional, You're Dysfunctional* by Wendy Kaminer

- *Maybe You Know My Kid* by Mary Fowler

- *Answers To Distraction* by Edward Hallowell, M.D. and John Ratey, M.D.

- *Fire Your Shrink!* by Michele Weiner-Davis

- *Fear and Loathing in Las Vegas* by Hunter S. Thompson

- *A.D.D. in Adults* by Lynn Weiss, Ph.D.

- *ADHD and Teens: A Parent's Guide for Getting Through the Tough Years* by Colleen Alexander-Roberts.

- *The Presence of the Past* by Rupert Sheldrake

INDEX